Emotional Mimicry in Social Context

In everyday life we actively react to the emotion expressions of others, responding by showing matching, or sometimes contrasting, expressions. Emotional mimicry has important social functions, such as signalling affiliative intent and fostering rapport, and is considered one of the cornerstones of successful interactions. This book provides a multidisciplinary overview of research into emotional mimicry and empathy and explores when, how, and why emotional mimicry occurs. Focussing on recent developments in the field, the chapters cover a variety of approaches and research questions, such as the role of literature in empathy and emotional mimicry, the most important brain areas involved in the mimicry of emotions, the effects of specific psychopathologies on mimicry, why smiling may be a special case in mimicry, whether we can also mimic vocal emotional expressions, individual differences in mimicry, and the role of social contexts in mimicry.

URSULA HESS is a professor in the Department of Psychology at the Humboldt University of Berlin.

AGNETA FISCHER is a professor in the Department of Social Psychology at the University of Amsterdam.

STUDIES IN EMOTION AND SOCIAL INTERACTION
Second Series

Series Editors

Keith Oatley
University of Toronto

Antony S. R. Manstead
Cardiff University

Titles published in the Second Series

The Psychology of Facial Expression, edited by James A. Russell and José Miguel Fernández-Dols

Emotions, the Social Bond, and Human Reality: Part/Whole Analysis, by Thomas J. Scheff

Intersubjective Communication and Emotion in Early Ontogeny, edited by Stein Bråten

The Social Context of Nonverbal Behavior, edited by Pierre Philippot, Robert S. Feldman, and Erik J. Coats

Communicating Emotion: Social, Moral, and Cultural Processes, by Sally Planalp

Emotions across Languages and Cultures: Diversity and Universals, by Anna Wierzbicka

Feeling and Thinking: The Role of Affect in Social Cognition, edited by Joseph P. Forgas

Metaphor and Emotion: Language, Culture, and Body in Human Feeling, by Zoltán Kövecses

Gender and Emotion: Social Psychological Perspectives, edited by Agneta H. Fischer

Causes and Consequences of Feelings, by Leonard Berkowitz

Emotions and Beliefs: How Feelings Influence Thoughts, edited by Nico H. Frijda, Antony S. R. Manstead, and Sacha Bem

Identity and Emotion: Development through Self-Organization, edited by Harke A. Bosma, and E. Saskia Kunnen

Emotional Mimicry in Social Context

Edited by

Ursula Hess

Department of Psychology, Humboldt University of Berlin

Agneta H. Fischer

Department of Social Psychology, University of Amsterdam

CAMBRIDGE
UNIVERSITY PRESS

University Printing House, Cambridge CB2 8BS, United Kingdom

Cambridge University Press is part of the University of Cambridge.

It furthers the University's mission by disseminating knowledge in the pursuit of
education, learning and research at the highest international levels of excellence.

www.cambridge.org
Information on this title: www.cambridge.org/9781107064478

First published 2016

A catalogue record for this publication is available from the British Library

Library of Congress Cataloguing in Publication data
Hess, Ursula, 1960– editor. | Fischer, Agneta, 1958– editor.
Emotional mimicry in social context / edited by Ursula Hess and Agneta Fischer.
Cambridge, United Kingdom : Cambridge University Press, 2016. | Series: Studies
in emotion and social interaction
LCCN 2015047196 | ISBN 9781107064478 (hardback)
LCSH: Emotions. | Imitation. | Emotions – Social aspects. | Social interaction. |
BISAC: PSYCHOLOGY / Social Psychology.
LCC BF531 .E4984 2016 | DDC 302–dc23
LC record available at http://lccn.loc.gov/2015047196

ISBN 978-1-107-06447-8 Hardback

Contents

List of figures   *page* vii
List of contributors   viii

Introduction: why and how we mimic emotions   1
Agneta H. Fischer and Ursula Hess

1 **On the sharing of mind**   7
   Keith Oatley

2 **The role of mimicry in understanding the emotions
   of others**   27
   Mariëlle Stel

3 **Revisiting the Simulation of Smiles model: the what,
   when, and why of mimicking smiles**   44
   Paula M. Niedenthal, Sebastian Korb, Adrienne
   Wood, and Magdalena Rychlowska

4 **The neuroscience of mimicry during social interactions**   72
   Leonhard Schilbach

5 **The social dimension as antecedent and effect
   of emotional mimicry**   90
   Ursula Hess, Isabell Hühnel, Job van der Schalk,
   and Agneta H. Fischer

6 **More than just a mirror: examining the cross-channel
   mimicry of emotional expressions**   107
   Skyler Hawk and Agneta H. Fischer

7 **Emotional mimicry: underlying mechanisms
   and individual differences**   125
   Marianne Sonnby-Borgström

8 **Mimicry, emotion, and social context: insights from
   typical and atypical humans, robots, and androids**   162
   Piotr Winkielman, Evan W. Carr, Bhismadev
   Chakrabarti, Galit Hofree, and Liam C. Kavanagh

v

9 The neurological basis of empathy and mimicry   192
Miriam Schuler, Sebastian Mohnke, and Henrik
Walter

**10 Conclusion: toward a better understanding
of emotional mimicry**   222
Ursula Hess and Agneta H. Fischer

Index   230

Figures

4.1 (a) Virtual scenario as shown in the instructions.
(b) Depiction of a self-directed, socially relevant facial
expression. (c) Depiction of an other-directed, arbitrary
facial movement. (d) Neural correlates of the perception
of self-directed facial expressions. (e) Neural correlates
of the perception of other-directed facial expressions.
(f) Neural correlates of the perception of arbitrary facial
movements (Taken from: Schilbach et al., 2013). *page 74*

4.2 Neural correlates of the perception of socially relevant
facial expressions related to the occurrence of facial
mimicry (Taken from Schilbach et al., 2008). 78

4.3 (a) Screenshot depicting an anthropomorphic virtual
character and three objects (grey squares). (b) Neural
correlates of joint attention. (c) Neural correlates
of non-joint attention. (d) Neural correlates of
other-initiated joint attention. (e) Neural correlates
of self-initiated joint attention (Taken from
Schilbach et al., 2013). 81

5.1 Example stick figure faces showing happiness,
anger, sadness, and fear. 98

5.2 Emotional mimicry to stick figures across conditions
and emotions. 100

7.1 A potential model illustrating the process involved
in emotional responding in a face-to-face
interaction situation. 128

9.1 Brain areas involved in the generation of an
empathic reaction. 205

9.2 Brain circuits for empathy and ToM. 207

10.1 Antecedents and consequences of mimicry and
reactive expressions. 225

Contributors

Evan W. Carr
University of California, San Diego

Bhismadev Chakrabarti
University of Reading

Agneta H. Fischer
University of Amsterdam

Skyler Hawk
The Chinese University of Hong Kong

Ursula Hess
Humboldt University of Berlin

Galit Hofree
University of California, San Diego

Isabell Hühnel
Humboldt University of Berlin

Liam C. Kavanagh
University of California, San Diego

Sebastian Korb
University of Geneva

Sebastian Mohnke
Charité – Universitätsmedizin Berlin

Paula M. Niedenthal
University of Wisconsin

Keith Oatley
University of Toronto

Magdalena Rychlowska
Cardiff University

Leonhard Schilbach
University Hospital Cologne

Miriam Schuler
Charité – Universitätsmedizin Berlin

Marianne Sonnby-Borgström
Malmö University

Mariëlle Stel
Tilburg University

Job van der Schalk
Cardiff University

Henrik Walter
Charité – Universitätsmedizin Berlin

Piotr Winkielman
University of California, San Diego

Adrienne Wood
University of Wisconsin

Introduction: why and how we mimic emotions

Agneta H. Fischer and Ursula Hess

Mimicry and its presumed neurological underpinnings in the form of mirror neurons have become a trending topic in the social, behavioural, and neurosciences during the past decades (e.g. Hess & Fischer, 2013). The notion that minds can be shared by subtly imitating others is a challenging idea that sparks our imagination. For ages, philosophers and scientists have been intrigued by the question of how we come to understand what others think. How can we read the minds of others, how can we know what they feel and predict how they will react, and how can we relate to their pain and suffering or join in their victories and pride? Understanding of and empathizing with others appear to form the basis for human bonding and positive social interaction. Whereas shared goals or interests may lead to temporary coalitions and cooperation, understanding others' feelings and perspectives provides the basis for long-term and enduring social bonds.

One crucial aspect of the sharing of minds is the communication of emotions. We cannot be involved in relationships without emotions. We feel and express emotions towards the people we care about, and if people do not elicit any emotions in us, this implies that we feel indifferent towards them. Thus we get angry, irritated, worried, sad, or proud with the people to whom we feel connected; the stronger our concerns, the stronger the emotions, whether negative or positive. Not only do people express their emotions, they also tend to share them with their friends, family and colleagues. The communication of emotions is thus part of many daily interactions as well. A cashier smiles when handing back change, nurses express sympathy to patients, and managers show enthusiasm to motivate employees. The study of emotional expressions has a long tradition in psychology, starting with Darwin and then the seminal work by Paul Ekman; yet, for many years the question mainly focused on observers' ability to recognize the facial signals of emotion sent by an expresser. In this line of research the perceiver remained passive.

1

Hatfield, Cacioppo, and Rapson (1994) were among the first to put the relationship between the perceiver and the perceived on the scientific agenda with the publication of their book *Emotional Contagion*. Emotional contagion is the sharing of emotional minds, and refers to the idea that we easily catch others' emotions. To illustrate the pervasiveness of this phenomenon, we only need to think about emotional crowds in panic, fright, or anger, or the pain we ourselves experience when watching the suffering of war victims and refugees on television. In their book Hatfield and colleagues identified several mechanisms that may lead to emotional contagion, of which mimicry has to date received most attention. Mimicry has been defined as the tendency to automatically imitate and synchronize facial expressions, vocalizations, postures, and movements with those of another person (see Hatfield et al., 1992). In other words, perceivers actively react to the emotional expressions of others and respond by showing matching – or sometimes contrasting – expressions. The tendency to mimic the expressions perceived in others can already be observed in small children and is assumed to have the important social functions of signalling affiliative intent and fostering rapport. For this reason, mimicry has been considered one of the cornerstones of successful and warm interactions.

Since then, an abundance of empirical research has been published on mimicry, investigating the determinants, boundaries, and effects of this phenomenon. We roughly distinguish between behavioural and emotional mimicry, the latter focusing on the mimicry of others' non-verbal behaviours that signal emotional meaning, such as a smile. The topic of the present volume is *emotional* mimicry. Several experts in this field reviewed the underlying processes and contextual boundaries of mimicry in order to better understand its functions in realizing the sharing of emotional perspectives. To date there is no clear picture regarding the conditions under which emotional mimicry is shown, or the situations in which it may be inappropriate. This is partly due to the fact that the literature on emotional mimicry is distributed over various subdisciplines in psychology and neuroscience. Thus, relevant studies have been published in diverse outlets across the domains of social psychology, emotions, neuroscience, biological psychology and psychophysiology, and even psycho-endocrinology. As a consequence the literature on this topic tends to be theoretically disjointed.

The aim of the present volume is to review and evaluate the state of the art in this research domain and to set out future directions. The only previous book addressing these issues, *Emotional Contagion* by Hatfield et al. (1994), was published more than 20 years ago, and since then many studies have been published and theoretical perspectives have been proposed. The present volume aims to reflect the state of the art on different aspects of mimicry, ranging from different factors and contexts affecting mimicry, different forms of mimicry (e.g. cross-channel mimicry), to the different functions of mimicry. The common thread in this volume is that emotional mimicry is a complex phenomenon influenced by context, usually a social exchange, which is crucial for when mimicry occurs and how it affects people.

Overview

Mimicry, empathy, and the sharing of mind

Mimicry is closely related to empathy, but there have been different ways in which this relation has been conceptualized. Mimicry can be seen as one of the causal paths to empathy (e.g. Hatfield et al., 1992), or as an early stage of empathy. In Chapter 1 Oatley refers to Donald (1991), who describes the mimetic stage as a crucial stage in the development of the mind, and as a preadaptation for language. This is also apparent in young children who mimic adults' facial expressions, signalling that they share the other's mind, before they are able to talk. Mimicry can thus be seen as an early stage in the development of empathy, preceding shared attention, shared intentions, and perspective taking. These are different paths all leading to the sharing of minds. Empathy is the sharing of emotions, which forms the building blocks of social life. Sharing of emotions is important for social coordination of plans in everyday life, but also for the appreciation of art, more specifically literature. Through art we identify with the protagonist and share life stories in films or novels.

Schuler, Mohnke, and Walter (Chapter 9) further differentiate between different forms of empathy, namely affective and cognitive empathy. Both forms of empathy differ from mimicry, although the neurological underpinnings are very similar. The core empathy regions comprise the AI (Anterior Insula) and ACC/MCC (Anterior and Medial Cingulate Cortex, XE "ACC/MCC"), which integrate information across various domains and allow selection of prospective responses. Two brain circuits, involving the mirror neuron system and the mentalizing system, have been associated with two routes to empathy, namely top-down and bottom-up. The first route involves more cognitive perspective taking, and the second route involves the mirror neuron system, eliciting automatic (mimicry) responses to affective stimuli. Although these routes can be distinguished, it should be clear that they are not independent of each other.

Not only do empathy and mimicry seem to have similar neurological underpinnings but individual differences in empathy can also be seen as determinant of individual differences in mimicry. In Chapter 7, Sonnby-Borgström reports evidence that individual differences in empathic ability, as measured with self-reports, are related to individual differences in the tendency to engage in facial mimicry. Studies of individuals with empathic disorders, such as ASD (Autistic Spectrum Disorder) or DBD (Disruptive Behaviour Disorder) also showed less mimicry when confronted with angry and sad faces. Mimicry has also been related to attachment behaviours, showing that insecurely attached children mimic positive emotions less often than securely attached children. The relation between empathy and mimicry is most likely bidirectional, however, because a variety of studies have also shown that mimicry affects liking, and bonding with the other person. Stel (Chapter 2) and Hess and colleagues (Chapter 5) describe studies showing that a priori attitudes influence mimicry, such that a positive attitude enhances mimicry, whereas a negative attitude decreases mimicry, but also that mimicking in turns increases positive attitudes, and thus may reinforce an empathic stance.

The relation between mimicry and empathy is therefore a close one. Most authors define empathy as a broad state of mind aimed at feeling or sharing with others, whereas mimicry is a more specific tendency to copy others' behaviour. We think it is important to differentiate the two concepts, while at the same time to acknowledge that they mutually influence each other.

Functions of emotional mimicry

Two functions of mimicry have traditionally been proposed and examined. The first is improving the understanding of others, which is discussed elaborately by Stel in Chapter 2. Several theories have provided explanations of this function, such as the Facial Feedback Hypothesis, the Perception-Behaviour link, and Embodiment theories, all suggesting that mimicry helps us to identify others' feelings. This seems particularly to be the case when others' feelings are not straightforward, and therefore difficult to unravel. In such cases differences between people who do or do not mimic are found. This is also evident from Chapter 3 by Niedenthal and colleagues who focus on smile mimicry. Their research on the role of smile mimicry has shown that participants whose mimicry is blocked are worse in detecting the distinction between true and false smiles. However, in general the results with regard to this function seem to be inconclusive. Whereas some studies found support for the facilitation or improvement of accuracy in recognizing others' emotions, other studies found no effects. Explanations for this inconsistency are discussed by Stel in Chapter 2.

A second function that has received much empirical support is the affiliation function: mimicry is assumed to lead to stronger and more positive social bonds. This is not only the case for smiling but also for negative emotions. Hess and colleagues review the evidence for social context effects of facial mimicry in Chapter 5 and show that mimicry is modulated by the social relational context in which it occurs. Individuals are more likely to mimic friends or people they like and less likely to mimic people they do not like or who are dissimilar to them. In addition, when individuals have the goal to cooperate, they are more likely to mimic others than when they are in competition. Indeed, Winkielman and colleagues (Chapter 8) further extend these social context effects of mimicry using human-like androids. This research shows that androids are mimicked but only in a cooperative and not in a competitive context. This research also emphasizes the human-bonding function, showing that the more human-like the android appears to be and the closer its presence, the more it was mimicked.

The nature of mimicry: underlying processes

Different theoretical approaches to explaining mimicry are reviewed in the various chapters. Most theories, such as the Matched Motor hypothesis, the Perception Action Model, and other variants of embodiment theory and simulation theory, assume that the observation of a facial expression elicits some form of internal simulation that is reflected in the activation of motor areas in the brain similar to the ones that are activated when one experiences the emotion oneself. Differences between these theoretical accounts relate to how the emotional signal is interpreted, what type of information needs to be processed, and at what level, in order for mimicry to occur. In Chapter 6 Hawk and Fischer discuss these different theoretical accounts extensively in order to explain the phenomenon of cross-channel mimicry, that is, the facial mimicry in response to auditory signals.

In contrast to views that assume an internal simulation of the perceived emotion, emphasizing self–other similarities, Schilbach (Chapter 4) proposes a second view that does not emphasize similarity with and matching of others' minds but instead an interactionist or enactive view of mimicry. In this account, knowledge of others' minds is required to support interpersonal coordination. He argues, in line with others in the volume, that mimicry based on the mirror neuron network (MNN) reflects the tight association between perception and premotor and motor areas in the brain, whereas mimicry based on the mentalizing network (MENT) is activated when socially relevant stimuli are processed more explicitly. Such a view is in line with our proposed Emotional Mimicry in Social Context model (see also Chapter 10, this book), which argues that emotional mimicry is not based on mere objective features of the face or the body but rather on the meaning and interpretation of these movements in a particular context.

In sum

These are just some of the many issues that are discussed in this volume. We hope that the volume will be useful and stimulate new research on the intriguing questions of how, why, and when we mimic others' emotions. Finally, we would like to thank all the authors for their enthusiasm to contribute to this volume, and we hope that they will enjoy the outcomes of this joint endeavour as much as we do.

References

Donald, M. (1991). *Origins of the modern mind*. Cambridge, MA: Harvard University Press.

Hatfield, E. C., Cacioppo, J. T., & Rapson, R. L. (1994). *Primitive Emotional contagion*. Cambridge: Cambridge University Press.

Hess, U., & Fischer, A. (2013). Emotional mimicry as social regulation. *Personality and Social Psychology Review, 17*, 142–157.

CHAPTER 1

On the sharing of mind

Keith Oatley

Sociality is central to being human and it depends on our ability to understand others, but not just in the way that we might understand something physical, like how to pick an apple from a tree. In this chapter, I draw together some threads of other chapters in the book and develop the idea that human sociality is based on emotions and that it involves sharing pieces of mind.

Empathy offers a clear example of emotion-based sharing of mind. As explained in Chapter 9 by Schuler and colleagues, it enables us to experience in our selves something of an emotion of another person. Singer et al. (2004) studied the phenomenon by monitoring the brains of respondents when they were themselves experiencing pain and when they were signalled that a loved one in another room was experiencing the same kind of pain. The anterior insula and the anterior cingulate cortex were activated in both cases. A piece of brain activation and a piece of mind were shared. De Vignemont and Singer (2006) explain that empathy, of this kind, occurs when someone has an emotion that is similar to that of another person, when one sees or imagines the other person having that emotion, and when one knows that the other is the source of one's own emotion.

In this chapter, I first discuss the sharing of mind in the emotions of day-to-day life, and then the sharing of pieces of mind in the form of works of art. In both cases, emotional mimicry, or emotional mirroring, can be involved: one person can share something of the emotions of others.

Evolution and everyday life

De Waal proposed what he calls the "Russian Doll" model of empathy in everyday life (De Waal & de Waal, 2007). Except for the one at the centre, Russian dolls are hollow and each contains another doll or dolls. In de Waal's model of empathy, each surrounding layer is built on and derives properties from the one inside it. The centre doll, the core, is emotional contagion: one individual matches an emotional state of another. This ability is ancient. It emerged with the evolution of mammals, perhaps earlier. Around this core, and based on it, is another doll, a layer of ability to feel concern for others, and hence to be able to care for them because of feeling something like their emotion. De Waal describes how this is frequently shown by our primate cousins, chimpanzees, both in attachment relationships and in friendships. The next doll, the next layer, he calls perspective taking. It enables people to adopt others' viewpoints, so that, for instance, they can help them in ways that they might need. This third layer is distinctively human, but it is based on the older abilities. Evolution does not usually discard pieces of structure it has installed. Instead, says de Waal, it builds on them, and this is what has happened in the series from state matching, to concern, to perspective taking.

The evolutionary line that led to humans is thought to have split off from the line that led to chimpanzees and bonobos about six million years ago. According to Lovejoy (1981), an important development for the human species was a modification of the usual primate arrangements in which sex was promiscuous and care for infants was provided by females. The change occurred among human forebears when sexual intercourse came to occur primarily in long-lasting couples, and when each male came to contribute economically to a single female and family. A human female and a male could come to share pieces of their minds in their ongoing cooperative relationship, as these pieces concerned sex and care for their joint offspring.

A mimetic stage

Donald (1991) pointed out a critical stage in the evolution of the human mind and called it "mimetic": the ability to copy what others are doing. It was associated with *homo erectus*, a hominid species that emerged about two million years ago. Donald sees this ability as primarily motor. He stresses, as an example, the culturally widespread imitative activity of dance. Nowadays, in the movies, dance is an icon of doing something that is active, enjoyable, and social. Donald also argues that mimetic ability is a preadaptation for language.

An important component of mimetic ability is the imitation of facial expressions. It emerges early in infancy, as shown by Meltzoff and Moore (1977), and it seems to occur only in humans. Meltzoff (1993) has argued that mimicry is a bridge to the shared mind. For him it means that the infant is able to understand that others are "like me". In turn, this leads to being able to share intentions and to the understanding of others that now, in cognitive developmental psychology, is called "Theory of Mind". In this book Stel, in Chapter 2, discusses how mimicry provides a basis for understanding others' emotions, and Hawk and Fischer, in Chapter 6, show how mimicry in one perceptual channel, for instance visual or auditory, can be the basis for more complete experiences of emotion that can also be expressed in broader ways.

The happiness that comes from smiling back at someone who smiles may be affected by proprioceptive aspects. Evidence for this comes from Strack, Martin, and Stepper (1988) who asked people to hold a pen in their mouth, and in this way to make an expression that was like smiling, though participants did not know that this was the effect they were having on themselves. The manoeuvre increased happiness. When they held a pen in their mouths, participants saw cartoons as more amusing. In the current book, Chapter 3 by Niedenthal and colleagues and Chapter 8 by Winkielman and colleagues offer discussions of embodiments of emotions and how they may be shared.

Shared intention

Beyond mimicry come the processes of shared attention (see e.g. Chapter 4 of this book, by Schilbach) and of shared intention. For instance, one person can learn to use a tool purposefully when he or she has seen it being used by someone else. On the whole, chimpanzees can neither demonstrate to others an activity that is a step towards a shared goal nor learn from such demonstrations (Povinelli & O'Neill, 2000). Important work on this issue has been done by Tomasello and his colleagues, who have compared the physical and social abilities of young human children and of apes. Herrmann, Call, Hernandez-Lloreda, Hare, and Tomasello (2007) and Tomasello and Herrmann (2010) have shown that human two-and-a-half-year-olds and their primate cousins of any age are about the same in their physical understanding, for instance of spatial layouts and transpositions, or of causality. The human children, however, were found to be far better than apes at social understanding. They can learn from a demonstration of how to solve a simple but non-obvious problem, they can understand communications of others, and they can follow the communicator's attention. They can also watch an intended action that miscarries and understand what the actor had intended to do.

Tomasello and Vaish (2012) argue that by the age of about one-and-a-half years, humans know that both they and others are agents, that is to say capable of acting in the world, and that they and the other are the same in this way. Tomasello and Rakoczy (2003) have called this "the real thing". They mean it's the most basic component of human sociality, and that it needs to be in place before children can acquire Theory of Mind. Consider how remarkable this kind of understanding is. To an eighteen-month-old child one can say: "See this crayon, you can draw a circle, like this. See?" And the child can use the crayon to produce a comparable result. Imagine you are a computer programmer working in artificial intelligence. Imagine what would it be to write a program to do this. It's not just a matter of producing a pattern of behaviour. It means being able to recognize the circle as the goal of an action intended to produce this result, and to generate a motor program capable first of conceptualizing the goal and then of achieving it. The actions to be programmed will include not only the concept of goal-directedness but grasping the crayon, guiding the hand, and them monitoring progress towards the goal, so that deviations from the conceptual goal-state are minimized.

One reason why the discovery of mirror neurons by Rizzolatti et al. (e.g. Rizzolatti, Fogassi, & Gallese, 2001) is regarded as so significant is that it offers a means that helps solve this problem. The discovery implies that our ability to perceive intended actions is based on knowing how to carry them out ourselves. A difficulty with this conception, as yet unsolved, is that although the initial discovery of mirror neurons was in monkeys, monkeys cannot themselves learn from being shown how to use a tool, or copy the behaviour of using a tool to achieve a goal.

Shifting, now, to pathology, Hobson, Lee, and Hobson (2007) have argued that people with autism are handicapped in the specific form of subjective interconnectedness in which they are able to identify with others, and to put themselves in the position of these others when they learn or demonstrate an action. They report a study in which, in the absence of a person called "Pete", 12 autistic and 12 non-autistic male adolescents were shown a series of actions by a person whom we can call Jim. Jim demonstrated each action to each participant and asked that when Pete came back into the room, the adolescent should show him what to do. Over six such actions, videotapes were made and analysed in terms of four indices: participants' emotional engagement in the tasks, their sharing of experience in joint attention, their communication of the style in which the action was originally demonstrated, and their ability to shift role to being the teacher. On this composite, except for one boy in the autistic group who scored the same as the lowest three participants in the non-autistic group, there was a complete separation between the two groups: the autistic boys were emotionally less involved, and far less able to engage with Pete, or to show him what to do.

We might say, then, that autism is a condition that involves emotions and mimicry, in which the complex bases of being able to learn intended actions from others, and of being able to enter others' minds to teach them about such actions, are only imperfectly available.

The social brain

A second stream of work relevant here is that of Dunbar (2004), who has found a strong correlation between the size of social groups in which different species of primates live and the size of the brain in these species. The most evolutionarily primitive of modern primates are lemurs, and they live in social groups of about nine. Monkeys live in larger social groups; the size of the social group of cebus monkeys is about 18. Chimpanzees live in social groups of about 50. For modern humans, the size of the social group – the number of people about whom one knows something of their life history and their personality – is about 150. Dunbar has found that with increasing size of the social group, there is an increase in the size of the cortex of the brain. So in lemurs the cortex is 1.2 times the size of the rest of the brain. In cebus monkeys it is 2.4 times. In chimpanzees it is 3.2 times. In humans it is 4.1 times. Dunbar's hypothesis is that increased brain size became necessary to house the mental models we make of others. So it's not just that we can know something of what others know, which is the usual subject matter of developmental studies of Theory of Mind. It is that we make mental models of the biographies of the people we know well, and the human brain is large because it needs to house many such models.

Chimpanzees cultivate friendly relationships by grooming. They sit quietly with another individual, cuddle, and sort through the other's fur for twigs and insects. In doing this they adopt the same posture, take part in the same activity, and build trust in the other. They do this for those in their social group to whom they feel close. Grooming is a cooperative activity of happily shared intention to maintain an affectionate relationship. Chimpanzees occupy about 20 per cent of their time in this way. Dunbar's argument (Dunbar, 2004) is that, as the size of the social group grew during primate evolution, so too would the amount of time necessary for grooming. A point was reached when this time reached about 30 per cent: the maximum a primate could afford and still do all the other things necessary for primate life. It was at this point that conversation arose. It was not that language arose and then this allowed conversation. Rather conversation arose – Dunbar calls it social grooming – and this required, and prompted the development of, spoken language.

Like grooming, conversation functions to form and maintain relationships. In modern humans, as Dunbar has found, some 70 per cent of conversation is about the plans and emotions of oneself and others one knows. Often, as Rimé (2009) has found, conversation involves sharing our emotions, not to diminish their intensity as was originally thought when the confiding of emotions started to be studied, but to form shared understandings of ourselves and others. In conversations, and in gossip, the models of others that we share with each other can come to be similar. The implication is that when we discuss our emotions, we share mental models such that the way in which we see ourselves is aligned with similarities to how others see us, in their mental models of us. If, in the moral domain, our model of our self veers too far from the models others have of us, we may feel shame or guilt. And, if such veering takes us very far from group norms, we or others may think us mentally ill.

Individual emotions and social emotions in everyday life

In an article that is perhaps the most important piece of theory on the cognitive functions of emotions, Simon (1967) pointed out that all human plans are limited in scope and that our models of the world, on which our plans are based, can never be complete. Hence the unexpected happens. Unexpectedness is multiplied because many of our plans involve others, whose intentions can be known only partially. As mentioned in the first section of this chapter, empathy is a prime example of the sharing of emotion, so an important question is how does it connect with cognitive theories that are based on arguments such as Simon's. One way is depicted by the communicative theory of emotions, of Oatley and Johnson-Laird (1987, 2014), which is one of half-a-dozen or so related and current cognitive theories of emotion. Oatley and Johnson-Laird have proposed that certain kinds of events that affect goals give rise to emotions. Events of these kinds have been reiterated during evolutionary time. They include the experience of doing well in a plan (happiness), suffering in relation to losses (sadness), responses being thwarted by another person (anger), and suchlike. These emotions can be thought of as basic and universal. They are heuristics that configure not only the individual cognitive system to deal somewhat appropriately with the reiterated kind of event, but also the relationships in which plans made jointly with others are based. In this scheme, empathy – experiencing of emotions that are shared with others with whom one interacts – becomes important for social coordination.

Let us see how this works for the emotion of happiness.

Happiness as a heuristic and as the emotion of cooperation

In research on emotions, people tend to think of happiness as the emotion that is pleasurable and positive. This is not wrong, but it misses two main aspects of the functional significance of this emotion.

The first aspect missed by the idea that happiness is the emotion that is pleasant is that emotions are heuristics for dealing with recurring kinds of events in a complex world. For happiness, the usual recurring kind of event is doing well in a plan, including a plan shared with someone else. It prompts the cognitive system to continue with the current train of action, and it configures both the individual system and the relationship to enable this. This is reflected in the experience of feeling encouraged and engaged in what we are doing. The experience that Csikszentmihalyi (1990) called "flow" is what happens when this engagement is complete.

The second important aspect of happiness that is missed by thinking that it is merely a nice feeling is that, as Oatley (2009) has argued, it is especially important in thinking about the sociality of emotions, and the ways this sociality can be based on mimicry and empathy. The social aspects of emotions can be thought of as scripts. The term "script" comes from the theatre. In a play or film, actors learn the words and, using these words, they enact emotionally based relationships with other characters. Emotion scripts are the other way round. They configure relationships and, as we interact with others in everyday life, we provide the words.

Happiness is the fundamental emotion and mood of cooperation, of expectation that a joint activity – be it a conversation, an arrangement, or a plan – will be able to go forward. So, when one person signals happiness, it's an invitation to cooperation, and the person to whom the signal is made not only feels happy, empathetically, but is also prompted towards cooperation. In this kind of activity, then, the individual mind is enlarged. It becomes a joint mind for which, in each individual, some parts are shared, including the specification of the top-level goal. In a conversation, this top-level goal might be the affectionate intention to spend time together and extend the relationship. In a plan, the pieces of shared mind also include the trustfully agreed details about what to do and how to do it. Several researchers are now arguing forcibly for the priority of relationship-forming aspects of emotions, over the merely individual aspects (Butler, 2011; Hess & Fischer, 2013).

Although, in terms of matching states, a smile tends to prompt another smile, following the idea of emotions as scripts it is better to think of smiles not just as states that might potentially be matched. As invitations into cooperative relationships, they are also gestures of trustfulness, and confidence in the other person. Thus, as Fridlund (1994) has argued, in this way we can understand the social functions of emotional displays not as outward expressions of something within, but as signals of social intentions. Along the same line of thought, Aubé (2009) has argued that emotions are commitment operators, that is to say, processes that link people together in mutual roles to which they are then committed for the duration of an emotion episode. A smile is a fundamental example. It has properties that are both evolutionarily ancient and foundational in child development. It enables the most characteristic and central of all human functions: being able to cooperate so that we can do together what we cannot do alone.

It is significant that in studies of emotion diaries by Oatley and Duncan (1992), in which we asked people to look out for episodes of emotion they would experience over a three- or four-day period, happiness was the most frequent type of emotion. When we used a different method, called experience sampling, which involved signalling people at random times and asking: "What is the most recent emotion you have felt", we found that happiness was recorded twice as frequently (Oatley, 1998) as other emotions. This method probably counts episodes of happiness more accurately than the method (used by Oatley and Duncan) in which people were asked to look out for incidents of emotion, and record the ones that were salient.

In this context, it may not be accidental that the facial expression of emotion that is most widely recognized – that is to say, the expression that is more or less universally agreed to be an evolutionary universal – is the smile (see e.g. Nelson & Russell, 2013). It is the social signal of cooperation. Whereas economists propose that people cooperate because they anticipate individual benefit from an exchange, they have things the wrong way round. We cooperate because we are human and social; individual economic benefit is a useful by-product. Yamagishi, Li, Tagagishi, Matsumoto, and Kiyonari (2014) have found that the proportion of people who interacted with others purely on the basis of self-interest, without regard for others, in prisoner's dilemma and dictator games, was only about 7 per cent.

In order to form a joint plan, each partner has to identify with the other as far as this plan is concerned. In terms of the joint goal, considerations for each partner are the same. The whole of human life, in families, in workplaces, in societies, is based on cooperation, on being able to do together what we cannot do alone. It requires the realization that we and others are agents. As discussed earlier, this property of the human mind is unique to humans. To make a plan or arrangement with others requires that the mood of happy cooperation is shared by both and that details of the plan are shared. Larocque and Oatley (2006) have shown that when something goes wrong in a joint plan, it is usually because, although the two partners thought their copies of the plan were the same, there was something different in them. Most tellingly, the difference was often that one or both partners had goals, apart from the agreed goals, that had not been explicitly shared with the partner, which would affect enactment of the shared plan.

Sadness and fear

Analyses of individual and social aspects, comparable to those for happiness, can be sketched for sadness and fear.

For sadness, the usual recurring event is failure in a plan or loss of a relationship. It sets the cognitive system into the mode of looking to see what went wrong to cause the loss or failure. In a study with Seema Nundy (see Oatley, 2002), we found that when a person is sad, the emotion sets them into a heuristic of what, in cognitive psychology, is called backwards chaining: starting with an event and reasoning backwards to understand its cause. If, again, we think in evolutionary terms we can see an adaptive advantage that when there has been a loss or failure in a plan, the cognitive system is set into a mode of this kind, because then it becomes possible to learn from the event.

One of the social effects of sadness is that other people tend to help, if they can. The effect can be seen in children, for example Hoffmann (2000), and the more cognitively advanced the child, the better he or she is at sharing the situation of the sufferer and knowing what might actually be helpful. For fear, the recurring event is danger; it configures the cognitive system to stop what it was doing, to be vigilant for any sign of danger, and to prepare to freeze, to avoid, to escape, or to fight (e.g. Gray, 1988). Interpersonally fear and anxiety configure relationships so that others too are sensitized to the danger, and they too become fearful or anxious. In this way, whole crowds of people can react similarly to shared dangers.

Anger

For anger, the recurring event is being thwarted by someone else in some important goal. The emotion configures relationships to be conflictual; it prompts the cognitive system to find ways of overcoming the obstacle that the other person has set, perhaps by defeating the other person. Feeling angry when we see someone is angry with us is an empathetic reaction, and it functions to set up a relationship: a conflictual one. People generally find the experience negative.

Although, moreover, conflict seems to be the opposite of sharing, two kinds of matter are shared. The first is the idea of hierarchy and of what is necessary to maintain oneself in the social group. In social life there are many hierarchies, which typically are associated with power: they include hierarchies in families, in occupational settings, and in social life. In each hierarchy, everyone knows both the general structure, and where he or she, and others are in the hierarchy. Also, membership of a social group requires knowledge of how to behave in that group in order to maintain one's selfhood and one's social position (see Hess et al., Chapter 5). As Averill (1982) has shown, anger occurs when people experience an attempt to lower, or displace, them from their position in a social structure, or when people experience their actions in a relationship or in a group, as devalued.

Second, in relation to anger, people learn and share not just one kind of role into which they have been cast but, where there are paired roles, they learn both, for instance oppressor and oppressed. Main and George (1985) observed 20 one-year-old to three-year-old children in day-care settings. Ten of these children had been abused, and ten were unabused. When one child became distressed, non-abused children responded with interest, with concern, with empathy, or with sadness. Abused children, however, responded differently. They reacted to their age-mate's distress with disturbing patterns that included fear, anger, and physical attacks. Their anger came not from an empathetic sharing of the current sad emotion of an age-mate, but from parents who had abused them when they themselves had been distressed. Now, in the day-care setting, they could take the role of the one being angry and attacking, a role they had learnt from a parent.

The nature of art

Until now in this chapter, I have mostly discussed the sharing of mind in day-to-day interaction. The issue can usefully be extended to consider engagement with works of art, which can be thought of as pieces of mind that have been externalized, so that they may be shared with others.

Lovejoy (1981) estimates that human abilities to share sex and child-rearing emerged about 2.5 million years ago or earlier. Abilities to share practical knowledge, such as how to make and use flint tools, date from about the same period (Semaw et al, 2003). Art involved a new kind of sharing – a certain kind of sharing of mind – and, as Mithen (1996) has pointed out, it emerged far more recently: within the last 100,000 years.

Among early signs of the emergence of art are shells, from 82,000 years ago, drilled to make beads that could be worn as necklaces (Bouzouggar et al., 2007); burial mounds from 40,000 years ago (Bowler et al., 2003); and cave paintings from 31,000 years ago (Chauvet, Deschamps, & Hillaire, 1996). Mithen calls such phenomena evidence of metaphor, and I think this is the right term. As he points out, in metaphor one thing is both itself and something else: a shell is a shell but also a bead of a necklace. From an elaborate burial, we may infer that someone is both dead and alive on another plane. In cave paintings, charcoal and paint marks are also a rhinoceros.

In thinking about the issue of mimicry in emotions, one needs to consider Aristotle's concept of mimesis, the central concept of his book *Poetics*. Its usual English translations include: imitation, copying, mimicry, and representation. They point to how a piece of art can reflect something in the world; as Shakespeare (1600/1981) put it, how it can hold "the mirror up to nature" (*Hamlet*, III, 2, l. 22). In the West, the idea has been a foundation of literary theory and indeed of artistic theory more generally.

Art is an invitation to share a piece of mind that has been externalized into a carefully fashioned object, such as a story or a painting. In this kind of sharing, as Turner (2011) has pointed out, cognitive blending can occur, as the piece of structure to be shared becomes associated with a piece of structure in the receiving mind, to generate relations such as simile, analogy, and allegory. Turner points out that, because the received structure and the receiving structure necessarily differ, the process of associating them can result in what he calls "double-scope blending". From the combined similarities and differences of the two structures, this kind of blending prompts the emergence of new properties – imaginations, insights, further explorations – that are not in either of the structures alone. Art is also based on emotions. One of the best theories of the psychology of art is by Collingwood (1938) and he proposes that art is the exploration of an emotion that is not yet understood, in a way that can be shared with others in a particular language, for instance of words or music or painting.

Identification

Written stories are less than 5,000 years old. Whereas metaphor is at the centre of all art, in literary art metaphor can be extended (Oatley, 2014). In hearing, reading, or watching a story, we ourselves can be metaphorical. We can remain ourselves and, by identification, become a literary character. We can become Elizabeth Bennet or Anna Karenina, and share something of such characters' minds.

One of the most informative studies of identification in narrative is by Trabasso and Chung (2004). They asked 20 people to watch two films: Alfred Hitchcock's *Vertigo* and Ridley Scott's *Blade Runner*. Each film was stopped at 12 points. At each stopping point, members of the first group were asked to say how well the protagonist was doing and how well the antagonist was doing in their intentions. Members of the second group of watchers were asked to say how they, themselves, were feeling in relation to the story at that point. When the first group of watchers said the protagonist was doing well, or the antagonist was doing badly, the ten people in the second group felt emotions such as happiness, satisfaction, and relief. When the protagonist was doing badly, or the antagonist was doing well, the watchers who reported on their own emotions felt anger, sadness, anxiety, and suchlike. Trabasso and Chung had demonstrated that identification in watching films is based on empathy. Although other modes of emotional experience, such as sympathy, occur in engagement with stories (see e.g. Oatley, 1994), identification with a protagonist is a principal mode of experience of emotion in stories. In the diary studies of Oatley and Duncan (1992) discussed earlier, 7 per cent of emotion episodes occurred as a result of reading, watching TV, and suchlike.

The term "identification" means to take on an aspect of another so that one becomes like that other. In mainstream psychology, the idea overlaps with empathy, imitation, sympathy, and emotional contagion. "Identification" is the term used by Hobson et al. (2007) in their explanation of the problem with which adolescents with autism have difficulty: sharing emotional involvement and intentions with others. In psychoanalysis, identification is the means by which personality is formed (Laplanche & Pontalis, 1980). In this context, Gallese (2009) has argued that it can be understood in terms of circuits of shared neural simulation that enable us to share the meanings of actions and emotions with others, in day-to-day life and in psychotherapy. In this essay I will use "identification" to include empathy and imitation, aspects of the subject matter of this book, and bear in mind, too, the idea that the process might be important in personality change.

Fiction as simulation

Psychology has been sneery about fiction because, in comparison with psychology's carefully valid and reliable descriptions of behaviour, it can seem arbitrary and biased: merely made up. But this is a misunderstanding. Despite the idea of art as *mimesis*, fiction is not description. It is simulation of selves in the social world (Oatley, 1999). As Halliwell (2002) has shown, though Aristotle's *mimesis* can mean imitation or copying, the Greek term had a second family of meanings, which in many ways is even more important. In this second sense, *mimesis* means world-building, or world-constructing, or simulation. When in a novel one identifies with a protagonist, one builds an imagined world of the story, one constructs a simulation and, within this simulation, one makes the protagonist's concerns one's own. In this way, the reader (or listener or watcher) shares something of the protagonist's mind, in particular the protagonist's intentions and aspirations. But – and here is the important aspect – a reader does not have the protagonist's emotions. The protagonist is, after all only symbolic, incapable of experience as such. As in the experiment by Trabasso and Chung (2004) discussed earlier, the reader experiences his or her own emotions in relation to the intentions he or she has taken on and the circumstances of the story. Let us put it like this: in their advice to writers, instructors and editors say that if, in a story, you find yourself writing, "She fell in love", you have blown it. What writers must do is to suggest to the reader how he or she might construct and run the story-simulation to feel love.

Written fiction, then, is a good way of coming to understand emotions of other cultures, including the cultures of the past, from sadness and despair at the loss of a friend in one of the world's most ancient stories

The Epic of Gilgamesh, down to shame in postcolonial novels such as J.M. Coetzee's *Disgrace*. Such effects occur partly because (as discussed earlier) recurring kinds of situations, such as making progress with a plan, suffering a loss, perceiving a danger, being thwarted by an antagonist, give rise to universal emotions, so that we can be moved by stories from many cultures. Narrative fiction is a set of simulations of people's intentions and their vicissitudes (Bruner, 1986). Emotion is at its centre because it too derives from intentions and their vicissitudes, in human situations of kinds that can occur in many cultures.

Effects of fiction

Recently, the psychological effects of reading fiction have been explored. It has been found that the more fiction people read, the better is their understanding of others (Mar, Oatley, Hirsh, dela Paz, & Peterson, 2006; Mar, Oatley, & Peterson, 2009). The direction of effect – that reading affects Theory-of-Mind – was confirmed by Kidd and Castano (2013). The effect occurs with preschool children, too. As Mar, Pickett, and Moore (2010) have shown, the more stories preschoolers had read to them, or that they watched in films, the better they were on five measures of theory-of-mind. Watching television had no such effect.

An important consideration in the understanding of others derives from attribution theory, and it is called the actor-observer effect (Jones & Nisbett, 1971). In this we tend see ourselves as affected by circumstance and tend to see others as acting out of fixed personality traits. An example is that if we almost trip over a toy on the floor, we see this in terms of the actor effect: due to the circumstance of the toy having been left where it shouldn't have been. If we see someone else do the same thing, we tend to see, from the position of an observer, that the person was clumsy.

The actor-observer effect means that there are different kinds of sharing of mind. When we make a mental model of someone else, we build that model around the other's personality traits, as reliable, as impulsive, as affectionate, or whatever it may be. With most people we know, we take on observer status that we can interact with them, and know in what kinds of plans and confidences we can trust them. It's an essential property of making mental models of others in our social world. In some circumstances, however, we need to understand others more empathetically, in a way that is closer to how they understand themselves. That is to say, we take on actor status, as if we were them. The sharing, here, is deeper; it's a kind of identification. It occurs with intimates such as spouses and close friends, and with children whom we are bringing up. The effect can occur, too, in the Western legal system, in which members of a jury have to construct a narrative of actions and events in order to reach a verdict (Hastie, 2008). This involves being able to understand how events and actions seemed from the point of view of the accused.

In literature, Flaubert made the very interesting advance, in *Madam Bovary*, of enabling us to experience the protagonist, Emma Bovary, simultaneously in terms of both a mental model (the observer effect) and empathetically from the inside (by identifying with her, in an actor effect). In *Middlemarch*, George Eliot arranged for readers to experience Casaubon, whom Dorothea marries, in terms of the observer effect, and see him in terms of his personality, as self-involved and mean-minded, and to identify with Dorothea empathetically, in the actor stance as the protagonist of the story.

Experience, consciousness, and fiction

So far I have argued for the sharing of emotions by empathy, for the sharing of intentions as when two people communicate to make a joint plan, and for the sharing of mental models of other, for instance in conversation. A piece of mind that can be held in common between two or more people, then, can include an emotion, a piece of information, and an attitude to this information. It is now widely accepted that rather than thinking of the mind as occurring entirely within a skull, we should think of it as extended (Clark & Chalmers, 1998). So a written shopping list – "broccoli, quinoa, dried apricots" – extends the mind by providing a piece of externalized memory. A piece of mind shared by two people is of much the same kind, for instance when two people agree that broccoli, quinoa, and apricots need to be bought. The sharing is based on the emotional mood of happiness, which, interpersonally, includes trust and cooperativeness. It includes the propositional information about what needs to be bought. And it includes an emotional attitude towards this information.

A recent theory of consciousness clarifies the sharing aspects of engaging with a work of artistic literature. Baumeister and Masicampo (2010) have presented evidence for the idea that consciousness is not generally the means for deciding what action to carry out next. It can have effects on decision-making and action, but over a longer term. Consciousness, they argue, is a simulation that relates past experience (including our models of others), the current social situation, and future goals and plans.

Similarly, when a writer offers us a story he or she has carefully worked on, it is an externalized piece of consciousness, a simulation. It is a piece of consciousness that can be shared. And indeed in reviews of novels, plays, and films, and in reading groups and other such discussions, we can see such sharing taking place. People share with each other their own versions of the consciousness externalized into a story.

Persuasion as compared with art

There are many different kinds of verbal communication in which some aspect of a message is meant to be shared. They include news broadcasts, e-mails, and so on. For the current argument, consider just two kinds of communication: those meant to be persuasive, which Aristotle considered in *Rhetoric*, and those that are artistic literature, which Aristotle considered in *Poetics*.

The intent of a great deal of verbally based communication is to persuade us to see, feel, and decide in the way that an author intends. Green and Brock (2005) have shown that being transported by a narrative is an especially good way of accomplishing persuasion. Van Laer, De Ruyter, Visconti, and Wetzels (2014) have reviewed a large number of studies, which show that people can be persuaded towards particular kinds of emotions and particular kinds of behavioural dispositions. Van Laer et al. conclude that "The more narrative transportation increases, the more story-consistent behavior increases" (p. 812). The effects occur in political speeches, in narratives told to juries, in advertising, and in propaganda. Religion, too, has comparable properties, with people being affected by the stories of religion and coming to share beliefs, and to enact shared ritual actions, or both. If we want to see extremes of sameness that can be accomplished by a concerted persuasion of mass media, we need only to look at certain newsreels from the twentieth century, of men dressed the same (in uniform), who march in the same way (in step), and who share a single purpose (of a nationalistic kind). Hogan (2009) has explained the role, in our lives, of persuasive stories of this political kind.

Some kinds of communication, however, are not kinds of persuasion. They are art. Djikic, Oatley, Zoeterman, and Peterson (2009) and Djikic, Oatley, and Carland (2012) have shown that narrative art can enable people to change their selfhood – their personality – not as an author might direct them, but in their own way.

In a letter dated 27 October 1888 to his mentor, Alexei Suvorin, Anton Chekhov wrote that for an artist there are two things that must not be confused: ". . . answering the questions and formulating them correctly. Only the latter is required of an author. There is not a single question answered in *Anna Karenina* . . . it is the duty of the court to formulate the questions correctly, it is up to each member of the jury to answer them according to his own preference" (Yarmolinsky, 1973, p. 117). In the same way, with the shared understandings of protagonists and other characters, and shared understanding of the circumstances, it is up to readers to understand the significance of the story, and when they change in themselves it is because they are disposed to change, and because of the particular significance they give to the story.

In reading groups, as Todd (2008) has found, there are often two phases of discussion. One is to reach a consensus on what happened in a novel, for instance in the plot. Once the group has come to share a common view of what happened, people tend to move to a second phase in which they talk about what it means for them.

With narrative art, which can include plays, novels, short stories, and films, there is both a shared part – the story and what happened in it – and a non-shared part, in which readers and spectators each make their own interpretations.

Conclusion

I have considered the ways in which pieces of minds can be shared and argued that emotion-based sharing derives from, and enhances, human sociality. Everyday social life as we know it, with its families, its friend-ships, its workplace collaborations, its technologies, would be impossible without the kind of sharing that is involved in theory-of-mind and empathy, based on certain kinds of mimicry. Distinctively, too, we humans also make and share art, which not only enhances our lives but increases our understandings of others and ourselves. Art is important because, although it is shared, it is not intended to achieve universal sameness, but distinctive and individual emotions and judgements. In a well-functioning society, there are both shared elements of mind and also individuality. If everything were shared, we would be shoals of fish. We would have sharedness, sameness, and togetherness, but no society.

References

Aristotle. (1954). *Aristotle: Rhetoric and poetics* (Ed. W.R. Roberts). New York: Random House (Original written circa 330 BCE).

Aubé, M. (2009). Unfolding commitments management: A systemic view of emotions. In J. Valverdu & D. Casacuberta (Eds.), *Handbook of research on synthetic emotions and sociable robotics: New applications in affective computing and artificial intelligence* (pp. 198–227). Hershey, PA: IGI Global.

Averill, J. R. (1982). *Anger and aggression. An essay on emotion.* New York, NY: Springer.

Baumeister, R. F., & Masicampo, E. J. (2010). Conscious thought is for facilitat-ing social and cultural interactions: How mental simulations serve the animal-culture interface. *Psychological Review, 117,* 94–71.

Bouzouggar, A., Barton, N., Vanhaeren, M., d'Errico, F., Collcutt, S., Higham, T., Hodge, E., Parfitt, S., Rhodes, E., Schwenninger, J., Stronger, C., Turner, E., Ward, S., Moutmir, A., & Stambouli, A. (2007). 82,000-year-old shell beads from North Africa and implications for the origins of modern human behavior. *Proceedings of the National Academy of Sciences of the USA, 104,* 9964–9969.

Bowler, J. M., Johnston, H., Olley, J. M., Prescott, J. R., Roberts, R. G., Shawcross, W., & Spooner, N. A. (2003). New ages for human occupation and climatic change at Lake Mungo, Australia. *Nature, 421*(6925), 837–840.

Bruner, J. (1986). *Actual minds, possible worlds.* Cambridge, MA: Harvard University Press.

Butler, E. (2011). Temporal Interpersonal Emotion System: The "TIES" that form relationships. *Personality and Social Psychology Review, 15,* 367–393.

Chauvet, J.-M., Deschamps, E., B., & Hillaire, C. (1996). *Dawn of art: The Chauvet cave.* New York: Abrams.

Clark, A., & Chalmers, D. (1998). The extended mind. *Analysis, 58,* 7–19.

Collingwood, R. G. (1938). *The principles of art.* Oxford: Oxford University Press.

Csikszentmihalyi, M. (1990). *Flow: The psychology of optimal experience.* New York: Harper Collins.

De Vignemont, F., & Singer, T. (2006). The empathetic brain: How, when, and why. *Trends in Cognitive Sciences, 10,* 435–441.

De Waal, F., & Waal, F. B. (2007). *Chimpanzee politics: Power and sex among apes.* JHU Press.

Djikic, M., Oatley, K., & Carland, M. (2012). Genre or artistic merit: The effect of literature on personality. *Scientific Study of Literature, 2,* 25–36.

Djikic, M., Oatley, K., Zoeterman, S., & Peterson, J. (2009). On being moved by art: How reading fiction transforms the self. *Creativity Research Journal, 21,* 24–29.

Djikic, M., Oatley, K., & Carland, M. (2012). Genre or artistic merit: The effect of literature on personality. *Scientific Study of Literature, 2,* 25–36.

Donald, M. (1991). *Origins of the modern mind.* Cambridge, MA: Harvard University Press.

Dunbar, R. I. M. (2003). The social brain: mind, language, and society in evolutionary perspective. *Annual Review of Anthropology, 32,* 163–181.

Dunbar, R. I. M. (2004). Gossip in evolutionary perspective. *Review of General Psychology, 8*(2), 100–110.

Fridlund, A. J. (1994). *Human facial expression: An evolutionary view.* San Diego: Academic Press.

Gallese, V. (2009). Mirror neurons, embodied simulation, and the neural basis of social identification. *Psychoanalytic Dialogues, 19,* 519–536.

Gray, J. A. (1988). The neuropsychological basis of anxiety. In C. G. Last & M. Hersen (Eds.), *Handbook of anxiety disorders* (pp. 10–37). New York: Pergamon Press.

Green, M. C., & Brock, T. C. (2005). Persuasiveness of narratives. In T. C. Brock & M. C. Green (Eds.), *Persuasion: Psychological insights and perspectives,* 2nd ed. (pp. 117–142). Thousand Oaks, CA: Sage.

Halliwell, S. (2002). *The aesthetics of mimesis: Ancient texts and modern problems.* Princeton, NJ: Princeton University Press.

Hastie, R. (2008). Conscious and non-conscious processes in jurors' decisions. In C. Engel & W. Singer (Eds.), *Better than conscious: Decision making, the human mind, and implications for institutions* (pp. 371–390). Cambridge, MA: MIT Press.

Herrmann, E., Call, J., Hernandez-Lloreda, M. V., Hare, B., & Tomasello, M. (2007). Humans have evolved specialized skills of social cognition: The cultural intelligence hypothesis. *Science, 317*, 1360–1366.

Hess, U., & Fischer, A. (2013). Emotional mimicry as social regulation. *Personality and Social Psychology Review, 17*, 142–157.

Hobson, R. P., Lee, A., & Hobson, J. A. (2007). Only connect? Communication, identification, and autism. *Social Neuroscience, 2*, 320–335.

Hoffman, M. L. (2000). *Empathy and moral development: Implications for caring and justice.* New York: Cambridge University Press.

Hogan, P. C. (2009). *Understanding nationalism: On narrative, cognitive science, and identity.* Columbus, OH: Ohio State University Press.

Jones, E. E., & Nisbett, R. E. (1971). *The actor and the observer: Divergent perceptions of the causes of behavior.* New York: General Learning Press.

Kidd, D. C., & Castano, E. (2013). Reading literary fiction improves theory of mind. *Science, 342*, 377–380.

Laplanche, J., & Pontalis, J.-B. (1980). *The language of psychoanalysis.* London: Hogarth Press.

Larocque, L., & Oatley, K. (2006). Joint plans, emotions, and relationships: A diary study of errors. *Journal of Cultural and Evolutionary Psychology, 3–4*, 246–265.

Lovejoy, C. O. (1981). The origin of man. *Science, 211*, 341–350.

Main, M., & George, C. (1985). Response of abused and disadvantaged toddlers to distress in playmates: A study in the daycare setting. *Developmental Psychology, 21*, 407–412.

Mar, R. A., Oatley, K., Hirsh, J., dela Paz, J., & Peterson, J. B. (2006). Bookworms versus nerds: Exposure to fiction versus non-fiction, divergent associations with social ability, and the simulation of fictional social worlds. *Journal of Research in Personality, 40*, 694–712.

Mar, R. A., Oatley, K., & Peterson, J. B. (2009). Exploring the link between reading fiction and empathy: Ruling out individual differences and examining outcomes. *Communications, 34*, 407–428.

Mar, R. A., Tackett, J. L., & Moore, C. (2010). Exposure to media and theory-of-mind development in preschoolers. *Cognitive Development, 25*, 69–78.

Meltzoff, A. N. (1993). The centrality of motor coordination and proprioception in social and cognitive development: From shared actions to shared minds. In G. J. P. Savelsbergh (Ed.), *The development of coordination in infancy* (pp. 463–496). Amsterdam: Elsevier.

Meltzoff, A. N., & Moore, M. K. (1977). Imitation of facial and manual gestures by human neonates. *Science, 198*, 75–78.

Mithen, S. (1996). *The prehistory of the mind: The cognitive origins of art and science.* London: Thames and Hudson.

Nelson, N. L., & Russell, J. A. (2013). Universality revisited. *Emotion Review, 5*, 8–15.

Oatley, K. (1994). A taxonomy of the emotions of literary response and a theory of identification in fictional narrative. *Poetics, 23*, 53–74.

Oatley, K. (1998). Emotion. *The Psychologist, 11,* 285–288.

Oatley, K. (1999). Why fiction may be twice as true as fact: Fiction as cognitive and emotional simulation. *Review of General Psychology, 3,* 101–117.

Oatley, K. (2002). Emotions and the story worlds of fiction. In M. C. Green, J. J. Strange & T. C. Brock (Eds.), *Narrative impact: Social and cognitive foundations* (pp. 39–69). Mahwah, NJ: Erlbaum.

Oatley, K. (2009). Communications to self and others: Emotional experience and its skills. *Emotion Review, 1,* 204–213.

Oatley, K. (2014). Worlds of the possible: Abstraction, imagination, consciousness. *Pragmatics and Cognition, 21,* 448–468.

Oatley, K., & Duncan, E. (1992). Incidents of emotion in daily life. In K. T. Strongman (Ed.), *International Review of Studies on Emotion* (Vol. 2, pp. 250–293). Chichester: Wiley.

Oatley, K., & Johnson-Laird, P. N. (1987). Towards a cognitive theory of emotions. *Cognition and Emotion, 1,* 29–50.

Oatley, K., & Johnson-Laird, P. N. (2014). Cognitive approaches to emotions. *Trends in Cognitive Sciences, 18,* 134–140.

Povinelli, D. J., & O'Neill, D. K. (2000). Do chimpanzees use their gestures to instruct each other? In S. Baron-Cohen, H. Tager-Flusberg, & D. Cohen (Eds.), *Understanding other minds: Perspectives from developmental cognitive neuroscience* (pp. 459–487). Oxford: Oxford University Press.

Rimé, B. (2009). Emotion elicits social sharing of emotion: Theory and empirical review. *Emotion Review, 1,* 60–85.

Rizzolatti, G., Fogassi, L., & Gallese, V. (2001). Neurophysiological mechanisms underlying the understanding and imitation of action. *Nature Reviews: Neuroscience, 2,* 661–670.

Semaw, S., Rogers, M. J., Quade, J., Sileshi, S., Rogers, M. J., Quade, J., Renne, P. R., Butler, R. F., Dominguez-Rodrigo, M., Stout, D., Hart, W. S., Pickering, T., & Simpson, S. W. (2003). 2.6-million-year-old stone tools and associated bones from OGS-6 and OGS-7, Gona, Afar, Ethiopia. *Journal of Human Evolution, 45,* 169–177.

Shakespeare, W. (1600). *Hamlet* (Ed. H. Jenkins). London: Methuen (current edition 1981).

Simon, H. A. (1967). Motivational and emotional controls of cognition. *Psychological Review, 74,* 29–39.

Singer, T., Seymour, B., O'Doherty, J., Kaube, H., Dolan, R. J., & Frith, C. (2004). Empathy for pain involves the affective but not sensory components of pain. *Science, 303,* 1157–1162.

Strack, F., Martin, L. L., Stepper, S. (1988). Inhibiting and facilitating conditions of the human smile: A nonobstrusive test of the facial feedback hypothesis. *Journal of personality and social psychology, 54*(5), 778–777.

Todd, Z. (2008). Talking about books: A reading group study. *Psychology of Aesthetics, Creativity, and the Arts, 2,* 256–263.

Tomasello, M., & Herrmann, E. (2010). Ape and human cognition: What's the difference. *Psychological Science, 19,* 3–8.

Tomasello, M., & Rakoczy, H. (2003). What makes human cognition unique? From individual to shared to collective intentionality. *Mind and Language, 18*, 121–147.

Tomasello, M., & Vaish, A. (2012). Origins of human cooperation and morality. *Annual Review of Psychology, 64*, 231–255.

Trabasso, T., & Chung, J. (2004). *Empathy: Tracking characters and monitoring their concerns in film*. Paper presented at the Winter Text Conference. Jackson Hole, WY.

Turner, M. (2011). The way we imagine. In P. Leverage, H. Mancing, R. Schweickert, & J. Marston (Eds.), *Theory of mind and literature* (pp. 41–61). Purdue: Purdue University Press.

Van Laer, T., De Ruyter, K., Visconti, L. M., & Wetzels, M. (2014). The extended transportation-imagery model: A meta-analysis of the antecedents and consequences of consumers' narrative transportation. *Journal of Consumer Research, 40*, 797–817.

Yamagishi, T., Li, Y., Tagagishi, H., Matsumoto, Y., & Kiyonari, T. (2014). In search of Homo Economicus. *Psychological Science, 25*, 1699–1711.

Yarmolinsky, A. (Ed.). (1973). *Letters of Anton Chekhov*. New York: Viking.

CHAPTER 2

The role of mimicry in understanding the emotions of others

Mariëlle Stel

In conversation with another person, abundant emotions such as happiness, sadness, anger, or fear may be expressed. People may react to the emotional expressions of others by smiling when another person smiles or feeling tears welling up in their eyes when the other person cries. People tend to mimic each other's behaviors, postures, speech, and emotional expressions. They even mimic emotional expressions when the expression is shown subliminally (Dimberg, Thunberg, & Elmehed, 2000). The question that will be addressed in the current chapter is to what extent mimicking these emotional expressions helps people to better understand the emotions of others. It is important to provide an answer to this question, as it would enhance our comprehension of one important function of mimicry, namely to facilitate emotional understanding. Emotional understanding is defined as people's ability to comprehend the emotions of others. One aspect of emotional understanding is recognizing which emotions are expressed. Another aspect is grasping how the other person may feel. This can be facilitated by actually experiencing the emotions oneself (affective empathy) or by understanding the person's situation and thoughts, which facilitates inferring how the other person is feeling (cognitive empathy). Mimicry might facilitate all these aspects.

The present chapter starts with an overview of the relevant theories that may provide an answer to these questions. Next, the chapter discusses empirical evidence in relation to the question whether mimicry enhances emotional understanding. Inconsistencies between studies will be reconciled and an interpretation will be provided as to whether and when mimicry facilitates emotional understanding.

Theories about the relation between mimicry and emotional understanding

The Perception-Behavior Link (which will be discussed more elaborately in Chapter 6, Hawk & Fischer) states that individuals tend to automatically mimic the emotional expressions they observe. Further, the Facial Feedback Hypothesis (Lipps, 1907; Tomkins, 1982) entails that activated facial muscles send signals to the brain, influencing one's emotions accordingly. Because feeling happy mostly co-occurs with smiling, happiness and smiling are strongly associated. Thus, putting on a smile should make people feel happier as a result. According to these two theories, people mimic and therefore express the same emotions as the person they observe, and thus should also feel the same emotions as the person they observe. These experienced emotions may in turn help them to understand the emotions of the other person.

This is also predicted by Embodiment Theory (e.g., Niedenthal, 2007), which implies that bodily states play a role in a person's affective and cognitive states via re-enactment of associated information (see also Chapter 6, Hawk & Fischer). This theory also suggests that adopting specific facial expressions activates corresponding affective as well as cognitive mental states. In sum, both the Facial Feedback Hypothesis and Embodiment Theory can explain why people tend to automatically catch the subjective feelings of another person (also referred to as *emotional contagion*) when they mimic their emotional expressions. Experiencing the same emotions as the other person may help to recognize which emotions are expressed and what the other person experiences. In other words, mimicking emotional expressions of others may help to understand the emotions of others.

Other theorists, however, have argued that catching other people's emotions – which promotes emotional understanding – is not facilitated by mimicking. Mimicry may just be a by-effect of experiencing these emotions oneself, rather than facilitating emotional understanding. It is conceivable that by listening to the story of another person, one catches his or her emotions without mimicry playing a facilitating role. In such cases, mimicry might just be a side effect of spreading activation or of communication (see also Hess & Fischer, 2013). First, when another person talks about a specific topic, one might catch the other person's emotions on the basis of verbal content. For example, stories about a splendid holiday may induce happiness merely as a result of the description of enjoyable activities, which the listener can imagine as being fun. As a result of imagining this happiness, people express their happiness with a smile. This way, people show a facial expression similar to the facial expression of the interaction partner, which is not necessarily due to mimicry, but may result from the spreading activation of feeling happy.

Another possible explanation for the relation between feeling an emotion and mimicking an emotion is that one might mimic the facial expressions of another person in order to communicate that one understands the emotions of the other person. Showing a facial expression similar to the other person's facial expression would be a deliberate signal to show that one cares and understands (e.g., Bavelas, Black, Lemery, & Mullett, 1986; Hess, Houde, & Fischer, 2014). This empathic reaction might show similarities to a mimicry reaction, but is not necessarily the same, making these reactions hard to disentangle.

In sum, according to these theories mimicry may be involved in emotional understanding. However, displaying mimicry does not necessarily mean that one is better able to feel the emotions of others. To provide an answer to the question of whether mimicry does or does not facilitate emotional understanding, we turn to the empirical evidence in the next section. I will discuss research in which the level of mimicry is manipulated, subsequently measuring its effects on emotion recognition and felt empathy. Furthermore, studies on the role of observers' characteristics and of context in the level of mimicry are presented and their implications for the function of mimicry in emotional understanding are discussed. Finally, evidence will be provided on whether mimicry is just a side effect of catching others' emotions.

Empirical evidence

Occurrence of mimicry

Before turning to empirical evidence on whether mimicry plays a role in understanding the emotions of others, it is important to discuss whether mimicry can indeed be observed for many discrete emotions. If not, this would suggest that mimicry does not play such a crucial role in understanding discrete emotions. Previous research has suggested that there is abundant evidence that people mimic emotional expressions like happiness and anger: People smile in reaction to smiling and frown in reaction to frowning. However, a limitation of the majority of studies on emotion mimicry of negative emotions like sadness, fear, and anger is that mimicry reactions have been found for activated muscles that are not emotion specific (i.e., also activated when experiencing another negative emotion). For instance the activation of the Corrugator Supercilii (the muscle that draws the eyebrows down and produces wrinkles on the forehead) is associated with sadness, anger, and fear (Brown & Schwartz, 1980). If emotion-specific mimicry is examined, there appears to be only limited evidence for mimicry of fear and disgust (for an overview, see Hess and Fischer, 2013).

In sum, people tend to mimic other people's emotional expressions, but this mimicry may occur at a more general level rather than at the level of specific emotions. Hess and Fischer (2013) suggested that people may not mimic specific movements, such as frowning, but the interpretation of these movements, which depends on the context as well. Thus, people may react with an anger mimicry when the frown is interpreted as an expression of anger, but with a concerned mimicry response when the frown is interpreted as an expression of concern.

Emotion recognition

Research testing whether emotion recognition is facilitated by mimicry shows mixed results. In several studies no relationship between mimicry and emotion recognition has been found. In a study by Blairy, Herrera, and Hess (1999), for example, participants were shown pictures of facial expressions displaying happiness, sadness, anger, fear, and disgust. Participants were instructed either to mimic these facial expressions or to show incompatible facial expressions. Participants were then asked to indicate for each expression to what extent it displayed happiness, sadness, anger, fear, disgust, contempt, and surprise. For each expression, participants' ratings were recoded as to whether they accurately recognized the posed emotional expression or not. Although the mimicry manipulation was successful, results showed that this manipulation did not affect the accuracy of recognizing the distinct emotions.

Hess and Blairy (2001) also investigated whether people's *spontaneous* mimicry reactions are related to the accuracy of recognizing emotions. Participants were shown short video fragments of 15 seconds, displaying persons who experienced happiness, sadness, anger, or disgust, and who showed at least one visible expression of this emotion. During the video, participants' spontaneous mimicry level was measured with facial electromyography (EMG). They measured accuracy of emotion recognition as did Blairy and colleagues (1999). Although participants spontaneously mimicked the displayed emotions (except for disgust), this mimicry did not help them in more accurately recognizing the emotions.

In another study on the effect of mimicry on emotion recognition, Oberman, Winkielman, and Ramachandran (2007) used a forced choice method. They found only limited evidence of the relation between mimicry and emotion recognition. In their study participants' spontaneous mimicry was either blocked or not. Mimicry was blocked by asking participants to either bite a pen (causing continuous activation across muscles) or to chew gum (causing continuous muscle activation around the lips). Participants were presented with facial emotional expressions for 500 milliseconds after which they indicated, using a forced choice method, whether the expression displayed was conveying happiness, sadness, fear, or disgust. Results showed that blocking mimicry interfered with the recognition of happiness. Furthermore, blocking mimicry with the bite manipulation, but not with the gum manipulation, reduced the recognition of disgust compared to the control condition. However, no effect of blocking mimicry was found for the recognition of sadness and fear.

Although these studies show limited or no evidence of the relation between mimicry and emotion recognition, there are several studies showing that the two are related. Niedenthal, Brauer, Halberstadt, and Innes-Ker (2001), for example, measured the speed at which participants could identify a change in emotion expression. They watched morph movies in which a facial expression changed from happiness to sadness and vice versa. Their task was to indicate when they saw a change in the facial expression. While performing this task, their facial expressions were either blocked (by using a pen in the mouth) or not blocked from mimicking. Participants were faster in detecting the change in emotional expression when they were not constrained to mimic compared to when they were.

In another experiment measuring speed of recognition, Stel and Van Knippenberg (2008) also showed that blocking mimicry interferes with emotion recognition. Participants were shown pictures of emotional facial expressions for 67 milliseconds. They were free to either mimic the expressions or not. For each emotional expression, they had to indicate – by pressing one of two keys – whether the displayed affect was positive or negative. Female participants who were constrained from mimicking were slower in the recognition of affect compared to female participants who were free to mimic.

A similar result was found in an experiment using participants with Botox injections. Neal and Chartrand (2011) showed that participants are less accurate in identifying the emotional expressions when they were unable to mimic these expressions due to the Botox injections. Specifically, all participants received a cosmetic treatment for facial wrinkles. They either received Botox, a fluid that paralyzes facial muscles, or Restylane, a dermal filler that does not block facial muscle feedback. Then, they were asked to identify emotions from pictures by choosing one out of a list of four adjectives that would best represent the depicted emotion. Importantly, the pictures only showed the eyes and the immediate surrounding area (Reading the Mind in the Eyes Test, Baron-Cohen, Wheelwright, Hill, Raste, & Plumb, 2001). The emotion recognition ability of people treated with Botox was worse compared to the people treated with Restylane. In sum, these studies suggest that blocking mimicry impairs emotion recognition.

This has also been found with respect to authenticity judgments of emotion, specifically happiness. People are more likely to accurately infer whether a smile is true or false when they are free to mimic these expressions compared to when mimicry was blocked (with a pen) (Maringer, Krumhumber, Fischer, & Niedenthal, 2011). The false and true smiles differed in onset of the smile, with a true smile having longer onset duration. When mimicking this longer onset duration of a true smile, participants rated the smile as more genuine than when mimicking the shorter onset duration of a fake smile. In the blocked mimicry condition there was no difference in ratings of genuineness. This suggests that mimicking true and false smiles helps in accurately recognizing whether the smile is genuine or not.

In an experiment by Stel, Van Dijk, and Olivier (2009), a seemingly contrasting finding was obtained. In this study, participants (listeners) talked to another participant who was either lying or telling the truth about whether (s)he had donated money to a good cause. The participants listened in three different conditions: they either received no mimicry instructions, or they were instructed to mimic or not to mimic during the conversation. Participants who were instructed not to mimic the expressions of the other person were more accurate in estimating whether the person was lying or not and in estimating the other person's true emotions (guilt and fear) compared to participants who were instructed to mimic and compared to participants who did not receive any mimicry instructions (and showed spontaneous mimicry). Thus, when other people display emotions that are not truly felt, mimicking these false emotional expressions does not help in understanding the true emotions experienced by this person.

Although the study of Maringer et al. (2011) shows that mimicry facilitates detecting truly felt emotions, the results of Stel et al. (2009) suggest the opposite, the results are not necessarily inconsistent. A possible way to reconcile the seemingly inconsistent results is assuming that people use the facial feedback caused by mimicry to infer the emotions of others. A true smile in the study of Maringer et al. is longer in onset duration, so participants receive longer feedback from the muscles associated with happiness, and thus may infer more genuine happiness than when they mimic a shorter onset duration. In the study by Stel et al., participants who lied were trying to inhibit their expressions of fear and guilt, which they experienced more than truth tellers and, possibly, tried to simulate other emotions. While mimicking these expressions of less fear and guilt, one may infer that the other person may not experience these emotions that strongly. Following this argumentation, both studies seem to show that when people mimic the emotions that the other person displays, they infer from their own emotions that the person is actually experiencing these emotions. This would lead to the conclusion that mimicry facilitates the facial recognition of emotions, but not the recognition of whether emotions are truly felt.

When looking at all the evidence on whether mimicry facilitates recognition of emotions that are expressed on the face, the results seem inconsistent: Some studies show no relationship (Blairy et al., 1999; Hess & Blairy, 2001; Oberman et al., 2007); whereas other studies do (Niedenthal et al., 2001; Neal & Chartrand, 2011; Stel & Van Knippenberg, 2008). When examining the differences between the studies showing or not showing a relationship between mimicry and emotion recognition, it becomes clear that mimicking does not help in the accuracy of recognizing the emotions when the emotions are clearly expressed (as in Blairy et al., 1999; Hess & Blairy, 2001; Oberman et al., 2007). Mimicry does facilitate emotion recognition in terms of the speed at which the emotions are recognized and/or in accuracy when the emotions displayed on the face are very subtle (as in Niedenthal et al., 2001; Maringer et al., 2011; Neal & Chartrand, 2011; Stel & Van Knippenberg, 2008). This makes sense as there may be other routes to recognize emotions (Stel & Van Knippenberg, 2008). When the emotion is clearly expressed on the face at least once, one can easily match this visual input with the stored knowledge about emotions. Therefore mimicry may not help in accurately recognizing these clear emotional expressions, especially when having sufficient time to do so. Mimicry, however, does make a difference when it comes to the speed with which individuals accurately identify the expressed emotion and in the accuracy when the emotions are expressed very subtly. In other words, mimicking these subtle expressions provides extra feedback about the emotions expressed. This, however, seems inconsistent with the findings that people do not seem to mimic specific emotions and movements (Hess & Fischer, 2013). However, as mentioned earlier, people do seem to mimic the interpretation of specific emotions and movements (Hess & Fisher, 2013), that may still provide extra feedback about the subtle emotions expressed.

Empathy

Affective empathy

Another aspect of understanding the emotions of others is whether someone experiences the emotions that the other person experiences. Feeling what others are feeling might also help in recognizing the other person's emotions and in better understanding what the other person is feeling emotionally. In the earlier described experiments, Blairy et al. (1999) and Hess and Blairy (2001) also measured to what extent participants reported to experience the same emotions as they observed on the pictures or in the short video fragments. Although evidence for emotional contagion was found (i.e., participants reported to experience more happiness after viewing happy facial expressions and more sadness after viewing sad facial expressions), the extent to which the emotions were felt was not related to their level of mimicry.

In these studies, however, only pictures or short video fragments (15 seconds) were shown. In a study by Stel, Van Baaren, and Vonk (Study 2, 2008) participants were presented with emotional expressions of longer duration. Participants watched a video of 3.5 minutes, observing a person displaying either positive or negative facial expressions. Additionally, participants were asked to either mimic or not mimic these facial expressions. Results showed that participants felt more positive after watching the positive facial expressions when they mimicked compared to when they did not mimic. The same was found for the negative expressions. In another study (Stel & Vonk, 2010), in which two (real) participants interacted for 4 minutes, these effects were replicated. When mimicry occurred during the interaction, participants felt more similar emotions (e.g., happiness, sadness, anger) than when mimicry did not occur.

Taken together, the results on affective empathy suggest that mimicry helps to feel what others are feeling, but the evidence to date advocates that this is limited to the exposure to emotional expressions for a longer period of time. When being exposed to emotional expressions for a short period of time, people do seem to catch the general emotion that is expressed, regardless of mimicry. Mimicking these emotional expressions for a longer time, however, may lead to a more exact match in what people are actually feeling with the emotions they observe. If one really wants to know how another person is feeling, more is needed than the mimicry of just a single display of an emotion.

Alternatively, it could be suggested that longer exposure to an emotion expression also provides more context. It is conceivable that information about a specific context may lead participants to mimic emotions differently (for instance, to mimic emotions only congruent with the context), which may help in experiencing the emotions of the other person. For example, when a person is talking about a sad event, this person may display sad expressions along with nervous or embarrassed smiles. Owing to the longer exposure to the sad story, people may be more likely to mimic only facial expressions that are congruent with the story (i.e., mimicking only sad expressions) or to mimic other emotional expressions in a way that is congruent with the interpretation in that specific context (i.e., mimicking the smile as a nervous/tense smile).

Cognitive empathy

Taking the perspective of another person generally helps to understand the emotions experienced by this person. Hawk, Fischer, and Van Kleef

(2011) suggested that mimicry and perspective taking could both be elicited when observing an emotional display. Mimicry and perspective taking may thus influence each other. Indeed, if mimicry would reinforce perspective taking, this could be another route to a better understanding of emotions. In Stel et al. (2008), in which participants mimicked an emotional person in a video, perspective taking was measured as well. Regardless of the valence of the mimicked emotion, participants reported that they took more perspective of the other person when they mimicked this person compared to when they did not mimic. This may, in part, be influenced by the increase in affective empathy, as affective and cognitive empathy tend to influence one another (Stel, 2005). Thus, both affective and cognitive empathy are increased by mimicry, which supports the idea that mimicry facilitates emotional understanding.

Observer's characteristics and context

Mimicry impairment

Another way to approach this issue is to look at people who have deficits in mimicry and/or in emotional understanding and at people who are more motivated to understand the emotions of others. If people with impaired mimicry have difficulties in emotional understanding also, this provides indirect support for the relationship between mimicry and emotional understanding.

A group of people having impairments in the ability to mimic is people with Möbius syndrome. People with Möbius syndrome are born with bilateral facial paralysis. As a result of this complete or near complete paralysis, they have an impairment in mimicry. Bogart and Matsumoto (2010) investigated whether people with Möbius syndrome also show an impairment in emotion recognition. People with and without Möbius syndrome were asked to indicate the emotion of clear expressions of happiness, anger, sadness, fear, disgust, and surprise. Results indicated no difference of emotion recognition abilities between people with and without Möbius syndrome. This suggests again that for clearly expressed emotions, mimicry does not facilitate recognition.

Another group of people with impairments in emotional understanding are people with Autistic Spectrum Disorders (ASD). People with ASD have problems understanding the emotions of others. Although they are capable of recognizing and categorizing facial expressions (Castelli, 2005; Spezio, Adolphs, Hurley, & Piven, 2007), they have difficulties in interpreting social and emotional signals and initiating and maintaining social relationships (e.g., American Psychiatric Association, 1994; Mehzabin & Stokes, 2011; Tantam, 2003). McIntosh, Reichmann-Decker, Winkielman, and Willbarger (2006) investigated whether the level of spontaneous mimicry is impaired in people with ASD. Participants with ASD and participants matched on chronological age, gender, and verbal ability were shown pictures of happy and angry expressions. Activity in the Zygomaticus Major region (associated with happiness) and the Corrugator Supercilii (associated with anger) was measured using EMG. Results showed that the spontaneous mimicry level of people with ASD was impaired for both anger and happiness compared to participants in the matched control group.

In another study with ASD patients, Stel, van den Heuvel, and Smeets (2008) compared participants with and without ASD to examine the impact of mimicry on their own subjective emotion reports. Participants did not receive any instructions regarding mimicry (and their spontaneous mimicry level was assessed) or were instructed to either mimic or not mimic while watching a video of a young male talking about going to an amusement park. After the video, participants' emotions were measured. Results showed that participants with ASD were capable of mimicry when asked to do so, but this mimicry did not result in feeling more similar emotions to the person expressed on the video. Participants in the control condition did feel more similar emotions in the mimicry than in the no mimicry condition. In another study (Stel, van den Heuvel, and Smeets, 2008; Study 3), it was suggested that the non-facilitating role of mimicry in experiencing similar emotions in people with ASD was because of impairment in their facial feedback mechanism. Holding a pen between the teeth (activating the muscles associated with smiling) resulted in more liking for pictures compared to holding a pen in their non-dominant hand (no smiling muscles activated) for participants in the control condition. However, this effect did not occur for participants with ASD (see Stel, van den Heuvel, and Smeets., 2008). McIntosh et al. (2006) further showed that the impairment in emotional understanding in people with ASD is related to impairment in spontaneous mimicry. Stel, van den Heuvel, and Smeets (2008), however, showed that instructing people with ASD to mimic does not increase the extent to which they catch the emotions of others due to impairment in the facial feedback mechanism as well.

Motivation

If mimicry facilitates emotional understanding, then people with more motivation to understand the emotions of others would be more likely to mimic the emotional expressions. Two studies by Hess, Philippot, and Blairy (1998) suggest that facial expressions are mimicked only when people are asked for an affective judgment (which emotion is expressed), not when other types of judgments are asked (for instance genuineness of the expression). In a similar vein, Cannon, Hayes, and Tipper (2009) showed that more muscle activation is present when making an emotional judgment of facial expressions than when making a color judgment. In their study, participants watched pictures of persons with happy or angry faces. These pictures were either yellow-tinted or blue-tinted and were presented for 1000 milliseconds followed by a blank screen for 1000 milliseconds. Half of the participants were asked to judge whether the expressed emotion on the face was happiness or anger, the other half was asked to judge whether the color of the face was yellow or blue. While doing so, activity in the Zygomaticus Major and Corrugator Supercilii region was measured. The authors found a general effect of greater activity in the Zygomaticus Major region when watching happy compared to angry faces and greater activity in the Corrugator Supercilii region when watching angry compared to happy faces. This mimicry effect was not different for the two types of judgments, but the authors did find that the overall muscle activity was lower when judging faces based on color compared to judgments based on emotion. This seems to suggest that when a person does not need to process the emotion, this results in overall lower facial muscle activity.

The results of Hess et al. (1998) and Cannon et al. (2009) are in line with studies showing that embodiment only occurs when the processing of the emotion is relevant for the task at hand, not when the judgment can be done without understanding the emotions (e.g., Niedenthal, 2007). Thus, facial expressions appear to be mimicked more when we are motivated to understand the emotional expression.

Taken together, although impairment in spontaneous mimicry is not related to recognition of clearly expressed emotions, it seems to result in impaired affective empathy. Furthermore, if individuals want to understand the emotions of others, they mimic more, implying that mimicry facilitates emotional understanding.

Mimicry-like reactions as a result of internal simulation

As suggested earlier, mimicry might not be the only route to understand the emotions of others. When an emotion is clearly expressed, people may recognize the emotion on the basis of visual input and the match with stored knowledge about the features of a happy expression. Functional imaging and lesion studies imply that recognition of emotion occurs in the right hemisphere. Adolphs, Damasio, Tranel, Cooper, and Damasio (2000) investigated brain areas related to the process of emotion recognition. They showed that recognizing emotions from faces that were visually presented resulted in activation in the right somatosensory-related cortices. They therefore argue that emotion recognition requires both visual representations of the expression and somatosensory representations of emotions that are associated with the expression. This argument implies that simulations play an important role in recognizing how the other person feels. As a result of this simulation, individuals may express emotions similar to those the other person is expressing. In other words, people show similar expressions not because they mimic these expressions but because these expressions are a result of internally simulating the emotions. This would also imply that simulating a specific emotion without observing the corresponding facial expression would lead to a facial reaction.

Hawk, Fischer, and Van Kleef (2012) demonstrated this by showing that individuals show corresponding facial expressions to vocal expressions without observing a facial expression. When hearing and reproducing vocalizations of happiness, sadness, anger, and disgust, participants tend to show facial expressions and report emotions congruent with what they hear. In other words, people tend to show mimicry-like reactions, without actually seeing the facial expressions. Magnée, Stekelenburg, Kemner, and de Gelder (2007) also demonstrated that people tend to respond with congruent facial reactions to vocal and bodily expressions of emotions. These mimicry-like reactions might be a result of somatosensory simulation.

As the context and expectations of people can influence how emotions are recognized and interpreted (Hess & Kirouac, 2000), people should show different facial expressions depending on the interpretation, and thus simulation, of the emotion. Studies indeed suggest that the expectation of a future interaction influences one's behavior accordingly (for instance, Cesario, Plaks, & Higgins, 2006). For example, Huntsinger, Lun, Sinclair, and Clore (2009) showed that participants matched their moods to the moods of their interaction partner before their actual interaction. Participants received information (e.g., demographics) about their future interaction partner in which the partner's mood was included. This mood was either positive or negative. Participants who were primed with affiliation were more likely to have a mood similar to the mood of the interaction partner: They felt more positive when they read about the interaction partner being in a positive mood and felt more negative when they read about the interaction partner being in a negative mood. This only occurred for participants who were motivated to affiliate (i.e., no effects were obtained for participants primed with social distance or participants in the control condition). This study suggests that when people are motivated to affiliate, they already match their moods on the basis of their expectation. As this mood matching occurred on the basis of a priori presented information about the other person's mood and before any actual interaction took place, this suggests that mood matching can occur without mimicry. It also implies that when these participants would engage in interaction with the other person, they are more likely to show facial expressions similar to the interaction partner because of having the same mood. This similarity in facial expressions might be interpreted as mimicry, but is actually because of experiencing similar emotions, making it more likely to have similar expressions as well.

The results of a study reported in Hess et al. (2014) also support the idea that people's expressive reactions are influenced by the interpretation, and not the observation of another person's emotion expression. Participants in their study watched persons with neutral facial expressions. They were told that the persons were feeling happy, sad, or angry. While watching the pictures of neutral faces, participants' Zygomaticus Major, Corrugator Supercilii, and Orbicularis Oculi activities were measured with EMG. The results showed that participants displayed congruent activity in their facial expressions depending on the emotions they thought the persons were experiencing (i.e., more Zygomaticus Major activity when thinking the person is feeling happy and more Corrugator Supercilii activity when thinking the person is feeling sad). Importantly, participants did not experience the emotions they expressed. Hence, the facial activation was not because of the emotions they felt themselves. This suggests that the mere imagination of the other person's emotions leads to a corresponding response in their facial expressions. These expressions cannot be because of mimicking, as the displayed facial expressions were neutral. Moreover, these effects were not found when trait descriptions were given together with the picture. Hess et al. suggest that the results can be explained in terms of the communicative function of mimicry. By mimicking the facial expressions of others, people signal that they understand the experienced emotions. This communicative function of mimicry can be regarded as another effect of understanding the emotions of others.

Bavelas et al. (1986) also referred to the communicative function of mimicry. In their study, people winced more when they had eye contact with victims in pain, and did not when their eyes had not met. Participants with increased wincing behaviors were also rated as more caring by naive observers. Bavelas and colleagues concluded that eye contact enhances mimicry reactions and that mimicry serves communication purposes. In line with this idea, Maurer and Tindall (1983) demonstrated that clients rated their counselor as being more empathic when their postures were more congruent. In sum, mimicry-like reactions may be the result of simulating the emotion felt by the other person or the result of communicating that people understand the emotions felt by the other person.

Conclusion

In sum, from the evidence reviewed earlier, we can conclude that mimicry plays an important role in understanding the emotions of others. More specifically, mimicry helps in recognizing the emotions of others, but only in fast recognition tasks or when the emotion expressions are subtle. Mimicry also facilitates cognitive and affective empathy, but only if there is sufficient exposure time, because catching another's feeling is impossible through a one-shot mimicry act. The studies of impairments on mimicry are in line with these findings showing that impairment in spontaneous mimicry is not related to recognition deficits for clearly expressed emotions, but it is related to impaired affective empathy. Finally, motivation to understand the emotions of others leads to more mimicry, and it may be suggested that this process also works vice versa, such that mimicry facilitates emotional understanding.

It is important to keep in mind that mimicry facilitates the understanding of the emotions that are expressed on the face. Thus, when a person is lying, mimicking these false expressions does not facilitate true understanding. Furthermore, people's interpretations of the expressions play a role in how emotions are mimicked. They mimic the emotion that they infer from the facial expressions. That is, people's cognitions play a role in targeting the to-be-mimicked expressions, which accordingly influence people's emotional understanding.

Finally, the fact that mimicry plays a role in emotional understanding does not mean that people need mimicry to understand others, as there are other routes to emotional understanding, for instance via somatosensory simulation. As a result of this internal simulation, people may show expressions that correspond with the simulated emotion. In conclusion, when understanding the emotions of others is difficult (because of speed or subtleness), participants extend their internal simulation to an external simulation of the other person's facial expressions (mimicry) to facilitate the understanding of the expressed emotions.

References

Adolphs, R., Damasio, H., Tranel, D., Cooper, G., & Damasio, A. R. (2000). A role for somatosensory cortices in the visual recognition of emotion as revealed by three-dimensional lesion mapping. *The Journal of Neuroscience, 20,* 2683–2690.

American Psychiatric Association. (1994). *Diagnostic and statistical manual of mental disorders,* 4th ed. Washington, DC: APA.

Baron-Cohen, S., Wheelwright, S., Hill, J., Raste, Y., & Plumb, I. (2001). The "reading the mind in the eyes" test revised version: A study with normal adults, and adults with Asperger syndrome or high-functioning autism. *Journal of Child Psychology and Psychiatry and Allied Disciplines, 42,* 241–251.

Bavelas, J. B., Black, A., Lemery, C. R., & Mullett, J. (1986). "I show how you feel": Motor mimicry as a communicative act. *Journal of Personality and Social Psychology, 50,* 322–329.

Blairy, S., Herrera, P., & Hess, U. (1999). Mimicry and the judgment of emotional facial expressions. *Journal of Nonverbal behavior, 23,* 5–41.

Bogart, K. R., & Matsumoto, D. (2010). Facial mimicry is not necessary to recognize emotion: Facial expression recognition by people with Moebius Syndrome. *Social Neuroscience, 5,* 241–251.

Brown, S. L., &. Schwartz, G. E. (1980). Relationships between facial electromyography and subjective experience during affective imagery. *Biological Psychology, 11,* 49–62.

Cannon, P., Hayes, A., & Tipper, S. (2009). An electromyographic investigation of the impact of task relevance on facial mimicry. *Cognition & Emotion, 23,* 918–929.

Castelli, F. (2005). Understanding emotions from standardized facial expressions in autism and normal development. *Autism, 9,* 428–449.

Cesario, J., Plaks, J. E., & Higgins, E. T. (2006). Automatic social behavior as motivated preparation to interact. *Journal of Personality and Social Psychology, 90,* 893–910.

Dimberg, U., Thunberg, M., & Elmehed, K. (2000). Unconscious facial reactions to emotional facial expressions. *Psychological Science, 11,* 86–89.

Hawk, S. T., Fischer, A. H., & van Kleef, G. A. (2011). Taking your place or matching your face: Two routes to empathic embarrassment. *Emotion, 11,* 502–513

Hawk, S. T., Fischer, A. H., & van Kleef, G. A. (2012). Face the noise: Embodied responses to nonverbal vocalizations of discrete emotions. *Journal of Personality and Social Psychology, 102,* 796–814.

Hess, U., & Blairy, S. (2001). Facial mimicry and emotional contagion to dynamic emotional facial expressions and their influence on decoding accuracy. *International Journal of Psychophysiology, 40,* 129–141.

Hess, U., & Fischer, A. (2013). Emotional mimicry as social regulation. *Personality and Social Psychology Review, 17,* 142–157.

Hess, U., & Kirouac, G., (2000). Emotion expression in Groups. In M. Lewis & J. Haviland-Jones (Eds.), *Handbook of emotion,* 2nd ed. (pp. 368–381). New York: Guilford Press.

Hess, U., Houde, S., & Fischer, A. (2014). Do we mimic what we see or what we know? In C. von Scheve & M. Salmela (Eds.), *Collective emotions* (pp. 94–107). New York: Oxford University Press.

Hess, U., Philippot, P., & Blairy, S. (1998). Facial reactions to emotional facial expressions: Affect or cognition? *Cognition and Emotion, 12,* 509–531.

Huntsinger, J. R., Lun, J., Sinclair, S., & Clore, G. L. (2009). Contagion without contact: Anticipatory mood matching in response to affiliative motivation. *Personality and Social Psychology Bulletin, 35,* 902–922.

Lipps, T. (1907). Das wissen von fremden ichen. In T. Lips (Ed.), *Psychologische Untersuchungen (Band 1)*. Leipzig: Engelmann.

Magnée, M. J. C. M., Stekelenburg, J. J., Kemner, C., & de Gelder, B. (2007). Similar facial electromyographic responses to faces, voices, and body expressions. *Neuroreport: For Rapid Communication of Neuroscience Research, 18,* 369–372.

Maringer, M., Krumhuber, E. G., Fischer, A. H., & Niedenthal, P. M. (2011). Beyond smile dynamics: Mimicry and beliefs in judgments of smiles. *Emotion, 11,* 181–187.

Maurer, R. E., & Tindall, J. H. (1983). Effect of postural congruence on client's perception of counselor empathy. *Journal of Counseling Psychology, 30,* 158–163.

McIntosh, D. N., Reichmann-Decker, A., Winkielman, P., & Wilbarger, J. L. (2006). When the social mirror breaks: Deficits in automatic, but not voluntary, mimicry of emotional facial expressions in autism. *Developmental Science, 9,* 295–302.

Mehzabin, P., & Stokes, M. (2011). Self-assessed sexuality in young adults with high functioning Autism. *Research in Autism Spectrum Disorders, 5,* 614–621.

Neal, D., & Chartrand, T. L. (2011). Embodied emotion perception: Amplifying and dampening facial feedback modulates emotion perception accuracy. *Social Psychological and Personality Science, 2,* 673–678.

Niedenthal, P. M. (2007). Embodying emotion. *Science, 18,* 1002–1005.

Niedenthal, P. M., Brauer, M., Halberstadt, J., & Innes-Ker, A. H. (2001). When did her smile drop? Facial mimicry and the influences of emotional state on the detection of change in emotional expression. *Cognition & Emotion, 15,* 853–864.

Oberman, L. M., Winkielman, P., & Ramachandran, V. S. (2007). Face to face: Blocking facial mimicry can selectively impair recognition of emotional expressions. *Social Neuroscience, 2,* 3–4.

Spezio, M. L., Adolphs, R., Hurley, R. S. E., & Piven, J. (2007). Abnormal use of facial information in high-functioning autism. *Journal of Autism and Developmental Disorders, 37,* 929–939.

Stel, M. (2005). *The social functions of mimicry: On the consequences and qualifiers of facial imitation*. Nijmegen: Prisma Print.

Stel, M. & van Knippenberg, A. (2008). The role of facial mimicry in the recognition of affect. *Psychological Science, 19,* 984–985.

Stel, M., Van Baaren, R. B., & Vonk, R. (2008). Effects of mimicking: Acting prosocially by being emotionally moved. *European Journal of Social Psychology, 38,* 965–976.

Stel, M., van den Heuvel, C., & Smeets, R. C. (2008). Facial feedback mechanisms in Autistic Spectrum Disorders. *Journal of Autism and Developmental Disorders, 38,* 1250–1258.

Stel, M., van Dijk, E., & Olivier, E. (2009). You want to know the truth? Then don't mimic! *Psychological Science, 20,* 693–699.

Stel, M., & Vonk, R. (2010). Mimicry in social interaction: Benefits for mimickers, mimickees and their interaction. *British Journal of Psychology, 101,* 311–323.

Tantam, D. (2003) The challenge of adolescents and adults with Asperger syndrome. *Child and Adolescent Psychiatric Clinics of North America, 12,* 143–163, vii–viii.

Tomkins, S. S. (1982). Affect theory. In P. Ekman (Ed.), *Emotion in the human face,* 2nd ed. (pp. 353–395). Cambridge: Cambridge University Press.

CHAPTER 3

Revisiting the Simulation of Smiles model: the what, when, and why of mimicking smiles

Paula M. Niedenthal, Sebastian Korb, Adrienne Wood, and Magdalena Rychlowska

Facial expressions accompany almost every social exchange, but there is more to them than meets the eye. Darwin believed that facial expressions are vestiges of solutions to long-past evolutionary challenges (Darwin, 1872); for instance, the lifted upper lip and wrinkled nose accompanying feelings of disgust probably evolved to help block or expel noxious smells or poisonous food. According to the Darwinian account, social animals, including our ancestors, began to use facial actions to communicate internal states and external dangers to others. Later, the communicative purpose of the facial movements eventually superseded the functional purpose (Darwin, 1872; Frith, 2009; Hess & Thibault, 2009).

However, the expressions of modern-day humans may still serve those original functions. For example, when individuals made facial expressions of fear (compared to neutral emotion), they executed more efficient eye movements in the localization of targets, their visual fields were subjectively larger, and their nasal volume and air velocity during inspiration increased. All of these reactions are useful in preparation for fighting or fleeing from a threat. In contrast, facial expressions of disgust appear to be associated with the constriction and slowing of such processes (Susskind et al. 2008; cf. Krusemark & Li, 2011) so that perception and ingestion of toxic or rotten objects can be minimized. Thus, expressive facial action can aid in generating the bodily responses that promote successful resolution of challenges to survival.

Still, human facial expressions are primarily communicative, and are a means to quickly convey status, motivation, affect, and other social information including the probability of cooperative or prosocial action (Anderson & Thompson, 2004; Brown, Palameta, & Moore, 2003; Scharlemann, Eckel, Kacelnik, & Wilson, 2001) and information about personality (Ames & Johar, 2009; Hareli & Hess, 2010; Harker & Keltner, 2001). Facial expressions also function as rewards (Matthews & Wells,

44

1999) and punishments (Blair, 1995) in learning (see also Blair, 2003; Gerull & Rappee, 2002; Mumme & Fernald, 1996). In this context there is lively debate about whether expressions of emotion are universal (Jack, Garrod, Yu, Caldara, & Schyns, 2012; Russell, 1994) and about how differences might be produced across individuals and across cultures (Elfenbein, Beaupré, Lévesque, & Hess, 2007; Wehrle, Kaiser, Schmidt, & Scherer, 2000). Whether expressions of emotion are innate or learned via socialization, it seems clear that typically developing individuals can usually accurately interpret and act on the facial expressions of others.

How do humans go about the complex task of deciphering the innumerable facial expressions they encounter? It may be that at any given moment in a social interaction, both the communicator *and* the perceiver produce facial expressions. The communicator, as described earlier, conveys an intention or emotion, while the perceiver produces visible or nonvisible corresponding facial expressions to decode the communicator's expression (e.g., Atkinson, 2007; Decety & Chaminade, 2003; Gallese, 2003, 2005; Keysers & Gazzola, 2007; Niedenthal, 2007; Niedenthal, Barsalou, Winkielman, Krauth-Gruber, & Ric, 2005; Winkielman, McIntosh, & Oberman, 2009). This theoretical proposition has a long history in philosophy and scientific psychology. Imitation of another person's facial expression of emotion, for example, was proposed by Theodor Lipps to be the basis of empathic responding (Lipps, 1903).

The present chapter explores how facial mimicry informs the perceiver about the emotion underlying another's facial movements. We adopt the hypothesis that mimicking a perceived facial expression facilitates embodied simulation of that expression and of the accompanying affective state. When we use the term "embodied simulation," we mean that a facial expression has triggered in the perceiver a simulation of a state in the motor, somatosensory, affective, and reward systems that is used by the perceiver to decode the expression's meaning. Thus, from this view, the perception of a facial expression is accompanied by some of the bodily and neural states associated with the expression and its corresponding emotion. The simulation is then used as the representation of meaning on which an interpretation or judgment is based. Facial mimicry should be an important part of this process.

In the present chapter, we review the empirical support for this position by using the human smile as a case study. We use as our theoretical platform the Simulation of Smiles model (SIMS; Niedenthal, Mermillod, Maringer, & Hess, 2010), a theory of how individuals decode the human smile, and then review research findings that test specific predictions of the model. We begin with a provisional definition of facial mimicry and a synopsis of the current challenges in its measurement. We then present neurological evidence of how mimicry unfolds in the brain and relates to perceptual processing of expression. The next issue discussed refers specifically to the smile and asks which smiles exist and *"what* do we mimic?" Indeed, the social–functional position of the SIMS model proposes that three classes of smile are used for "love, sympathy, and war" (Rychlowska et al., 2014, p. 1), or for the social tasks of rewarding behavior, creating and maintaining social bonds, and constructing or maintaining social hierarchies. We review new evidence in support of this social–functional account.

The second question we explore is *"when* do we mimic?" Mimicry is not always necessary or dominant in facial expression processing because other inputs can guide the decoding of facial expression of emotion (see Niedenthal et al., 2010, for details). The SIMS model holds that one sufficient trigger of facial mimicry is eye contact. We present novel data addressing this hypothesis. One of the SIMS model's key claims points to the utility of mimicry for decoding smiles. The final question is *"why* do we mimic?" The SIMS model asserts that mimicry is especially useful for distinguishing between the subtle meanings of different smiles. Evidence in favor of this claim is reported.

In sum, this chapter focuses on the nature, the role and the triggers of facial mimicry in smile processing. Before addressing these questions, however, we need to agree on a definition of facial mimicry and set out the open questions in the extant research in this area.

Facial mimicry: challenges of definition and measurement

Anyone who catches themselves smiling while watching a person smile on TV or unintentionally imitating a friend's odd facial expression in order to determine what she is feeling "knows" they have engaged in facial mimicry. Photos that capture persons mirroring one another with a very specific type of (gaping or silly) smile seem to "document" facial mimicry. But the scientific definition of this imitation process remains elusive or at the very least debatable, and measurement follows closely along in being suboptimal most of the time. First, mimicry is difficult to distinguish from having a parallel emotional reaction or reacting emotionally to the perceived face as a stimulus (e.g., Hess & Fischer, 2013; Moody, McIntosh, Mann, & Weisser, 2007). Furthermore, however defined, mimicry is a response to a stimulus and both the stimulus and response unfold over a particular time course. How, in theory, should those time courses match or overlap? What is the time lag over which a smile response to a perceived smile constitutes mimicry rather than an emotional reaction? Finally, facial expressions combine different facial units or features. Does facial mimicry involve complete matching of all relevant facial actions with a precise degree of intensity? These questions all await fuller scientific treatment.

Past research has often defined mimicry as any activity on the perceiver's face that matches some or all of the expression on the target's face. In our most recent work (e.g., Korb, With, Niedenthal, Kaiser, & Grandjean, 2014; Rychlowska et al., 2014), we operationalize mimicry in a different way, namely in terms of the correlation over time in the activation of major action units in the *communicator's* face and the *perceiver's* face. Clearly, the more precise our measurement of the matching between the stimulus and the response can be, the more certain we can be that a response constitutes facial mimicry. Capturing correspondence (or the lack of it) is one of the main challenges in the research on facial mimicry. In the present chapter we adopt a working definition of mimicry based on this criterion and propose that *a perceiver's facial response is mimicry if it temporally and physiologically matches the target's expression.* We do not hold that mimicry has to activate all the facial muscles involved with the same intensity as in the target's face, but we do expect similar patterns of facial muscle activations. In other words, facial mimicry may sometimes only involve producing a "trace" version of the target's expression.

In the SIMS model (Niedenthal et al., 2010), facial mimicry involves, sequentially, (1) the *perception* of a facial expression of emotion, (2) the partial simulation (i.e., *production*) of the perceived expression, and (3) the processing of one's own facial feedback. The visual and somatosensory information is then integrated to help interpret another person's emotional expression. It can thus be assumed that facial mimicry recruits, at the very least, neural structures involved in (1) basic visual perception of emotional faces, (2) the production, and (3) the somatosensation of facial movements. The precise neural bases of automatic facial mimicry are, to date, not completely understood. Nevertheless, insights about the brain structures relevant for facial mimicry may be obtained by focusing on what we know about the neural bases of the *perception* and *production* of facial expressions, which is our aim for the next section.

The neural bases of facial mimicry

The neural circuitry underlying the perception of facial expressions is complex and debated. Accumulating evidence points to a very extensive and distributed neural network, including cortical and subcortical areas, and multiple feed-forward and feedback connections (Adolphs, 2002a, 2002b; Haxby et al., 2001; Vuilleumier & Pourtois, 2007). A more limited set of subcortical structures including the amygdala has been suggested to underlie quick, simple, and unconscious processing of emotional faces

(De Gelder, Vroomen, Pourtois, & Weiskrantz, 1999; LeDoux, 1996; Morris, Ohman, & Dolan, 1999). This so-called low road may be of particular interest in relation to facial mimicry, since the quick and spontaneous occurrence of facial mimicry implies its need for an even faster – although simplistic – stimulus perception in the first place.

In addition, the right somatosensory cortices have been proposed to support the recognition of facial expressions based on a large sample of patients with focal lesions (Adolphs, Damasio, Tranel, Cooper, & Damasio, 2000) and based on the impairing effects of transcranial magnetic stimulation (TMS) over the right somatosensory cortex on speed and accuracy of emotion recognition (Pitcher, Garrido, Walsh, & Duchaine, 2008; Pourtois et al., 2004). These brain areas are likely to be involved in the facial feedback occurring during facial mimicry.

One can assume that the production of automatic facial mimicry utilizes parts of the same neural circuitry involved in the production of spontaneous facial expressions of emotion (i.e., that are not caused by the perception of another's expression). Of specific interest here is the discovery of a double dissociation between volitional facial paresis (VFP) and emotional facial paresis (EFP), suggesting that voluntary and spontaneous facial movements stem from partly distinct neural structures (Hopf, Muller-Forell, & Hopf, 1992). In EFP the capacity to show emotional facial expressions (e.g., smiling at a joke) is impaired or lost, while the ability to contract facial muscles voluntarily is spared. EFP has been reported following lesions of the thalamus, the striatocapsular area, the frontal subcortical white matter, the insula, the medial frontal lobe including the supplementary motor area (SMA), or the dorsolateral pontine tegmentum area (Hopf et al., 1992; Iwase et al., 2002; Morecraft, Stilwell-Morecraft, & Rossing, 2004). Moreover, EFP also occurs in patients with Parkinson's disease (Gazzaniga & Smylie, 1990).

In contrast, VFP causes difficulties in the production of voluntary movements of the (mostly contralateral) facial muscles, without impairing a person's emotional facial expressions. VFP is commonly observed with lesions of the contralateral primary motor cortex (M1) and/or the lateral premotor cortex (LPMC) or along the corticobulbar tract descending to the facial nucleus (Hopf et al., 1992). However, a case of VFP in the lower right face has also been reported in conjunction with a vascular lesion of the left SMA (Jox, Bruning, Hamann, & Danek, 2004). In line with this, tracing studies in nonhuman primates suggest that the SMA contributes to the planning and execution of voluntary facial movements. Two areas of the cingulate cortex may also be involved in the production of spontaneous, emotional facial expressions (Korb & Sander, 2009; Morecraft et al., 2004; Morecraft & Van Hoesen, 1998).

In sum, neurological and neuroanatomical studies suggest that the production of spontaneous emotional facial expressions relies on the basal ganglia and other subcortical areas, the medial frontal lobe including cingulate motor cortices, and the insula. In contrast, voluntary facial movements rely mostly upon M1 and other motor cortices located laterally on the hemispheres. The role of the SMA is uncertain, because this structure has been implicated in both voluntary and spontaneous facial expressions. Finally, the separation of the brain systems for the production of voluntary and spontaneous facial expressions may not be as strict, since voluntary motor commands generated in M1 can receive emotional "coloring" when passing through the brain stem (Korb & Sander, 2009).

The neural bases of the production of spontaneous and voluntary facial expressions were also investigated using brain-imaging techniques such as functional magnetic resonance imaging (fMRI). Iwase et al. (2002) reported correlations between Zygomaticus Major activation during spontaneous smiling and activity of the bilateral SMA and left putamen. Zygomaticus Major activation during voluntary smiling correlated with brain activity in the bilateral M1 and again the SMA. Importantly, the SMA activation was stronger in the voluntary than spontaneous condition. A study by Wild et al. (2006) found increased activity in the primary sensorimotor cortices and the SMA during voluntary smiling. Spontaneous smiling, on the other hand, led to increased activation in the temporal poles, hippocampi, amygdala, parahippocampal gyri, the left frontal operculum, and the thalamus. Hennenlotter et al. (2005) report that voluntary smiles are associated with widespread activations in cortical sensorimotor and premotor areas (including the pre-SMA, the anterior cingulate cortex [ACC], M1, and the primary sensorimotor cortex [S1]), the insula, subcortical structures (putamen, thalamus, globus pallidus, dorsal amygdala), and the cerebellum. However, participants' facial movements were not measured, and the production of posed and spontaneous smiles was not compared. Similarly, Schilbach, Eickhoff, Mojzisch, & Vogeley (2008) did not measure facial movements in the fMRI, but examined facial mimicry in a separate EMG study, using the same stimuli and paradigm. They report greater activation in the left precentral motor area as well as in other areas not related to motricity (e.g., posterior cingulate cortex) in response to avatars displaying socially relevant (e.g., smiling) compared to arbitrary (e.g., blowing the cheeks) facial expressions. Schilbach and colleagues' suggestion that spontaneous facial mimicry is partially rooted in the lateral motor and premotor areas seems to contradict most of the neurological and brain-imaging literature reviewed here.

Overall, neuroimaging studies of voluntary vs. spontaneous facial movements confirm the findings from patients' studies, that is, that lateral somatomotor areas including M1 support mainly voluntary facial movements, while spontaneous facial expressions recruit rostro-medial motor cortices (SMA, cingulate motor areas) and subcortical structures like the basal ganglia. Interestingly, while cases of both EFP and VFP have been reported in combination with SMA lesions, brain-imaging studies rather suggest a role for the SMA in the planning and execution of voluntary facial expressions.

To the best of our knowledge, facial mimicry has not been directly measured in patients with either VFP or EFP. A limited number of brain-imaging studies, however, have recorded brain activity related to the voluntary and/or spontaneous mimicry of facial expressions. Lee, Josephs, Dolan, and Critchley (2006) asked participants to voluntarily imitate certain facial movements. They report greater activation of the bilateral motor and premotor cortices as well as the right inferior frontal gyrus during the intentional imitation of sad, angry, and happy faces. These findings confirm the importance of the lateral motor cortices for the production of voluntary facial movements, and suggest a role for the right inferior frontal gyrus in the voluntary imitation of emotional facial expressions. They cannot, however, inform us about the neural correlates of automatic facial mimicry.

Likowski et al. (2012) induced facial mimicry in the fMRI using pictures of avatar faces displaying a neutral, happy, sad, or angry expression, and simultaneously recorded participants' facial EMG from the left Corrugator Supercilii and Zygomaticus Major muscles. Focusing on a large set of a priori defined regions of interest, significant correlations were found between Zygomaticus Major and brain activation to happy faces in the right caudate, left cerebellum, right inferior frontal gyrus (IFG), left posterior cingulate cortex, right supplementary motor area), and right medial temporal gyrus (MTG). Corrugator Supercilii activity, on the other hand, correlated with brain activity to angry faces in the left cerebellum, and in the right hemisphere with the IFG, hippocampus, insula, SMA, and superior temporal sulcus (STS). The study by Likowski and colleagues thus found Zygomaticus Major reactions to happy expressions and Corrugator Supercilii reactions to angry faces to be correlated with activations in the right IFG, the right SMA, and the left cerebellum. The observed differences between emotions may suggest that the neural correlates of facial mimicry vary depending on the emotion perceived. Interestingly, only some of the areas reported here (e.g., the SMA, caudate) coincide with the sites of brain lesions reported in cases of EFP.

In summary, fMRI studies of direct facial mimicry (as opposed to non-mimicking facial expressions) suggest that both voluntary and spontaneous facial mimicry require the right inferior frontal gyrus. In addition, voluntary mimicry activates the lateral motor cortices bilaterally, whereas spontaneous mimicry may activate the right SMA and the left cerebellum. Finally, findings by Likowski et al. suggest that spontaneous mimicry of happiness correlates with activity in the caudate, posterior cingulate, and MTG, whereas mimicry of anger activates the hippocampus, insula, and STS.

Consistent with the SIMS model, the reviewed research suggests that facial mimicry engages both motor and somatosensory areas of the brain (Niedenthal et al., 2010). At the neural level, facial mimicry could unfold as follows: (1) An initial, basic, and unconscious visual perception of another person's facial expression and gaze may take place in subcortical circuits involving the amygdala. Indeed, facial mimicry can occur even in the absence of conscious face perception (Dimberg, Thunberg, & Elmehed, 2000; Mathersul, McDonald, & Rushby, 2013; Neumann, Schulz, Lozo, & Alpers, 2014). (2) Spontaneous motor commands – generated mostly subcortically, but also in cingulate motor areas, the SMA, and parts of the mirror neuron system – produce facial mimicry of the perceived facial expression. This assumption is based on studies with patients, on tracing studies in nonhuman primates, and in recent brain-imaging studies (Hopf et al., 1992; Likowski et al., 2012; Morecraft et al., 2004; Morecraft & Van Hoesen, 1998). In contrast, the original proposition of the SIMS was that motor and premotor cortices lying on the lateral walls of each hemisphere, known to allow voluntary movements of the mostly contralateral facial muscles, also underlie the production of spontaneous facial mimicry. (3) The proprioceptive feedback of this facial mimicry is processed by (right) somatosensory areas of the brain, as suggested by impaired expression recognition after inhibition (TMS) or lesion of these areas (Adolphs et al. 2000; Pitcher et al., 2008; Pourtois et al., 2004). (4) Simultaneously, a more precise analysis of the perceived expression takes place in visual, and associative, cortices through feed-forward and feedback loops (Lamme, Super, & Spekreijse, 1998). (5) Finally, an integration of the visual perception and somatosensory processing of one's own facial mimicry, together with contextual knowledge, may take place in higher associative cortices.

This circuitry is thought to underlie the production of all spontaneous facial mimicry, although differences between facial expressions are also expected. The predictions of the SIMS model for understanding the neural basis of mimicking specific categories of smiles will be the subject of future research. In the next section we will ask *what* types of functional smiles are available to be mimicked.

What smiles do we mimic?

The SIMS model, developed as a theory of embodied simulation in the processing of facial expression, focuses on the human smile as a sort of case study. Studying human smiles is useful for a better understanding of the functions of facial mimicry. Among other grounds for this claim, the most important is that smiles are unique in their ability to express a wide range of social messages, such as joy, contempt, politeness, embarrassment, and threat (see LaFrance, 2011; Niedenthal et al., 2010, for a review). Empirical evidence links emotional contagion and mimicry of smiles to the perception and processing of these facial expressions (Korb, With, Niedenthal, Kaiser, & Grandjean, 2014; Krumhuber, Likowski, & Weyers, 2013; Manera, Grandi, & Colle, 2013; Maringer, Krumhuber, Fischer, & Niedenthal, 2011; Rychlowska et al., 2014; Schneider, Hempel, & Lynch, 2013) and shows that smiles elicit strong, easily measurable facial responses (Oberman, Winkielman, & Ramachandran, 2007). The complexity of smiles and the amplitude of their mimicry make the study of these facial expressions especially promising for a better understanding of the functions of facial mimicry. It is also crucial to develop working and empirically validated typologies of smiles.

One such typology is proposed by the SIMS model, which groups smiles according to their social functions. The proposed functions that these facial expressions accomplish are (1) rewarding self and other, (2) maintaining social bonds, and (3) negotiating social hierarchies. Smiles that serve such functions are called *pleasure, affiliative,* and *dominance* smiles, respectively. They reflect internal states and emotions of the smiler, but also communicate social motives and behavioral intentions.

Pleasure smiles are closely related to the so-called *true* or *enjoyment* smiles, and reflect internal states elicited by positive social or sensory experience. Their main function is to communicate pleasure, thus rewarding oneself and others. The category of pleasure smiles is homogeneous and well defined compared to the two other classes (Frank, Ekman, & Friesen, 1993). The category of affiliative smiles may include different subclasses, such as polite, embarrassed, or greeting smiles. These smiles promote the creation and maintenance of social bonds (Cashdan, 1998; Fischer, Becker, & Veenstra, 2012; Fridlund, 1991, 2002) and communicate positive social motives other than joy. Finally, dominance smiles show and maintain social or moral status (perceived, not necessarily sanctioned), and thus help to define one's position in a given hierarchy. This category of smiles may involve displays of contempt (Ekman, 1992), derision (Carranza, Prentice, & Larsen, 2012), and pride (Tracy & Robins, 2007). Unlike pleasure and affiliative smiles, dominance smiles are predicted to convey and elicit negative feelings.

Initial evidence supporting this typology was provided by a cross-cultural study conducted in nine countries in North America, Europe, Asia, and the Pacific Rim (Niedenthal et al., 2013). We assessed the endorsement of motives and feelings associated with smiling in these countries. A factor analysis revealed a structure consistent with the three smile types proposed by the SIMS model – that is, participants' responses grouped into clusters corresponding to reward, bonding, and hierarchy-managing functions. The findings therefore motivated us to investigate the patterns of facial activity characterizing these displays.

To this end, we used a data-driven approach combining a flexible computer graphic platform and the technique of reverse correlation (Generative Face Grammar, GFG; Yu, Garrod, & Schyns, 2012; Jack et al., 2012). The technique generates predictions about individuals' mental representations of facial expressions without being influenced by researchers' expectations. We created a large number ($N = 2400$) of videos representing random facial expressions of realistic 3-D models. Each of them contained smiling (*lip corner puller*; also called action unit [AU] 12, in the Facial Action Coding System [FACS]; Ekman, Friesen, & Hager, 2002) and combined it with 1 to 4 other AUs. We also varied 6 temporal parameters controlling the time course of each facial expression (Rychlowska et al., 2014).

The experiment involved untrained observers from France and the United States. Participants first read definitions of the three smiles and the corresponding situations. Examples of situations included learning about getting hired in somebody's dream job (pleasure smile), thanking somebody for their help in a store (affiliation smile), and crossing paths with an enemy after winning an important prize (dominance smile). After reading the instructions, participants completed a multi-session online study. They viewed the 2,400 random smiles and categorized them as instances of pleasure, affiliative, and dominance smiles, or no smile. We then used participants' responses to extract the patterns of facial activity – including a precise description of the AUs – corresponding to each of the functional smiles, and synthesized videos corresponding to the new prototypes for the smiles of pleasure, affiliation, and dominance.

The representations of French and American participants were significantly correlated, suggesting the validity and generalizability of our findings. The three categories of smiles were also related to different patterns of facial activity. Pleasure smiles involved bilateral and symmetrical action of the Zygomaticus Major muscle (AU 12) and eyebrow flashes (AU 2). Lip stretching (AU 20), pressing (AU 24), and dimpler activity (AU 14) were typical of affiliative smiles. These smiles also involved bilateral Zygomaticus Major activity, though less consistently than pleasure smiles. Dominance smiles were asymmetric (AU 12L) and involved displays of disgust (AU 10) and cheek raising (AU 6).

The psychological–perceptual validity of reconstructed smile proto-types was assessed in three recognition studies. In these experiments, new untrained observers classified the prototypes as pleasure, affiliation, and dominance smiles, and associated them with corresponding social motives. All the studies yielded similar results. Participants were very accurate in distinguishing and classifying dominance and enjoyment smiles. Affiliative smiles, however, were confounded with pleasure smiles. Both smiles were also associated with prosocial motives, that is, communicating positive emotions and friendly intentions. Future studies will focus on the facial action units that distinguish affiliative smiles from pleasure smiles and on identifying possible subtypes of the former cate-gory – such as embarrassment, polite, or greeting smiles.

The prototypes of smiles created with the technique of GFG do not represent *actual* instances of smiles described in the SIMS model. Instead, they can be interpreted as collections of indicators about facial actions relevant to these smiles. That is, a naturally occurring affiliative smile may involve a combination of some but not all of the relevant action units (AUs 12, 20, 24, 14). Though not ecological per se, the models provide a framework for identifying and describing naturalistic smiles of plea-sure, dominance, and affiliation.

The typology of the three social–functional smiles provides a paradigm for testing the influences of the social context to a greater extent than the classic distinction between true and false smiles. It also offers the opportunity to test the mimicry of smiles perceived as *negative* facial expressions (Huang & Galinski, 2010). Another important question is related to the brain regions involved in the perception and processing of the social–functional smiles. A better understanding of the morphology and the time course of the enjoyment, affiliative, and dominance smiles will allow a precise investigation of the underlying neural structures.

We have defined facial mimicry, discussed the brain regions involved in embodied simulation, and laid out a novel approach to categorizing smile types. Now that we have a better understanding of the *what* of mimicry, we will explore *when* mimicry is more likely to occur.

When do we mimic smiles?

The SIMS model posits that people can use multiple processes to decode facial expression. These are not necessarily mutually exclusive; people automatically recruit different processes depending on the demands of the task (Adolphs, 2002a; Atkinson, 2007; Kirouac & Hess, 1999). One process involves the integration of low-level perceptual cues, such as the visibility of teeth in a smile, and the matching of the resulting information to mental representations of expression prototypes. The neural basis of this strategy seems to be the occipito-temporal cortices (Adolphs, 2002a). Such a pattern-matching process may be preferable for lower demand tasks, such as the classification of prototypical expressions into basic categories (Buck, 1984).

Indeed, Dailey, Cottrell, Padgett, and Adolphs (2002) trained a neural network computer model to classify six basic emotion expressions – anger, happiness, disgust, fear, sadness, and surprise – and demonstrated that prototypical expressions are inherently "categorical" in nature. Thus, the morphology of each of these prototypical expressions is unique enough that even a machine will classify slight variations of a given emotion, such as anger, as belonging to the same "angry" category. Smith, Cottrell, Gosselin, and Schyns (2005) similarly suggest that configurations of muscles that have emerged during phylogenetic development of the human species maximize differences between the six basic emotional expressions and lead to efficient recognition of these expressions.

While the proposed pattern-matching route to emotion processing is an efficient way to distinguish between basic categories of expressions, different processes may be required to interpret less prototypic, perhaps more realistic, emotion expressions. In such cases, we propose that perceivers call on various sources of nonvisual information, such as conceptual emotion knowledge about the expresser and the social situation (Kirouac & Hess, 1999; Niedenthal, 2008). For example, faces provide information about the sex, age, and race of the other person, and people possess expectations and stereotypes about how members of these social groups react emotionally (Hess, Adams, & Kleck, 2005). Such knowledge about emotion has been shown to exert effects early in the processing of ambiguous facial expressions (e.g., Halberstadt & Niedenthal, 2001; Halberstadt, Winkielman, Niedenthal, & Dalle 2009; Hess & Thibault, 2009).

Both the *perceptual* visual pattern-matching route, which lends itself to more categorical perception of expressions (Calder, Young, Perrett, Etcoff, & Rowland, 1996), and the conceptual knowledge-based route, which applies beliefs and stereotypes, may fail to distinguish the subtle meanings of the thousands of possible variations in facial expressions. We therefore propose that when the perceived facial expression is complex, ambiguous, or particularly relevant for the observer, its correct recognition will rely on embodied simulation processes, including mimicry.

This proposal still requires reference to possible behavioral mediators, of course. According to SIMS, eye contact is one candidate trigger to facial mimicry. A collection of imaging studies suggests that activation in certain brain regions increases specifically in response to the perception of eye contact, which in turn modulates concurrent cognitive and behavioral responses, underscoring the importance of rapidly detecting eye contact and responding appropriately (for a review see, Senju & Johnson, 2009). Recent evidence also suggests that faces achieving eye contact are localized more rapidly than faces with averted gaze and that eye contact is processed outside of conscious awareness (Stein, Senju, Peelen, & Sterzer, 2011). Being the target of another's gaze increases the tendency to approach (Hietanen, Leppanen, Peltola, Linna-aho, & Ruuhiala, 2008), and the responses of the mirror neuron system (suggested to be a possible substrate of facial mimicry) seem more likely to occur when the actor is facing the perceiver, which signals social relevance of the observed action (Kilner, 2006).

Early evidence for the role of eye contact in mimicry showed that mimicry of pained expressions increases when the perceiver can see the eyes of the victim (Bavelas, Black, Lemery, & Mullett, 1986). More recently, Schrammel and colleagues (2009) demonstrated that, when viewing emotional expressions, participants' Zygomaticus Major muscle activity was higher for happy than for angry or neutral faces, and, most importantly, that this effect was stronger under conditions of eye contact. Furthermore, angry faces elicited more negative affect and happy faces elicited more positive affect following eye contact, relative to the no-eye-contact condition.

Similarly, Rychlowska and colleagues (2012) used EMG to measure participants' Zygomaticus Major activation in response to smiling faces with averted and direct eye gaze and found evidence for greater facial mimicry when eye contact was achieved. Soussignan et al. (2012) employed dynamic avatars to manipulate eye gaze and emotion expression while measuring several facial muscles with EMG. The authors found that participants showed greater mimicry for anger and happiness with direct eye contact but mimicked fear faces more with averted gaze. A fear face directed at an object in the environment signals a threat to both the actor and the perceiver and is arguably more evocative than a fear expression directed at the perceiver. This finding suggests that embodied simulation of certain emotion expressions is more adaptive when eye contact does not occur. Such functional specificity needs to be taken into consideration as SIMS is applied to other expressions beyond smiles.

In support of this emotion-specific account of eye contact, Adams and Kleck (2003, 2005) found that eye contact increased the recognition accuracy and perceived intensity of so-called approach-oriented emotions (i.e., anger and happiness). Such findings are neither completely consistent with nor contradictory to the present SIMS account, as processing of facial expressions does not always require embodied simulation. When a prototypic expression is judged via simple perceptual analysis (Adolphs, 2002a), eye contact can contribute to accurate recognition, providing information about social relevance, category of emotion, or social status (Driskell, Olmstead, & Salas, 1993).

It is worth mentioning that the SIMS prediction regarding eye contact is that it is a *sufficient but not necessary* trigger of embodied simulation. It is thus unsurprising that eye contact is not necessary for embodied simulation to occur, such as when people mimic fearful faces with averted gaze (Soussignan et al., 2012). This is obviously adaptive, as it is often useful to know the emotional state of people who do not, or cannot, achieve eye contact. For instance, embodied simulation of pain can occur when only a target's body part is visible (Singer et al., 2004). Future research may demand a revision of the current model by showing eye contact to *not* be sufficient by itself – for instance, eye contact may not overcome a lack of social motivation. Eye contact may turn out to be a moderator, rather than a cause, of embodied simulation and mimicry, but that remains an empirical question at this time.

Importantly, just as people do not mimic everyone equally (see Stel, Chapter 2, and Hess et al., Chapter 5), it appears that people do not look at all eyes to the same extent. Social categories, for instance, may moderate the role of eye contact (Adams, Pauker, & Weisbuch, 2010), and eye contact can sometimes feel threatening or risky (Ellsworth & Carlsmith, 1973). For instance, White individuals make eye contact less with Black compared to White interlocutors (McConnell & Leibold, 2001; Penner, 1971). Kawakami and colleagues (2012) presented participants with the faces of in-group and out-group individuals simultaneously, in both a minimal group paradigm and a cross-race context, and found that subjects attended more to the eyes of in-group than out-group members.

We extended the paradigm from Kawakami and colleagues in our own laboratory and found the in-group bias for eye contact was moderated by the target's emotion. Participants viewed video clips of "in-group" and "out-group" faces morphing from happiness to sadness or from sadness to happiness while their eye gaze was recorded with an eye tracker. When the emerging emotion was sadness, participants looked more at the eyes of in-group members than of out-group members, but when the emerging emotion was happiness, they actually tended to look more at the eyes of out-group members compared to in-group members. This finding converges with facial mimicry data from Bourgeois and Hess (2008), who demonstrated that people mimic in-group sadness more than out-group sadness, but mimic out-group and in-group happiness equally. Together these studies suggest that when engaging with the emotional state of another person is especially costly, as may be the case with sadness, people will avoid achieving eye contact with out-group members, and will therefore mimic them less than in-group members. Sharing and acknowledging a target's happiness, on the other hand, is low-cost and can boost affiliation and positive affect, so perhaps people are less motivated to avoid out-group members' smiles.

While a causal relationship between eye contact and simulation cannot currently be drawn, the studies mentioned here suggestively provide support for the SIMS model prediction that if people are less motivated to know or acknowledge the emotional state of another, such as a disliked out-group member, they may simply avoid eye contact and thereby avoid embodied simulation. Experiments that manipulate social context while studying the role of eye contact in triggering mimicry are invaluable, as they may indirectly manipulate the routes that participants use to decode facial expressions. If future research more decisively demonstrates the importance of eye contact for emotion processing, it will inform a variety of real-world applications, from intergroup conflict interventions to therapy for people with autism. We will now present recent data substantiating the claim that facial mimicry supports recognition of subtle differences in expressions, particularly smiles.

Why do we mimic smiles?

The SIMS model holds that mimicry of smiles of pleasure, affiliation, and dominance guides the decoding of such smiles in cases in which social or cultural context does not discourage perceptual exploration of the face (i.e., achieving eye contact) or transparency (i.e., visible mimicry, which signals that the expression has been perceived). Most of the research that has tested the role of mimicry in smile recognition, though, has been conducted using a different set of smiles, namely "true" and "false" smiles, largely because this is the only typology of smiles for which validated stimuli have been readily available.

Initial evidence for the role of mimicry in decoding true and false smiles was reported in a set of studies by Maringer and colleagues (2011). There, participants saw videos of animated agents expressing "true" and "false" dynamic smiles that had been created and validated in prior work (Krumhuber, Manstead, & Kappas, 2007). Half of the participants could mimic the smiles normally. The mimicry of the remaining participants was disrupted; they were instructed to hold a pen between their teeth and lips. The task for all participants was to rate how genuine they thought the smiles were. Results showed that participants who could mimic the smiles judged true ones to be more genuine than false ones. This difference was, however, not observed when participants' mimicry was inhibited. In that condition, participants rated both types of smile as equally genuine.

Recent research in our laboratory has extended and improved on the demonstration of Maringer and colleagues. In particular, Rychlowska and colleagues (2014) introduced and validated the use of a plastic mouthguard to more uniformly inhibit facial mimicry. When inserted, the mouthguard slightly stretches the mouth and cheeks, keeps the mouth in a stable position, and reduces facial movements without requiring the active attention of the wearer. Thus, mouthguards should effectively inhibit or at least disrupt the dynamics of facial mimicry. In their first study, Rychlowska and colleagues showed videos of true and false smiles to participants with and without mouthguards, and measured the activation of their Zygomaticus Major muscles using EMG. In order to compare the activation of participants' Zygomaticus Major activity in the mouthguard condition to the activation of participants without mouthguards (i.e., differences in their ability to mimic the smiles), we compared EMG responses of the participants to the smile dynamics of the stimuli videos, extracted with the Computer Expression Recognition Toolbox (CERT; Littlewort et al., 2011). Analyses revealed that the pattern of Zygomaticus Major activation of participants who were wearing mouthguards was not correlated with the facial action of the stimuli as quantified by CERT, whereas a strong positive correlation between the two was observed for participants without mouthguards.

Over two studies the mouthguard technique was then used to block facial mimicry in a third of the participants while they rated true and false smiles on scales of genuineness. A second group of participants in both studies wore no mouthguard, while a third group wore no mouthguard but held a "stress ball" in their non-dominant hand as they performed the same smile-decoding task. The stress ball condition was added to the design of these studies to control for the possibility that blocking facial mimicry with a physical inhibitor such as a pen or a mouthguard is inherently distracting. That is, it is possible that the mimicry-blocked participants in the Maringer study were less accurate in decoding true and false smiles because they were distracted by the pen-in-the-mouth manipulation. Findings showed that individuals who could mimic the smiles, even if they were also holding a squeeze ball, rated true smiles as significantly more genuine than false smiles. This was not the case for the participants whose facial mimicry was inhibited. For these individuals the true and false smiles seemed equally genuine, indicating that facial mimicry is indeed a mechanism for accurate decoding of smiles.

Related findings have been reported by Manera and colleagues (2013). The researchers tested participants' performance on judging static photographs as instances of true and false smiles, defined as the presence and absence, respectively, of the Duchenne marker. This performance varied significantly as a function of participants' tendency to experience emotional contagion, measured with a self-report trait questionnaire (Doherty, 1997). Susceptibility to emotional contagion for *negative emotions*, such as fear, anger, and sadness, predicted more accurate judgments of smile genuineness. But higher levels of susceptibility to emotional contagion for *positive emotions* (happiness, love) predicted lower recognition performance, because such participants categorized more false smiles as sincere. Manera and colleagues (2013) did not directly assess or manipulate the facial reactions of the participants. Still, when combined with Rychlowska et al.'s (2014) demonstration of the role mimicry plays in smile genuineness judgments, it is entirely possible that individual tendencies to produce overt or covert facial mimicry might have been the mechanism underlying differences in participants' judgments.

Despite the findings that implicate facial mimicry in the decoding of smiles, strong mediational evidence is still lacking. For example, Korb and colleagues (2014) presented participants with different types of precisely constructed synthetic smiles and recorded participants' facial EMG while they rated smile authenticity. As expected, and consistent with the findings just presented, smile intensity and participants' facial mimicry predicted judgments of authenticity. But Korb and colleagues did not find evidence of mediation. That is, statistically controlling for participants' facial mimicry did not significantly change the difference in ratings of smile genuineness. Also, a recent study by Slessor et al. (2014) showed that the time course of facial reactions to enjoyment and non-enjoyment smiles differs in young and older adults. Such differences in facial mimicry, however, did not predict participants' ratings of smile genuineness. Furthermore, when Stel, van Dijk, and Olivier (2009) instructed participants to intentionally mimic or avoid mimicking their interaction partners while deciding whether the partner was lying, they found that participants were better at detecting deception when they were intentionally avoiding mimicry. Such findings complicate even more the function of mimicry in authenticity judgments and highlight the need for future studies exploring the effects of *automatic* versus *voluntary* facial mimicry.

Given the conflicting literature, it appears that strong conclusions cannot yet be drawn about the mediational role of facial mimicry in the decoding of smile genuineness. However, concerns about the exact definition and measurement of mimicry (see the next section) make the difficulty in drawing conclusions at this time rather unsurprising.

Conclusions

In this chapter we have examined new evidence for a theory of how individuals decode the human smile, the SIMS model (SIMS; Niedenthal, Mermillod, Maringer, & Hess, 2010). We first defined what we mean by "facial mimicry" and addressed some of the challenges researchers face in trying to operationalize that phenomenon. We then summarized the existing understanding of how perception of facial expressions involves embodied simulation and facial mimicry by looking at data from neuroscience. We next examined the question, "what smiles can we mimic?" We provided some new findings in favor of a social–functional typology of the SIMS model that propose at least three classes of smile, those used to solve the social tasks of rewarding behavior, creating and maintaining social bonds, and constructing and maintaining social hierarchies. Findings from both cross-cultural studies and experiments using a new perceptual boot-strapping platform provide support for this view. Next, we addressed the question, "when do we mimic?" Because the SIMS model holds that mimicry is not always necessary for the decoding of facial expression such as the smile, we proposed that eye contact may be an automatic trigger of facial mimicry. Studies addressing this hypothesis, while suggestive, are far from conclusive. Thus, future research that takes to heart challenges in examining facial mimicry raised in the initial sections of the chapter will be required to clarify the role of eye contact and also to explore other conditions under which facial mimicry might spontaneously occur.

Finally, we explored the question, "why do we mimic?" One of the SIMS model's central hypotheses is that mimicry can be used to decode smiles. We presented new findings regarding the prediction that mimicry is useful for distinguishing between the meanings of different smiles, and in particular true and false smiles. Future research will need to test the same hypothesis with new smile stimuli representing the three classes of smiles outlined in the SIMS model and described here.

As researchers continue to test the specific predictions set forth in the SIMS model, emerging evidence may demand that we revise the model, replace it with a better one, or combine it with other existing models. For instance, the recent model of Emotional Mimicry in Social Context (Hess & Fischer, 2013) proposes that mimicry is an emotional rather than matched motor response, subserving specific social functions. Namely, it facilitates bonding, enhances similarity, and acts as a "social glue" (Chartrand & Bargh, 1999; Van der Schalk et al., 2011; Yabar & Hess, 2007). Such a view is consistent with the extant evidence that people show congruent facial reactions either in affiliative contexts or when affiliation is not excluded – as for example in experimental paradigms in which stimulus faces are presented without additional information and thus, as a potential in-group. On the other hand, facial reactions are less congruent during interactions with competitors or disliked out-group members (Herrera, Bourgeois, & Hess, 1998; Lanzetta & Englis, 1989; Likowski, Mühlberger, Seibt, Pauli, & Weyers, 2011; Weyers, Mühlberger, Kund, Hess, & Pauli, 2009). Moreover, mimicking negative expressions per se is argued to be socially dysfunctional. Such an explanation is consistent with the evidence that people mimic frowns to a lesser extent than they mimic smiles (Hinsz & Tomhave, 1991) and with the mixed findings concerning mimicry of negative expressions. The latter seem to elicit reactive rather than imitative facial reactions (see Hess & Fischer, 2013, for details).

This social–functional perspective on mimicry is not contradictory to embodied simulation accounts such as SIMS (Adolphs, 2002a; Niedenthal, 2007; Niedenthal et al., 2010; Oberman et al., 2007), according to which facial imitation is part of a larger process that involves re-experiencing the perceived expression (and corresponding emotion) in the self to promote its interpretation. Combined, these theoretical frameworks can generate specific predictions about the conditions under which observers will mimic and internally simulate the expressions they see. Given that it is possible to judge facial displays using other, less costly strategies, (see previous sections for details), deep processing involving facial mimicry should mostly occur when a given facial expression is interpreted as an emotional signal and when it is interpreted as relevant for the observer. Thus, observers should mimic facial expressions when they are motivated to share others' emotions or to understand the meaning of the displays they see. Still, the exact role of facial mimicry in judgments of facial expressions, as well as its proposed social–functional role, needs to be explored in further studies.

In addition, in order to advance the SIMS and other theories of facial mimicry, great advances are needed in the measurement of all steps involved in perceiving and responding to faces. In order to quantify mimicry, a researcher needs to know what, exactly, is perceived by the observer. Probing the perceiver's perceptual input can be challenging. One issue is related to the way facial expression stimuli have been constructed. In previously published research, some but not all facial stimuli have been coded by humans or quantified by facial expression recognition software. In the case of the smile, researchers for whom the smile is not specifically under study may use stimuli with no prior effort to validate the expression. Thus, claims about the action units that constitute the expression may not be empirically based. If the stimuli have not been objectively described, then a measurement of perceivers of those expressions cannot be carried out systematically.

Another problem is that what a perceiver sees may depend upon where on the face she is looking. Most concepts of mimicry include assumptions about what the facial expression is (i.e., that it is valid; and as noted earlier this might not be the case) and about what the perceiver is looking at (i.e., the entire face). Perceivers may not explore the faces of all individuals in the same way, so what they see may not be equivalent. Recently researchers are using measurement techniques such as eye-tracking to quantify gaze patterns during face perception (e.g., Schrammel, Pannasch, Graupner, Mojzisch, & Velichkovsky, 2009). They can also use boot-strapping procedures to assess the perceptual characteristics that are used by an individual or type of individual in building their percepts (Smith et al., 2005).

Finally, there is the issue of top-down effects in perception. Applying labels to percepts modulates fundamental aspects of perception (Lupyan & Ward, 2013). This is especially important in the study of mimicry because labeling appears to affect low-level aspects of face perception (Halberstadt, Winkielman, Niedenthal, & Dalle, 2009). If a person believes an objectively neutral face to be angry, his or her "mimicry" may not resemble the objective expression but may instead involve an anger expression. Scientific research on facial mimicry will need to reveal the conditions under which perception is vulnerable to top-down influences in order to construct situations in which such vulnerability is reduced. Ultimately, however, these influences cannot always be treated as error; top-down effects are systematic processes in the perception of facial expression of emotion and they moderate, if not determine, what an individual could possible mimic.

In sum, facial mimicry seems ubiquitous, automatic, and useful. Further exploration of the temporal aspects of mimicry-related processes, their exact functions, their neural underpinnings, and their moderating factors will do more than explain how we recognize facial expressions. It will aid interventions for populations ranging from facial palsy patients to people with autism. It will also provide insight into the evolution of emotions and their expressions. Furthermore, it will inform research on embodied cognition more broadly and perhaps emphasize the fundamental role the body plays in cognitive processes. However, as always, empirical demonstration will have to outweigh intuition in fully characterizing facial mimicry, embodied simulation, and their social functions.

References

Adams, R. B., Jr., & Kleck, R. E. (2003). Perceived gaze direction and the processing of facial displays of emotion. *Psychological Science, 14*(6), 644–647.

Adams, R. B., Jr., & Kleck, R. E. (2005). Effects of direct and averted gaze on the perception of facially communicated emotion. *Emotion*, 5(1), 3–11.

Adams, R. B., Pauker, K., & Weisbuch, M. (2010). Looking the other way: The role of gaze direction in the cross-race memory effect. *Journal of Experimental Social Psychology* 46(2), 478–481.

Adolphs, R. (2002a). Recognizing emotion from facial expressions: Psychological and neurological mechanisms. *Behavioral and Cognitive Neuroscience Reviews*, 1(1), 21–62.

Adolphs, R. (2002b). Neural systems for recognizing emotion. *Current Opinion in Neurobiology*, 12(2), 169–177.

Adolphs, R., Damasio, H., Tranel, D., Cooper, G., & Damasio, A. R. (2000). A role for somatosensory cortices in the visual recognition of emotion as revealed by three-dimensional lesion mapping. *Journal of Neuroscience*, 20(7), 2683–2690.

Ames D. R., & Johar, G. V. (2009). I'll know what you're like when I see how you feel: How and when affective displays influence behavior-based impressions. *Psychological Science*, 20(5), 586–593.

Anderson, C., & Thompson, L. L. (2004). Affect from the top down: How powerful individuals' positive affect shapes negotiations. *Organizational Behavior and Human Decision Processes*, 95(2), 125–139.

Atkinson, A. P (2007). Face processing and empathy. In *Empathy in mental illness*, 360–385. Cambridge: Cambridge University Press.

Bavelas, J. B., Black, A., Lemery, C. R., & Mullett, J. (1986). "I show how you feel": Motor mimicry as a communicative act. *Journal of Personality and Social Psychology*, 50(2), 322–329.

Blair, R. J. (1995). A cognitive developmental approach to morality: Investigating the psychopath. *Cognition*, 57, 1–29.

Blair, R. J. (2003). Facial expressions, their communicatory functions and neuro-cognitive substrates. *Philosophical Transactions of the Royal Society of London*, 358, 561–572.

Bourgeois, P., & Hess, U. (2008). The impact of social context on mimicry. *Biological Psychology*, 77(3), 343–352.

Brown, W. M., Palameta, B., & Moore, C. (2003). Are there nonverbal cues to commitment? An exploratory study using the zero-acquaintance video presentation paradigm. *Evolutionary Psychology*, 1, 42–69.

Buck, R. (1984). *The communication of emotion* (pp. 101–105). New York: Guilford Press.

Calder, A. J., Young, A. W., Perrett, D. I., Etcoff, N. L., & Rowland, D. (1996). Categorical perception of morphed facial expressions. *Visual Cognition*, 3(2), 81–118.

Cashdan, E. (1998). Smiles, speech, and body posture: How women and men display sociometric status and power. *Journal of Nonverbal Behavior*, 22(4), 209–228.

Carranza, E, Prentice, D. A., & Larsen, J. T. (2012). *Derisive response to dominance and deviance*. Manuscript in preparation.

Chartrand, T. L., & Bargh, J. A. (1999). The chameleon effect: The perception-behavior link and social interaction. *Journal of Personality and Social Psychology, 76,* 893–910.

Dailey, M. N., Cottrell, G. W., Padgett, C., & Adolphs, R. (2002). EMPATH: A neural network that categorizes facial expressions. *Journal of cognitive neuroscience, 14*(8), 1158–1173.

Darwin, C. (1872/1998). *The expression of the emotions in man and animals.* New York/Oxford: Oxford University Press.

Decety, J., & Chaminade, T. (2003). Neural correlates of feeling sympathy. *Neuropsychologia, 41*(2), 127–138.

De Gelder, B., Vroomen, J., Pourtois, G., & Weiskrantz, L. (1999). Non-conscious recognition of affect in the absence of striate cortex. *Neuroreport, 10*(18), 3759–3763.

Dimberg, U., Thunberg, M., & Elmehed, K. (2000). Unconscious facial reactions to emotional facial expressions. *Psychological Science, 11*(1), 86–89.

Doherty, R. W. (1997). The emotional contagion scale: A measure of individual differences. *Journal of Nonverbal Behavior, 21,* 131–154.

Driskell, J. E., Olmstead, B., & Salas, E. (1993). Task cues, dominance cues, and influence in task groups, *Journal of Applied Psychology, 78*(1), 51–60.

Ekman, P. (1992). *Telling lies: Clues to deceit in the marketplace, politics, and marriage.* New York: WW Norton & Company.

Ekman, P., Friesen, W. V., & Hager, J. C. (Eds.). (2002). *Facial action coding system* [E-book]. Salt Lake City, UT: Research Nexus.

Elfenbein, H. A., Beaupré, M. G., Lévesque, M., & Hess, U. (2007). Toward a dialect theory: Cultural differences in the expression and recognition of posed facial expressions. *Emotion, 7*(1), 131–146.

Ellsworth, P., & Carlsmith, J. M. (1973). Eye contact and gaze aversion in an aggressive encounter. *Journal of Personality and Social Psychology, 28*(2), 280–292.

Fischer, A. H., Becker, D., & Veenstra, L. (2012). Emotional mimicry in social context: The case of disgust and pride. *Frontiers in Emotion Science, 3,* 475.

Frank, M. G., Ekman, P., & Friesen, W. V. (1993). Behavioral markers and recognizability of the smile of enjoyment. *Journal of Personality and Social Psychology, 64,* 83–93.

Fridlund, A. (1991). The sociality of solitary smiling: Potentiation by an implicit audience. *Journal of Personality and Social Psychology, 60,* 229–240.

Fridlund, A. J. (2002). The behavioral ecology view of smiling and other facial expressions. In M. H. Abel (Ed.), *An empirical reflection on the smile* (pp. 45–82). New York: Ewin Mellen Press.

Frith, C. (2009). *Making up the mind: How the brain creates our mental world.* Malden, MA: Blackwell Publishing.

Gallese, V. (2003). The roots of empathy: The shared manifold hypothesis and the neural basis of intersubjectivity. *Psychopathology, 36,* 171–180.

Gallese, V. (2005). Being like me: Self-other identity, mirror neurons, and empathy. In S. Hurley & H. Chater (Eds.), *Perspectives on imitation: From neuroscience to social science. Vol. 1: Mechanisms of imitation and imitation in animals* (pp. 101–18). Cambridge, MA: MIT Press.

Gazzaniga, M. S., & Smylie, C. S. (1990). Hemispheric mechanisms controlling voluntary and spontaneous facial expressions. *Journal of Cognitive Neuroscience, 2*(3), 239–245.

Gerull, F. C., & Rappee, R. M. (2002). Mother knows best: Effects of maternal modeling on the acquisition of fear and avoidance behaviour in toddlers. *Behavior Research and Therapy, 40,* 279–287.

Gosselin, F., & Schyns, P. (2001). Bubbles: A new technique to reveal the use of visual information in recognition tasks. *Vision Research, 41,* 2261–2271.

Halberstadt, J., & Niedenthal, P. M. (2001). Effects of emotion concepts on perceptual memory for emotional expressions. *Journal of Personality and Social Psychology, 81,* 587–598.

Halberstadt, J., Winkielman, P., Niedenthal, P., & Dalle, N. (2009). Emotional conception: How embodied emotion concepts guide perception and facial action. *Psychological Science, 20,* 1254–61.

Hareli, S., & Hess, U. (2010). What emotional reactions can tell us about the nature of others: An appraisal perspective on person perception. *Cognition and Emotion, 24,* 128–140.

Harker, L., & Keltner, D. (2001). Expressions of positive emotion in women's college yearbook pictures and their relationship to personality and life outcomes across adulthood. *Journal of Personality and Social Pscyhology, 80,* 112–124.

Haxby, J. V., Gobbini, M. I., Furey, M. L., Ishai, A., Schouten, J. L., & Pietrini, P. (2001). Distributed and overlapping representations of faces and objects in ventral temporal cortex. *Science, 293*(5539), 2425–2430.

Hennenlotter, A., Schroeder, U., Erhard, P., Castrop, F., Haslinger, B., Stoecker, D., … Ceballos-Baumann, A. O. (2005). A common neural basis for receptive and expressive communication of pleasant facial affect. *Neuroimage, 26*(2), 581–591.

Herrera, P., Bourgois, P., & Hess, U. (1998, September 23–27). *Counter mimicry effects as a function of racial attitudes.* Paper presented at the 38th Annual Meeting of the Society for Psychophysiological Research, Denver, CO.

Hess, U., & Fischer, A. (2013). Emotional mimicry as social regulation. *Personality and Social Psychology Review, 17,* 142–157.

Hess, U., & Thibault, P. (2009). Darwin and emotion expression. *American Psychologist, 64,* 120–128.

Hess, U., Adams, R. B., Jr., & Kleck, R. E. (2005). Who may frown and who should smile? Dominance, affiliation, and the display of happiness and anger. *Cognition and Emotion, 19,* 515–36.

Hietanen, J. K., Leppanen, J. M., Peltola, M. J., Linna-aho, K., & Ruuhiala, H. J. (2008). Seeing direct and averted gaze activates the approach–avoidance motivational brain systems. *Neuropsychologia, 46,* 2423–2430.

Hinsz, V. B., & Tomhave, J. A. (1991). Smile and (half) the world smiles with you, frown and you frown alone. *Personality and Social Psychology Bulletin, 17,* 586–592.

Hopf, H. C., Muller-Forell, W., & Hopf, N. J. (1992). Localization of emotional and volitional facial paresis. *Neurology, 42*(10), 1918–1923.

Huang, L., & Galinski, A. D. (2010). No mirrors for the powerful: Why dominant smiles are not processed using embodied simulation. *Behavioral and Brain Sciences, 33*, 448–448.

Iwase, M., Ouchi, Y., Okada, H., Yokoyama, C., Nobezawa, S., Yoshikawa, E., ... Watanabe, Y. (2002). Neural substrates of human facial expression of pleasant emotion induced by comic films: A PET study. *Neuroimage, 17*(2), 758–768.

Jack, R. E., Garrod, O. G. B., Yu, H., Caldara, R., & Schyns, P. G. (2012). Facial expressions of emotion are not culturally universal. *PNAS, 109*, 7241–7244.

Jox, R., Bruning, R., Hamann, G., & Danek, A. (2004). Volitional facial palsy after a vascular lesion of the supplementary motor area. *Neurology, 63*(4), 756–757.

Kawakami, K., Williams, A., Sidhu, D., Vilaythong, O., Choma, B. L., Rodriguez-Bailon, R., et al. (2012). *Windows to the Soul: Preferential Attention to the Eyes of Ingroup Members*.

Keysers, C., & Gazzola, V. (2007). Integrating simulation and theory of mind: From self to social cognition. *Trends in Cognitive Science, 11*, 194–196.

Kilner, J. M. (2006). Modulation of the mirror system by social relevance. *Social Cognitive and Affective Neuroscience, 1*, 143–148.

Kirouac, G., & Hess, U. (1999). Group membership and the decoding of non-verbal behavior. In *The social context of nonverbal behavior* (pp. 182–210). Cambridge University Press.

Korb, S., & Sander, D. (2009). The neural architecture of facial expressions. In D. Sander & K. R. Scherer (Eds.), *The Oxford companion to emotion and the affective sciences* (pp. 173–175). New York: Oxford University Press.

Korb, S., With, S., Niedenthal, P., Kaiser, S., & Grandjean, D. (2014). The perception and mimicry of facial movements predict judgments of smile authenticity. *PLoS ONE 9*(6): e99194, http://doi:10.1371/journal.pone.0099194

Krumhuber, E. G., Likowski, K. U., & Weyers, P. (2013). Facial mimicry of spontaneous and deliberate Duchenne and non-Duchenne smiles. *Journal of Nonverbal Behavior*, 1–11.

Krumhuber, E., Manstead, A. S. R., & Kappas A. (2007). Temporal aspects of facial displays in person and expression perception. The effects of smile dynamics, head-tilt and gender. *Journal of Nonverbal Behavior, 31*, 39–56, http://doi:10.1007/s10919–006–0019-x.

Krumhuber, E., Manstead, A. S. R., Cosker, D., Marshall, D., Rosin, P. L., & Kappas, A. (2007). Facial dynamics as indicators of trustworthiness and cooperative behavior. *Emotion, 7*(4), 730–735.

Krusemark, E. A., & Li, W. (2011). Do all threats work the same way? Divergent effects of fear and disgust on sensory perception and attention. *Journal of Neuroscience, 31*, 3429–3434.

LaFrance, M. (2011). *Lip service: Smiles in life, death, trust, lies, work, memory, sex, and politics*. New York: W.W. Norton & Company.

Lamme, V. A., Super, H., & Spekreijse, H. (1998). Feedforward, horizontal, and feedback processing in the visual cortex. *Current Opinion in Neurobiology, 8*, 529–535.

Lanzetta, J. T., & Englis, B. G. (1989). Expectations of cooperation and competition and their effects on observers' vicarious emotional responses. *Journal of Personality and Social Psychology, 56*, 543–554.

LeDoux, J. (1996). *The emotional brain.* New York: Simon & Schuster.

Lee, T. W., Josephs, O., Dolan, R. J., & Critchley, H. D. (2006). Imitating expressions: Emotion-specific neural substrates in facial mimicry. *Social Cognitive and Affective Neuroscience, 1*, 122–135.

Likowski, K. U., Mühlberger, A., Seibt, B., Pauli, P., & Weyers, P. (2011). Processes underlying congruent and incongruent facial reactions to emotional facial expressions. *Emotion, 11*, 457–467, http://doi:10.1037/a0023162.

Likowski, K. U., Mühlberger, A., Gerdes, A. B. M., Wieser, M. J., Pauli, P., & Weyers, P. (2012). Facial mimicry and the mirror neuron system: Simultaneous acquisition of facial electromyography and functional magnetic resonance imaging. *Frontiers in Human Neuroscience, 6*, 214.

Lipps, T. (1903). Einfühlung, innere Nachahmung, and Organempfindungen. *Archiv für die gesamte Psychologie, 2*, 185–204.

Littlewort, G., Whitehill, J., Wu, T., Fasel, I., Frank, M., Movellan, J., & Bartlett, M. (2011). The computer expression recognition toolbox (CERT). *2011 IEEE International Conference on Automatic Face & Gesture Recognition (FG 2011)*, 298–305.

Lupyan, G., & Ward, E. J. (2013). Language can boost otherwise unseen objects into visual awareness. *Proceedings of the National Academy of Sciences*, http://doi:10.1073/pnas.1303312110.

Manera, V., Grandi, E., & Colle, L. (2013). Susceptibility to emotional contagion for negative emotions improves detection of smile authenticity. *Frontiers in Human Neuroscience, 7*, http://doi:10.3389/fnhum.2013.00006.

Maringer, M., Krumhuber, E. G., Fischer, A. H., & Niedenthal, P. M. (2011). Beyond smile dynamics: Mimicry and beliefs in judgments of smiles. *Emotion, 11*, 181–187.

Mathersul, D., McDonald, S., & Rushby, J. A. (2013). Automatic facial responses to briefly presented emotional stimuli in autism spectrum disorder. *Biological Psychology, 94*(2), 397–407.

Matthews, G., Wells, A. (1999). The cognitive science of attention and emotion. In T. Dalgleish, M. J. Power (Eds.), *Handbook of cognition and emotion* (pp. 171–192). Chichester, UK: Wiley

McConnell, A. R., & Leibold, J. M. (2001). Relations among the implicit association test, discriminatory behavior, and explicit measures of racial attitudes. *Journal of Experimental Social Psychology, 37*, 435–442, http://doi:10.1006/jesp.2000.1470.

Mondillon, L., Niedenthal, P. M., Gil, S., & Droit-Volet, S. (2007). Imitation and in-group versus out-group members' facial expressions of anger: A test with a time perception task. *Social Neuroscience, 2*, 223–237.

Moody, E. J., McIntosh, D. N., Mann, L. J., & Weisser, K. R. (2007). More than mere mimicry? The influence of emotion on rapid facial reactions to faces. *Emotion, 7*, 447–457.

Morecraft, R. J., & Van Hoesen, G. W. (1998). Convergence of limbic input to the cingulate motor cortex in the rhesus monkey. *Brain Research Bulletin, 45*(2), 209–232.

Morecraft, R. J., Stilwell-Morecraft, K. S., & Rossing, W. R. (2004). The motor cortex and facial expression: New insights from neuroscience. *Neurologist, 10* (5), 235–249.

Morris, J. S., Ohman, A., & Dolan, R. J. (1999). A subcortical pathway to the right amygdala mediating "unseen" fear. *Proceedings of the National Academy of Sciences of the United States of America, 96*(4), 1680–1685.

Mumme, D. L., & Fernald, A. (1996). Infants' responses to facial and vocal emotional signals in a social referencing paradigm. *Child Development, 67*, 3219–3237.

Neumann, R., Schulz, S. M., Lozo, L., & Alpers, G. W. (2014). Automatic facial responses to near-threshold presented facial displays of emotion: Imitation or evaluation? *Biological Psychology, 96*, 144–149, http://doi:10.1016/j.biopsycho.2013.12.009.

Niedenthal, P. M. (2007). Embodying emotion. *Science, 316*(5827), 1002–1005, http://doi:10.1126/science.1136930.

Niedenthal, P. M. (2008) Emotion concepts. In M. Lewis, J. M. Haviland-Jones, & L. F. Barrett (Eds.), *Handbook of emotion*, 3rd ed. (pp. 587–601). New York: Guilford Press.

Niedenthal, P. M., Brauer, M., Halberstadt, J. B., & Innes-Ker, Å. H. (2001). When did her smile drop? Facial mimicry and the influences of emotional state on the detection of change in emotional expression. *Cognition & Emotion, 15*, 853–864, http://doi:10.1080/02699930143000194.

Niedenthal, P. M., Mermillod, M., Maringer, M., & Hess, U. (2010). The simulation of smiles (SIMS) model: Embodied simulation and the meaning of facial expression. *Behavioral and Brain Sciences, 33*, 417–433, http://doi:10.1017/S0140525X10000865.

Niedenthal, P. M., Barsalou, L. W., Winkielman, P., Krauth-Gruber, S., & Ric, F. (2005). Embodiment in attitudes, social perception, and emotion. *Personality and Social Psychology Review, 9*, 184–211.

Niedenthal, P. M., Rychlowska, M., Miyamoto, Y., Matsumoto, D., Hess, U., Gilboa-Schechtman, E., ... Masuda, T. (2013). *Historical homogeneity, emotional expressiveness and the social functions of smiles.* Manuscript in preparation.

Oberman, L. M., Winkielman, P., & Ramachandran, V. S. (2007). Face to face: Blocking facial mimicry can selectively impair recognition of emotional expressions. *Social Neuroscience, 2*, 167–178, http://doi:10.1080/17470910701391943.

Penner, L. A. (1971). Interpersonal attraction toward a black person as a function of value importance. *Personality: An International Journal*, 175–187.

Pitcher, D., Garrido, L., Walsh, V., & Duchaine, B. C. (2008). Transcranial magnetic stimulation disrupts the perception and embodiment of facial expressions. *Journal of Neuroscience, 28*(36), 8929–33.

Pourtois, G., Sander, D., Andres, M., Grandjean, D., Reveret, L., ... Vuilleumier, P. (2004). Dissociable roles of the human somatosensory and superior temporal cortices for processing social face signals. *European Journal of Neuroscience, 20*(12), 3507–3515.

Russell, J .A. (1994). Is there universal recognition of emotion from facial expression? A review of the cross-cultural studies. *Psychological Bulletin, 1994,* 102–141.

Rychlowska, M., Zinner, L., Musca, S. C., & Niedenthal, P. M. (2012). From the eye to the heart: Eye contact triggers emotion simulation. *Proceedings of the 4th Workshop on Eye Gaze in Intelligent Human Machine Interaction.*

Rychlowska, M., Jack, R., Garrod, O. G. B., Schyns, P. G., & Niedenthal, P. (2014). What's in a smile? Specific facial actions combine with zygomaticus major in expressions of pleasure, affiliation and dominance. Manuscript in preparation.

Rychlowska, M., Canadas, E., Wood, A., Krumhuber, E. G., Fischer, A., & Niedenthal, P. M. (2014). Blocking mimicry makes true and false smiles look the same. *PloS One,* http://doi:10.1371/journal.pone.0090876.

Scharlemann, J. P. W., Eckel, C. C., Kacelnik, A., & Wilson, R. K. (2001). The value of a smile: game theory with a human face. *Journal of Economic Psychology, 22,* 617–640.

Schilbach, L., Eickhoff, S. B., Mojzisch, A., & Vogeley, K. (2008). What's in a smile? Neural correlates of facial embodiment during social interaction. *Social Neuroscience, 3,* 37–50.

Schneider, K. G., Hempel, R. J., & Lynch, T. R. (2013). The "poker face" just might lose you the game! The impact of expressive suppression and mimicry on sensitivity to facial expressions of emotion. *Emotion, 13,* 852–866.

Schrammel, F., Pannasch, S., Graupner, S. T., Mojzisch, A. & Velichkovsky, B. M. (2009). Virtual friend or threat? The effects of facial expressions and gaze interaction on psychophysiological responses and emotional experience. *Psychophysiology, 46,* 922–931.

Senju, A., & Johnson, M. H. (2009). Atypical eye contact in autism: Models, mechanisms and development. *Neuroscience & Biobehavioral Reviews, 33,* 1204–1214, http://doi:10.1016/j.neubiorev.2009.06.001.

Singer, T., Seymour, B., O'Doherty, J., Kaube, H., Dolan, R. J., & Frith, C. D. (2004). Empathy for pain involves the affective but not sensory components of pain. *Science, 303,* 1157–1162.

Slessor, G., Bailey, P. E., Rendell, P. G., Ruffman, T., Henry, J. D., & Miles, L. K. (2014). Examining the time-course of young and older adults' mimicry of enjoyment and non-enjoyment smiles. *Emotion, 14*(3), 532.

Smith, M. L., Cottrell, G., Gosselin, F. & Schyns, P. G. (2005). Transmitting and decoding facial expressions of emotions. *Psychological Science, 16,* 184–189.

Soussignan, R., Chadwick, M., Philip, L., Conty, L., Dezecache, G., & Grèzes, J. (2012). Self-relevance appraisal of gaze direction and dynamic facial expressions: Effects on facial electromyographic and autonomic reactions. *Emotion, 13*(2), 330, http://doi:10.1037/a0029892.

Stein, T., Senju, A., Peelen, M. V., & Sterzer, P. (2011). Eye contact facilitates awareness of faces during interocular suppression. *Cognition, 119,* 307–311.

Stel, M., van Dijk, E., & Olivier, E. (2009). You want to know the truth? Then don't mimic! *Psychological Science, 20*(6), 693–699, http://doi:10.1111/j.1467–9280.2009.02350.x.

Susskind, J. M., Lee, D. H., Cusi, A., Feiman, R., Grabski, W., Anderson, A. K. (2008). Expressing fear enhances sensory acquisition. *Nature Neuroscience, 11,* 843–850.

Tracy, J. L., & Robins, R. W. (2007). The prototypical pride expression: Development of a nonverbal behavior coding system. *Emotion, 7*(4), 789–801, http://doi:10.1037/1528–3542.7.4.789.

Van der Schalk, J., Doosje, B., Hawk, S., Fischer, A., Wigboldus, D., & Rotteveel, M. (2011). Convergent and divergent responses to emotional displays of ingroup and outgroup. *Emotion, 11*(2), 286–298.

Vuilleumier, P., & Pourtois, G. (2007). Distributed and interactive brain mechanisms during emotion face perception: Evidence from functional neuroimaging. *Neuropsychologia, 45*(1), 174–194.

Wehrle, T., Kaiser, S., Schmidt, S. & Scherer, K. R. (2000). Studying the dynamics of emotional expression using synthesized facial muscle movements. *Journal of Personality and Social Psychology, 78*(1), 105–119.

Weyers, P., Mühlberger, A., Kund, A., Hess, U., & Pauli, P. (2009). Modulation of facial reactions to avatar emotional faces by nonconscious competition priming. *Psychophysiology, 46,* 328–335.

Wild, B., Rodden, F. A., Rapp, A., Erb, M., Grodd, W., & Ruch, W. (2006). Humor and smiling: Cortical regions selective for cognitive, affective, and volitional components. *Neurology, 66*(6), 887–893.

Winkielman, P., McIntosh, D. N., & Oberman, L. (2009). Embodied and disembodied emotion processing: Learning from and about typical and autistic individuals. *Emotion Review, 2,* 178–190.

Yabar, Y., & Hess, U. (2007). Display of empathy and perception of out-group members. *New Zealand Journal of Psychology, 36,* 42–50.

Yu, H., Garrod, O. G. B., & Schyns, F. (2012). Perception-driven facial expression synthesis. *Computers and Graphics, 36,* 152–162.

CHAPTER 4

The neuroscience of mimicry during social interactions

Leonhard Schilbach

Successful interpersonal communication depends to a large extent upon the exchange of non-verbal information (e.g. Mehrabian, 1971). The face is known to be of particular importance in this context because facial expressions not only convey information about the emotional state of others but may also reflect their appraisal of a given situation (Darwin, 1872; Erickson & Schulkin, 2003; Frijda & Tcherkassof, 1997; Kaiser & Wehrle, 2001). Apart from these more passive aspects of face perception, the perception of facial expressions can directly affect human observers and elicit responses from them: specifically, perceivers across the human lifespan spontaneously imitate the facial gestures of others (e.g. Meltzoff & Moore, 1977; Dimberg, 1990; Lang, Greenwald, Bradley, & Hamm, 1993; Dimberg & Thunberg, 1998).

This phenomenon of facial responses that occur automatically in a human observer's face in response to seeing facial expressions of a perceived other has been described as *facial mimicry*. It has also been suggested that these facial reactions are consistent with how subjects perceive the stimuli and their own emotions, therefore, constituting a form of "physiological linkage" or socio-emotional contagion (Dimberg, 1982; Dimberg, Thunberg, & Elmehed, 2000; Wallbott, 1991), that may impact on the selection of consequent response patterns and could also be of considerable importance for interpersonal communication (Niedenthal, Barsalou, Winkielman, Krauth-Gruber, & Ric, 2005). In other words, this automatic form of facially mediated social contagion might allow us to "live in someone else's facial expressions" (Merleau-Ponty, 1964). Conversely, reductions in involuntary facial reactions (e.g. due to conditions resulting in facial paralysis) may have a detrimental effect on the quality of interpersonal communication (Cole, 2001; Oberman, Winkielman & Ramachandran, 2007). Other more recent studies targeting the functional relevance of this phenomenon have focused on emotional mimicry in an interactive setting and have demonstrated that mimicry reactions are dependent upon social context (cf. Hess & Bourgeois, 2010; Fischer, Becker, & Veenstra, 2012; Hess & Fischer, 2013).

In spite of the phenomenon's undisputed importance for interpersonal interaction and communication, there is still widespread dispute about what mimicry should be taken to reflect on a conceptual level. Some have argued that embodied cognition theories suggest that mimicry reflects an internal simulation of a perceived emotion and could thereby facilitate the understanding of others' mental states (e.g. Oberman et al., 2007; Niedenthal, Mermillod, Maringer, & Hess, 2010). This reading is often linked to varieties of "simulation theory" or other simulationist accounts of social cognition, which describe how we can obtain a *"first-person grasp"* on the motor goals and intentions of other individuals (e.g. Rizzolatti & Sinigaglia, 2010). In contrast to this view, which emphasizes similarities in self- and other-related processes that are needed to bridge the gap between minds, it has been argued that from an interactionist or enactive view of social cognition, interpersonally coordinated and responsive behaviour could be seen as constituting "knowledge" of other minds (e.g. Schilbach et al., 2013). Furthermore, it has been suggested that neuroscientific approaches may help to provide further insights into the mechanisms and nature of mimicry responses. In this chapter, the existing neuroscience literature with regard to mimicry is therefore reviewed, while putting special emphasis on the modulatory impact of gaze cues on mimicry reactions as relevant during ongoing social interactions (see also Niedenthal et al., Chapter 3).

The neural correlates of imitation and facial mimicry

In spite of a great wealth of neuroimaging literature pertaining to face perception (Blair, 2003; Haxby, Hoffmann, & Gobbini, 2002) as well as imitation and the "mirror neuron system" (MNS; Iacoboni et al., 1999; Rizzolatti, Fogassi, & Gallese, 2001), the neural correlates of automatically occurring, involuntary facial reactions in response to certain stimuli are not equally well researched. Previous neuroimaging studies suggest the involvement of "mirror neurons" for emotional facial actions: a largely similar neural network is activated when subjects either passively view or deliberately imitate static pictures of facial expressions of basic emotions (Carr, Iacoboni, Dubeau, Mazzioatta, & Lenzi, 2003) and dynamic depictions of smiling and frowning expressions (Leslie, Johnson-Frey, & Grafton, 2004). Lee, Josephs, Dolan, and Critchley (2006) specifically looked at the perception and imitation of facial expressions that index emotions (as compared to "ingestive" facial movements) and were able to show that imitation leads to enhanced activity in right inferior frontal cortex, a pattern not found for passive viewing (Lee et al., 2006). In spite of these interesting findings, it must be noted that these studies focused on the intentional, voluntary imitation of facial behaviour and not on its

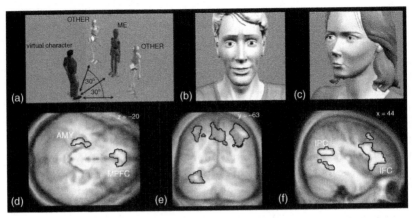

Figure 4.1 (a) Virtual scenario as shown in the instructions. (b) Depiction of a self-directed, socially relevant facial expression. (c) Depiction of an other-directed, arbitrary facial movement. (d) Neural correlates of the perception of self-directed facial expressions. (e) Neural correlates of the perception of other-directed facial expressions. (f) Neural correlates of the perception of arbitrary facial movements (Taken from: Schilbach et al., 2013).

spontaneous, involuntary occurrence in response to seeing facial behaviour. Here, a study by Wild, Erb, Eyb, Bartels, and Grodd (2003) is most relevant and has demonstrated that the involvement of the medial basotemporal lobe might facilitate the occurrence of automatic, involuntary facial movements in response to the perception of facial expressions. Taken together, activity change in different brain areas can, hence, be assumed to contribute to the neural network subserving facial mimicry.

To further investigate and delineate the behavioural and neural correlates of facial mimicry, we performed a series of studies (Schilbach et al., 2006; Mojzisch et al., 2008; Schilbach, Eickhoff, Mojzisch, & Vogeley, 2008), in which participants were asked to imagine being part of a scenario with three others, only one of whom was visible (Figure 4.1a), and were shown short video sequences depicting this virtual character, who showed either socially relevant facial expressions or arbitrary facial movements. Furthermore, it was varied whether or not the virtual character looked directly at the participant (Figure 4.1b) or towards the right or left in the direction of an invisible agent (Figure 4.1c).

Participants were asked to rate for all conditions whether they felt that the virtual character had expressed an intention to initiate a social interaction.

The behavioural results from these studies demonstrate that participants did not have difficulties in differentiating socially relevant from arbitrary facial behaviour. In spite of the explicit instruction to "put themselves into the shoes of the other," participants interestingly demonstrated a bias towards giving socially relevant facial expressions a higher rating when they were self- rather than other-directed. In parallel to this, results of the neuroimaging analysis demonstrated significant differences in activation patterns subserving the perception of socially relevant facial expressions depending upon whether these expressions were self- or other-directed: while self-directed facial expressions led to a differential increase of neural activity in the ventral portion of medial prefrontal cortex and the amygdala (Figure 4.1d), other-directed facial expressions resulted in a differential recruitment of medial and lateral parietal cortex (Figure 4.1e). Our findings, therefore, demonstrate that even though the perception of socially relevant non-verbal cues from an observer's point of view recruits brain regions that have been linked to visuo-spatial processing, the perception of identical, self-directed stimuli activate brain regions that have been linked to emotional and evaluative processing (Schilbach et al., 2006).

With regard to the different brain regions implicated, the amygdala is known to be a crucial hub of the so-called limbic system and has been linked to serving various integrative sensory and emotional functions by attaching biological and social significance to stimuli (e.g. Gamer & Buchel, 2009; Muscatell et al., 2010). The ventral portion of medial prefrontal cortex is also known to be relevant for emotional processing and has been related to "outcome monitoring" (cf. Amodio & Frith, 2006). More generally, emotions are known to be an important driving force for interpersonal behaviour and a "short hand" that guides decision-making processes (e.g. Frijda, 1986; Damasio, 2010). As outlined above, simulationist accounts of social cognition suggest that emotions are crucial for interpersonal perception, because they allow an observer to share the feeling state of another individual (Preston & de Waal, 2002). Apart from this more conventional view of how emotions might contribute to social cognition, an interactionist account views emotional responses not only as a way of perceiving emotional states in others but also as a way of being engaged with and being moved by others, which could contribute to the understanding of the bodily intentionality of the other in terms of bodily responsiveness. Being responsive to the socially relevant, expressive behaviour of others in this way could provide and bias possibilities for (inter-) action by motivating behaviour and soliciting activity.

Interestingly, the neuroimaging data also demonstrated that the perception of arbitrary facial movements irrespective of whether they are directed towards oneself or someone else activated right inferior frontal and inferior parietal cortices (Figure 4.1f). These brain regions are commonly described as important nodes of the so-called mirror neuron system (MNS), which is often thought to provide an understanding of the intentions that govern actions irrespective of whether these are own actions or someone else's actions (e.g. Rizzolatti & Sinigaglia, 2010). Here, an important suggestion has been that mirror neurons may only play a role in situations when the action and its stereotypic context are highly familiar (e.g. Brass et al., 2007). In our study, however, MNS brain regions respond more strongly to arbitrary facial movements than to socially relevant ones, which appear to contradict the idea that the MNS only plays a role in familiar situations. On the contrary, an arbitrary facial movement – with which one may be less familiar than with socially relevant facial expressions, which are more frequently encountered – also leads to the recruitment of the MNS. This finding could be understood in terms of a prediction error signal (Pelphrey et al., 2003; Schippers & Keysers, 2011) and might be relevant to associative learning processes that have recently been discussed as an alternative account of the development and modulation of activity in the MNS (Heyes, 2010).

More specifically, one could argue for a role for the MNS beyond mere motor resonance: rather than suggesting that mirror neuron activity constitutes a simulation routine which gives us access to the first-person perspective of the other (Rizzolatti & Sinigaglia, 2010), a case could be made for an understanding of the MNS on the enactive view of cognition, which would suggest that activity in these regions might be more closely related to the ability to perceive social affordances, that is, the possibilities for interaction provided by others, in terms of an activation of motor programs that could allow for interpersonal coordination of behaviour (Gangopadhyay & Schilbach, 2012). In line with this proposal, both reactive and anticipatory aspects of social mimicry should exist. A recent study by Heerey and Crossley (2013) has provided evidence for this distinction between reactive (rather than simulationist) and predictive mechanisms of behavioural reciprocity during social interactions: not only do participants smile "back" at others reactively but they also anticipate their partners' expression and they do so substantially more when anticipating genuine as compared to polite smiles. Future research in social neuroscience could use adequate mathematical models to investigate the computational mechanisms that may underlie reactive and predictive processes during social interaction and could relate model predictions to brain activity changes in the motor and/or MNS to differentiate their contributions to facial mimicry during social interaction. Such investigations could help to provide further support for an interactionist or enactive view of social cognition that emphasizes the importance of social interactions for the emergence and modulation of

MNS activity (cf. Heyes, 2010) and might offer a more parsimonious account for actions that people perform jointly as these often involve complementary rather than imitative actions (cf. Gallagher, 2007; Kourtis et al., 2010).

In a follow-up experiment to the above described fMRI study, the paradigm was used while recording eye-movements, pupil size, and facial electromyography (EMG). The results from this follow-up study show that attention allocation, as assessed by fixation duration, was specifically related to the perception of self-directed stimuli. EMG measurements demonstrated that facial activity was influenced by the perception of socially relevant facial expressions and showed spontaneous, involuntary facial responses (Mojzisch et al., 2006). Using the temporal information from the EMG study, we then re-analysed the fMRI data to investigate the neural correlates of the observed facial mimicry responses. This re-analysis was performed to investigate whether automatically occurring facial mimicry relies upon differential neuronal activity in the MNS or the motor system alone or whether other brain regions known to be involved in social cognition would make up the neural network subserving this phenomenon. Drawing upon functional imaging data (Schilbach et al., 2006) and the temporal information from the follow-up EMG investigation using exactly the same experimental paradigm (Mojzisch et al., 2006), we are able to show that specific neural activations do pertain to the time window of our stimulus sequence in which facial mimicry occurs. The findings show that specific brain activations are related to the occurrence of involuntary facial movements in human observers in response to the perception of socially relevant facial expressions shown by perceived others. These activations comprise but extend beyond classical motor regions (face motor area) and include other brain centres such as the cingulate cortex, the precuneus, hippocampus, and the dorsal midbrain (Figure 4.2).

Differential neural activity related to facial mimicry in response to the perception of socially relevant facial expressions regardless of whether these are self- or other-directed was observed in the motor system, namely the left pre-central gyrus. More precisely this activation was located in the inferior part, that is, the face representation, of the primary motor cortex. This area has not only been shown to be differentially active in fMRI studies targeting the voluntary production of facial movement and expressions (Dresel et al., 2005; Hanakawa, Parikh, Bruno, & Hallett, 2005) but has also been shown to be automatically activated during the perception of emotional vocalizations (e.g. laughter), thereby potentially preparing facial gestures in response to the stimuli (Warren et al., 2006). It is also interesting to note that subjects in the study by Warren and colleagues are described as reporting an urge to produce a facial

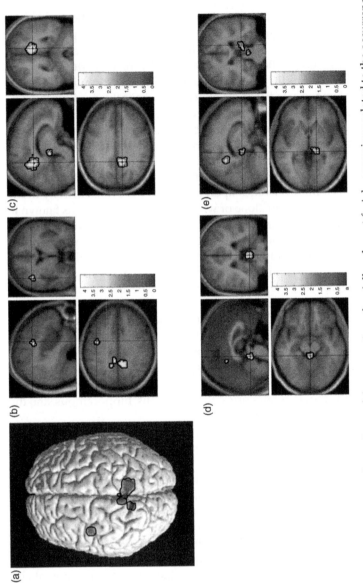

Figure 4.2 Neural correlates of the perception of socially relevant facial expressions related to the occurrence of facial mimicry: (a) overview of activations*; (b) left precentral cortex activation (_42,_4, 38); (c) posterior cingulate cortex activation (12,_48, 32); (d) midbrain activation (0,_36,_14); (e) right hippocampus activation (16,_32, 0). *Activations in (a) are shown as overlay rendered onto SPM template; Activations in (b) to (e) are shown as section overlay onto mean structural image of the analysed subjects after normalization (Taken from Schilbach et al., 2008).

expression when exposed to emotive auditory stimuli, which bears a strong resemblance to the phenomenon of facial mimicry.

As suggested above, there might be several benefits to instantiating an involuntary, embodied component as part of a reaction to a stimulus: first of all, it might help to add an affective, body-based component to the appraisal of a given situation. Furthermore, perceptual-motor links might also facilitate motor responses by altering the organism's state of action readiness. Facially embodied reactions, in particular, might have evolved to serve communicative functions by making a feeling state accessible to others, thereby immediately entering into reciprocal relations with the perceived other. Indeed, it has been suggested that it might be this very evolutionary heritage of interpersonal coupling that conjoins human beings (Cole, 2001). While in adults these automatic facial reactions can be suppressed and do not necessarily translate into a visible change in facial appearance, evidence from developmental psychology demonstrates that this mechanism and its automatic manifestation is important from birth onwards and fosters infant–caretaker attachment (e.g. Meltzoff & Moore, 1977).

On the basis of the results described earlier, it can be concluded that both premotor and motor areas of the brain can be automatically engaged by the perception of socially relevant actions. It has been proposed that activation of premotor areas can be understood as belonging to the MNS, which is known to play an important role both in the production and perception of intentional motor behaviour (Grèzes, Armony, Rowe, & Passingham, 2003; Likowski et al., 2012; Rizzolatti et al., 2001). Intriguingly, primary motor areas are also activated differentially when we perceive facial actions, for which the production would rely on these activations. Consequently, there seems to be a close link between the visual representation of face-based cues and its corresponding motor representation that lends support to the idea that the process of perceiving faces always includes an enactive element through which we engage with and respond to stimuli instead of a mere "passive" perception of face-based cues (Schilbach et al., 2013).

Apart from activity change in the extended MNS, the neural correlates of facial mimicry also include activation of the posterior aspects of cingulate cortex and the precuneus (Figure 4.2). The posterior cingulate cortex and precuneus are considered to be part of the so-called mentalizing network (MENT), which is often thought to contribute to social cognition by providing more explicit processing of stimuli. Consistently, posterior cingulate cortex has been connected to processes in which emotional experiences trigger memory retrieval (Maddock, Garrett, & Buonocuore, 2001, 2003), which is in concordance with the idea that the recognition of the affective content of gestures (including facial expressions) is shaped by sharing and forming memories of experiences in interpersonal interaction. Consistently, posterior cingulate cortex has been shown to be activated in studies of empathy and forgiveness as well as self-reflection and self-referential processing (Carr et al., 2003; Iacoboni et al., 2004; Schilbach et al., 2012; Timmermans, Schilbach, Pasquali, & Cleeremans, 2012).

Taken together, regions of the motor system (primary motor cortex), the limbic system (amygdala), and the MENT network appear to play a role during the perception of and automatic responding to socially relevant facial expressions. While activity in motor cortex might help to generate a representation of the action which under the influence of the midbrain and medial temporal lobe may, in fact, translate to mimicking that behaviour oneself, involvement of the mentalizing network might contribute to social cognition by processing the differentiation of self and other. In dyadic interaction, both mechanisms are crucially important as a person's facial expression might highlight their internal state, but could also refer to some object or might be expressive of their assessment of the other's behaviour or the interaction itself.

The neural correlates of gaze-based social interaction and the modulatory effect of gaze on mimicry

While the studies described earlier provide some important insights into automatic processes that are relevant for social understanding, they have not assessed the behavioural and neurophysiological correlates of social cognition during real-time interaction. Recent conceptual developments, however, suggest that doing so may be of crucial importance and could help to shed light on this "blind spot" of social neuroscience research (Pfeiffer, Timmermans, Vogeley, Frith, & Schilbach, 2013; Schilbach et al., 2013). Indeed, important differences between situations of social observation and social interaction exist. For instance, within social interaction, interactors mutually and directly influence each other and may hold different roles during the interaction.

To establish an experimental paradigm that allows participants to be part of an ongoing social interaction in the constrained neuroimaging setting, we have devised a setup that makes use of eye-tracking data obtained from participants to control an anthropomorphic virtual character's gaze behaviour in real time, making it "responsive" to the human observer's gaze (Pfeiffer, Vogeley & Schilbach, 2013; Wilms et al., 2010). This setup, therefore, allows participants to experience their own eye-movements as having an effect on the gaze behaviour of a (virtual) other, similar to how this would occur in real-life situations. Importantly, this setup allows to investigate phenomena whose emergence necessarily

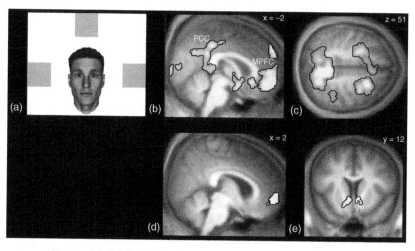

Figure 4.3 (a) Screenshot depicting an anthropomorphic virtual character and three objects (grey squares). (b) Neural correlates of joint attention. (c) Neural correlates of non-joint attention. (d) Neural correlates of other-initiated joint attention. (e) Neural correlates of self-initiated joint attention (Taken from Schilbach et al., 2013).

depends upon social interaction, its reciprocity and whose underlying psychological processes and neural mechanisms may differ depending upon the roles interactants hold during interaction, namely those of being "initiator" or "responder" during the interaction.

Based on the hypothesis that differences in the neural basis of joint attention, that is, looking at something together with someone, could be related to the reciprocity of social interaction (as compared to previous social neuroscience attempts to investigate the neural correlates of joint attention by means of tasks in which participants are mere observers of gaze cues; e.g. Williams, Waiter, Perra, Perrett, & Whiten, 2005; Materna, Dicke, & Thier, 2008), the interactive eye-tracking setup was used to conduct an fMRI study, in which participants interacted with a virtual other while undergoing neuroimaging (Schilbach et al., 2010). Experimental variations consisted of initiating vs. following the gaze of the virtual character when fixating objects shown on the stimulus screen (Figure 4.3a). Results demonstrate recruitment of the MENT for joint attention to an object, regardless of whether or not this was initiated by the participant or the (virtual) other (Figure 4.3b). Conversely, looking at an object different from the one inspected by the virtual other led to recruitment of a more lateralized fronto-parietal network (Figure 4.3c) resembling the neural network, which has been associated with the control of attention and eye-movements (Corbetta, Patel, & Shulman, 2008; Pierrot-Deseilligny, Milea, & Muri, 2004).

In summary and in spite of participants always fixating an object on the stimulus screen, the underlying brain activity appears to be markedly different depending upon whether or not the participant was doing this "together" with a virtual other or not. Doing so in coordination with the virtual character resulted in a differential increase of neural activity in a network whose activity has been associated with the human ability for grasping another person's mental states, their communicative intentions and for using an internally oriented mode of cognizing to contextualize aspects of a situation (Schilbach et al., 2008, 2012). Importantly, the MENT was activated as a result of participants naturally coordinating their gaze with that of the other without any explicit instruction to assess her mental states. Our findings, therefore, seem to contradict the proposal that the MENT is exclusively responsible for reflective and more explicit social cognition (cf. Keysers & Gazzola, 2007). On the contrary, this network is also activated as a result of interpersonal coordination in social interaction, which was also experienced as more pleasant and less effortful than doing the opposite of what the virtual character was doing (cf. Schnell et al., 2011).

Our findings, therefore, raise the intriguing possibility that activity changes in the MENT can occur as a result of (gaze-based) social interaction. To us it is tempting to think of this finding as paralleling the suggestions of Heyes (2010) with respect to the MNS, giving rise to the hypothesis that similar associative mechanisms might play a role in the case of the MENT. In a similar line of thought, Behrens and colleagues have demonstrated that social prediction error signals – when learning from the behaviour of or advice provided by others – are coded by MENT components, which they describe as evidence for the argument that higher-order social cognitive mechanisms may rely on simple associative processes (Behrens, Hunt, Woolrich & Rushworth, 2008). Similarly, future research in social neuroscience could investigate the development and changes in neural networks, that is, the neural plasticity related to and induced by real-time social interactions, thereby helping to understand how particular functions actually develop in particular areas of the brain or brains of interactants (cf. Westermann et al., 2007) and how they are related to phenomena of interpersonal coupling on the behavioural level.

Results of the fMRI study on joint attention also demonstrated differences in the neural correlates depending upon whether joint attention was self- or other-initiated: whereas following someone else's gaze to engage in joint attention resulted in the recruitment of the anterior portion of medial prefrontal cortex (Figure 4.3d), directing someone else's gaze towards an object activated the ventral striatum, an important part of the functional neuroanatomy of reward processing (Figure 4.3e).

In light of ratings of subjective experience also obtained from participants during a post-scan questionnaire – which indicated that they enjoyed looking at objects more "together with" the virtual other – the latter finding, interestingly, appeared to be related to the hedonic aspects of experiencing self-initiated joint attention (Schilbach et al., 2010). This seems to be in line with the idea that social interaction may involve collaborative and affiliative motives, the fulfilment of which is experienced as rewarding, possibly relying upon an "intrinsic" motivation of humans for sharing of experiences (Tomasello, 2009). Furthermore, these findings demonstrate how basic motivation- or reward-related signals may play a key role in the establishment and maintenance of social relations and the display of mimicry responses (e.g. Panksepp, Herman, Vilberg, Bishop, & DeEskinazi, 1980; Haffey, Press, O'Connell, & Chakrabarti, 2013). Our findings are in line with seminal findings of the "chameleon effect," that is, being imitated leads to positive feelings (Chartrand & Bargh, 1999), and neuroimaging results, which suggest that the neural correlate of such effects is localized to reward-related neurocircuitry (Kühn et al., 2010).

Finally, recent investigations have begun to target the effects of social priming on mimicry responses based on the idea that the subtlety and sophistication of mimicry in social contexts may reflect a social top-down response modulation (STORM), which could help to enhance one's own social standing (Wang & Hamilton, 2012). Wang and Hamilton (2012) pit their model against simulationist accounts of mimicry (e.g. Pickering & Garrod, 2004; Niedenthal et al., 2010) and accounts that suggest that mimicry is merely an epiphenomenon, and review evidence from social psychology to support the STORM model. Furthermore, they provide new empirical evidence gathered by making use of a novel social stimulus – response compatibility (SRC) paradigm, in which participants are asked to open (or close) their hand in response to hand-opening (or hand-closing) stimuli of an actress, who either established direct gaze before performing the hand action or not: the results demonstrate that eye gaze rapidly and specifically modulates the mimicry of the hand actions as indexed by reaction time differences between actions following direct as compared to averted gaze in the congruent, but not the incongruent condition. These behavioural studies were followed up by an fMRI study to investigate the putative interactions between MNS and MENT XE "mentalizing network" and in order to test whether information was passed on to MENT from the MNS (consistent with the simulationist account of mimicry) or vice versa (as suggested by the STORM model). The fMRI results showed that performing the social SRC task activated the MNS, whereas observation of direct gaze and inhibition of mimicry both engaged a part of the MENT. In a second step of the neuroimaging analysis, dynamic causal modelling (DCM) was used to investigate the effective connectivity between the brain regions of the two systems, that is, how brain regions exert causal influence over each other to produce activity changes. Results of the DCM analysis demonstrate strong intrinsic connectivity strength from medial prefrontal cortex to inferior frontal gyrus and from medial prefrontal cortex to superior temporal sulcus. Second, when participants performed the task, the connectivity strength from superior temporal sulcus to inferior frontal gyrus increased, suggesting that these regions implement the visuo-motor mapping for the task. Finally, the interaction of direct gaze and mimicry enhanced the connection strength from medial prefrontal cortex to superior temporal sulcus, which suggests that medial prefrontal cortex is the originator of the gaze-mimicry interaction and that it modulates sensory input to the MNS as proposed by the STORM model.

Future research could help to address whether social priming is equally effective for different types of mimicry (e.g. hand actions as compared to facial mimicry) and could include two-person investigations by means of dual eye-tracking and virtual-reality-based setups to provide a quantification of interpersonal processes (Barisic et al., 2013; Pfeiffer, Vogeley, & Schilbach, 2013). Also, future research could assess how changing the reward value of social interactions will affect mimicry responses in normal populations and individuals with social interaction and communication deficits, such as autism spectrum disorder (Haffey et al., 2013), and whether group-specific differences in mimicry responses are the result of dysfunctions of bottom-up or top-down modulations of mimicry.

Conclusions

Successful interpersonal communication depends to a large extent upon the exchange of non-verbal information. One particularly remarkable aspect of non-verbal behaviour during social interaction is interpersonal alignment or mimicry as humans have a tendency to unconsciously imitate and mimic others' behaviour. In the past, spontaneous mimicry has been a key topic in social psychology research, which has provided evidence for the consequences of the "chameleon effect," namely that mimicry has positive consequences on social interaction by increasing liking and affiliation between interactants.

More recently, cognitive neuroscience has started to investigate the neurobiological correlates of mimicry responses and has provided evidence for the involvement of different brain systems that contribute to the neural network subserving mimicry. On one hand, cognitive neuroscience suggests that mimicry is based on the MNS, which provides a tight perceptual-motor link whereby the observation of an action leads to the activation of the motor representation of that action. Furthermore, studies have shown that the motor system itself may also play an important role by realizing a pre-reflective, embodied response to socially relevant stimuli, which might serve evaluative and communicative functions, particularly in the case of facial mimicry. On the other hand, medial temporal and midbrain areas are differentially engaged during mimicry and could provide important emotional and mnestic contributions as well as a facilitation of non-volitional movements. Additionally, areas of the MENT or "default mode network" of the brain are engaged during mimicry and may have important top-down modulatory effects on perceptual-motor systems to make them context-sensitive.

Most importantly, involuntary muscle activity in response to the perception of socially relevant stimuli and its neural correlates may not only serve processing or evaluative functions, but may promote interpersonal alignment and reciprocal engagement with others. It may be these mechanisms of perceptual-motor interaction that in the context and history of social interactions constitute a form of "direct" access to other people's minds, while at the same time producing behavioural responses visible to the interaction partner, which help to sustain the process of interaction.

References

Amodio, D. M., & Frith, C. D. (2006). Meeting of minds: The medial frontal cortex and social cognition. *National Review of Neuroscience, 7*, 268–277.

Barisic, I., Timmermans, B., Pfeiffer, U. J., Bente, G., Vogeley, K., & Schilbach, L. (2013). In it together: Using dual eyetracking to investigate real-time social interactions. *Proceedings from SIGCHI Conference on Human Factors in Computing Systems.*

Behrens, T. E., Hunt, L. T., Woolrich, M. W., & Rushworth, M. F. (2008). Associative learning of social value. *Nature, 456*(7219), 245–249.

Blair, R. J. (2003). Facial expressions, their communicatory functions and neuro-cognitive substrates. *Philosophical Transactions of the Royal Society of London. Series B: Biological Sciences, 358*(1431), 561–572.

Brass, M., Schmitt, R. M., Spengler, S., & Gergely, G. (2007). Investigating action understanding: Inferential processes versus action simulation. *Current Biology, 17*(24), 2117–2121.

Carr, L., Iacoboni, M., Dubeau, M. C., Mazziotta, J. C., & Lenzi, G. L. (2003). Neural mechanisms of empathy in humans: A relay from neural systems for imitation to limbic areas. *Proceedings of the National Academy of Science, 100*(9), 5497–5502.

Chartrand, T. L., & Bargh, J. A. (1999). The chameleon effect: The perception-behavior link and social interaction. *Journal of Personality and Social Psychology, 76*(6), 893–910.

Cole, J. (2001). Empathy needs a face. *Journal of Consciousness Studies, 8*(5–7), 51–68.

Corbetta, M., Patel, G., & Shulman, G. L. (2008). The reorienting system of the human brain: From environment to theory of mind. *Neuron, 58*(3), 306–324.

Damasio, A. (2010). *Self comes to mind.* New York: Pantheon.

Darwin, C. (1872). *The expression of the emotions in man and animals.* London: Murray.

Dimberg, U. (1982). Facial reactions to facial expressions. *Psychophysiology, 19,* 643–6647.

Dimberg, U. (1990). Facial electromyography and emotional reactions. *Psychophysiology, 27,* 481–494.

Dimberg, U., & Thunberg, M. (1998). Rapid facial reactions to emotional facial expressions. *Scandinavian Journal of Psychology, 39*(1), 39–45.

Dimberg, U., Thunberg, M., & Elmehed, K. (2000). Unconscious facial reactions to emotional facial expressions. *Psychological Science, 11*(1), 86–89.

Dresel, C., Castrop, F., Haslinger, B., Wohlschlaeger, A. M., Hennenlotter, A., & Ceballos-Baumann, A. O. (2005). The functional neuroanatomy of coordinated orofacial movements: Sparse sampling fMRI of whistling. *Neuroimage, 28,* 588–597.

Erickson, K., & Schulkin, J. (2003). Facial expressions of emotion: A cognitive neuroscience perspective. *Brain and Cognition, 52*(1), 52–60.

Fischer, A. H., Becker, D., & Veenstra, L. (2012). Emotional mimicry in social context: The case of disgust and pride. *Frontiers in Emotion Science, 3,* 475.

Frijda, N. H. (1986). *The emotions.* London: Cambridge University Press.

Frijda, N. H., & Tcherkassof, A. (1997). Facial expressions as modes of action readiness. In J. A. Russel & J. M. Fernandez-Dols (Eds.), *The psychology of facial expression* (pp. 78–102). New York: Cambridge University Press.

Gallagher, S. (2007). Simulation trouble. *Social Neuroscience, 2,* 353–365.

Gamer, M., & Buchel, C. (2009). Amygdala activation predicts gaze toward fearful eyes. *Journal of Neuroscience, 29*(28), 9123–9126.

Gangopadhyay, N., & Schilbach, L. (2012). Seeing minds: A neurophilosophical investigation of the role of perception-action coupling in social perception. *Social Neuroscience, 7*(4), 410–423.

Grezes, J., Armony, J. L., Rowe, J., & Passingham, R. E. (2003). Activations related to "mirror" and "canonical" neurones in the human brain: An fMRI study. *Neuroimage, 18*(4), 928–937.

Haffey, A., Press, C., O'Connell, G., & Chakrabarti, B. (2013). Autistic traits modulate mimicry of social but not nonsocial rewards. *Autism Research, 6*(6), 614–620.

Hanakawa, T., Parikh, S., Bruno, M. K., & Hallett, M. (2005). Finger and face representations in the ipsilateral precentral motor areas in humans. *Journal of Neurophysiology, 93*(5), 2950–2958.

Haxby, J. V., Hoffman, E. A., & Gobbini, M. I. (2002). Human neural systems for face recognition and social communication. *Biological Psychiatry, 51*(1), 59–67.

Heerey, E. A., & Crossley, H. M. (2013). Predictive and reactive mechanisms in smile reciprocity. *Psychological Science, 24*(8), 1446–1455.

Hess, U., & Bourgeois, P. (2010). You smile-I smile: Emotion expression in social interaction. *Biological Psychology, 84*(3), 514–520.

Hess, U., & Fischer, A. (2013). Emotional mimicry as social regulation. *Personality and Social Psychology Review, 17*(2), 142–157.

Heyes, C. (2010). Where do mirror neurons come from? *Neuroscience and Biobehavioral Review, 34*(4), 575–583.

Iacoboni, M., Lieberman, M. D., Knowlton, B. J., Molnar-Szakacs, I., Moritz, M., Throop, C. J., et al. (2004). Watching social interactions produces dorsomedial prefrontal and medial parietal BOLD fMRI signal increases compared to a resting baseline. *Neuroimage, 21*(3), 1167–1173.

Iacoboni, M., Woods, R. P., Brass, M., Bekkering, H., Mazziotta, J. C., & Rizzolatti, G. (1999). Cortical mechanisms of human imitation. *Science, 286* (5449), 2526–2528.

Kaiser, S., & Wehrle, T. (2001). Facial expressions as indicators of appraisal processes. In K. R. Scherer, A. Schorr., & T. Johnstone (Eds.), *Appraisal processes in emotions: Theory, methods, research* (pp. 285–300). New York: Oxford University Press.

Keysers, C., & Gazzola, V. (2007). Integrating simulation and theory of mind: From self to social cognition. *Trends in Cognitive Science, 11*(5), 194–196.

Kourtis, D., Sebanz, N., & Knoblich, G. (2010). Favouritism in the motor system: Social interaction modulates action simulation. *Biological Letters, 6*(6), 758–761.

Kuhn, S., Muller, B. C., van Baaren, R. B., Wietzker, A., Dijksterhuis, A., & Brass, M. (2010). Why do I like you when you behave like me? Neural mechanisms mediating positive consequences of observing someone being imitated. *Social Neuroscience, 5*(4), 384–392.

Lang, P. J., Greenwald, M. K., Bradley, M. M., & Hamm, A. O. (1993). Looking at pictures: Affective, facial, visceral, and behavioral reactions. *Psychophysiology, 30*(3), 261–273.

Lee, T. W., Josephs, O., Dolan, R. J., & Critchley, H. D. (2006). Imitating expressions: Emotion-specific neural substrates in facial mimicry. *Social Cognition and Affective Neuroscience, 1*(2), 122–135.

Leslie, K. R., Johnson-Frey, S. H., & Grafton, S. T. (2004). Functional imaging of face and hand imitation: Towards a motor theory of empathy. *Neuroimage, 21*(2), 601–607.

Likowski, K. U., Muhlberger, A., Gerdes, A. B., Wieser, M. J., Pauli, P., & Weyers, P. (2012). Facial mimicry and the mirror neuron system: Simultaneous acquisition of facial electromyography and functional magnetic resonance imaging. *Frontiers in Human Neuroscience, 6*, 214.

Materna, S., Dicke, P. W., & Thier, P. (2008). Dissociable roles of the superior temporal sulcus and the intraparietal sulcus in joint attention: A functional magnetic resonance imaging study. *Journal of Cognitive Neuroscience, 20*(1), 108–119.

Mehrabian, A. (1971). *Silent messages*. Belmont, CA: Wadsworth.

Meltzoff, A. N., & Moore, M. K. (1977). Imitation of facial and manual gestures by human neonates. *Science, 198*(4312), 75–78.

Merleau-Ponty, M. (1964). *The primacy of perception*. Evanston, IL: Northwestern University Press.

Mojzisch, A., Schilbach, L., Helmert, J. R., Pannasch, S., Velichkovsky, B. M., & Vogeley, K. (2006). The effects of self-involvement on attention, arousal, and facial expression during social interaction with virtual others: A psychophysiological study. *Social Neuroscience, 1*(3–4), 184–195.

Muscatell, K. A., Addis, D. R., & Kensinger, E. A. (2010). Self-involvement modulates the effective connectivity of the autobiographical memory network. *Social Cognition and Affective Neuroscience, 5*(1), 68–76.

Niedenthal, P. M., Barsalou, L. W., Winkielman, P., Krauth-Gruber, S., & Ric, F. (2005). Embodiment in attitudes, social perception, and emotion. *Personality and Social Psychology Review, 9*(3), 184–211.

Niedenthal, P. M., Mermillod, M., Maringer, M., & Hess, U. (2010). The Simulation of Smiles (SIMS) model: Embodied simulation and the meaning of facial expression. *Behavioral and Brain Sciences, 33*(6), 417–433; discussion 433.

Oberman, L. M., Winkielman, P., & Ramachandran, V. S. (2007). Face to face: Blocking facial mimicry can selectively impair recognition of emotional expressions. *Social Neuroscience, 2*(3–4), 167–178.

Panksepp, J., Herman, B. H., Vilberg, T., Bishop, P., & DeEskinazi, F. G. (1980). Endogenous opioids and social behavior. *Neuroscience and Biobehavioral Review, 4*(4), 473–487.

Pelphrey, K. A., Singerman, J. D., Allison, T., & McCarthy, G. (2003). Brain activation evoked by perception of gaze shifts: The influence of context. *Neuropsychologia, 41*(2), 156–170.

Pfeiffer, U. J., Vogeley, K., & Schilbach, L. (2013). From gaze cueing to dual eye-tracking: Novel approaches to investigate the neural correlates of gaze in social interaction. *Neuroscience and Biobehavioral Review, 37*(10 Pt 2), 2516–2528.

Pfeiffer, U. J., Timmermans, B., Vogeley, K., Frith, C. D., & Schilbach, L. (2013). Towards a neuroscience of social interaction. *Frontiers in Human Neuroscience, 7*, 22.

Pickering, M. J., & Garrod, S. (2004). Toward a mechanistic psychology of dialogue. *Behavioral and Brain Sciences, 27*(2), 169–190; discussion 190.

Pierrot-Deseilligny, C., Milea, D., & Muri, R. M. (2004). Eye movement control by the cerebral cortex. *Current Opinion Neurology, 17*(1), 17–25.

Preston, S. D., & de Waal, F. B. (2002). Empathy: Its ultimate and proximate bases. *Behavioral and Brain Sciences, 25*(1), 1–20; discussion 20.

Rizzolatti, G., & Sinigaglia, C. (2010). The functional role of the parieto-frontal mirror circuit: Interpretations and misinterpretations. *Nature Reviews Neuroscience, 11*(4), 264–274.

Rizzolatti, G., Fogassi, L., & Gallese, V. (2001). Neurophysiological mechanisms underlying the understanding and imitation of action. *Nature Reviews Neuroscience, 2*(9), 661–670.

Schilbach, L., Eickhoff, S. B., Mojzisch, A., & Vogeley, K. (2008). What's in a smile? Neural correlates of facial embodiment during social interaction. *Social Neuroscience, 3*(1), 37–50.

Schilbach, L., Bzdok, D., Timmermans, B., Fox, P. T., Laird, A. R., Vogeley, K., et al. (2012). Introspective minds: Using ALE meta-analyses to study commonalities in the neural correlates of emotional processing, social & unconstrained cognition. *PLoS One, 7*(2), e30920.

Schilbach, L., Timmermans, B., Reddy, V., Costall, A., Bente, G., Schlicht, T., et al. (2013). Toward a second-person neuroscience. *Behavioral and Brain Sciences, 36*(4), 393–414.

Schilbach, L., Wilms, M., Eickhoff, S. B., Romanzetti, S., Tepest, R., Bente, G., et al. (2010). Minds made for sharing: Initiating joint attention recruits reward-related neurocircuitry. *Journal of Cognitive Neuroscience, 22*(12), 2702–2715.

Schilbach, L., Wohlschlaeger, A. M., Kraemer, N. C., Newen, A., Shah, N. J., Fink, G. R., et al. (2006). Being with virtual Others: Neural correlates of social interaction. *Neuropsychologia, 44*(5), 718–730.

Schippers, M. B., & Keysers, C. (2011). Mapping the flow of information within the putative mirror neuron system during gesture observation. *Neuroimage, 57*(1), 37–44.

Schnell, K., Bluschke, S., Konradt, B., & Walter, H. (2011). Functional relations of empathy and mentalizing: An fMRI study on the neural basis of cognitive empathy. *Neuroimage, 54*(2), 1743–1754.

Timmermans, B., Schilbach, L., Pasquali, A., & Cleeremans, A. (2012). Higher order thoughts in action: Consciousness as an unconscious re-description process. *Philosophical Transactions of the Royal Society of London. Series B: Biological Sciences, 367*(1594), 1412–1423.

Tomasello, M. (2009). *Why we cooperate*. Cambridge, MA: MIT Press.

Wallbott, H. G. (1991). Recognition of emotion from facial expression via imitation? Some indirect evidence for an old theory. *British Journal of Social Psychology, 30*(Pt 3), 207–219.

Wang, Y., & Hamilton, A. F. (2012). Social top-down response modulation (STORM): A model of the control of mimicry in social interaction. *Frontiers in Human Neuroscience, 6*, 153.

Warren, J. E., Sauter, D. A., Eisner, F., Wiland, J., Dresner, M. A., Wise, R. J., et al. (2006). Positive emotions preferentially engage an auditory-motor "mirror" system. *Journal of Neuroscience, 26*(50), 13067–13075.

Westermann, G., Mareschal, D., Johnson, M. H., Sirois, S., Spratling, M., & Thomas, M. (2007). Neuroconstructivism. *Developmental Science, 10*(1), 75–83.

Wild, B., Erb, M., Eyb, M., Bartels, M., & Grodd, W. (2003). Why are smiles contagious? An fMRI study of the interaction between perception of facial affect and facial movements. *Psychiatry Research, 123*(1), 17–36.

Williams, J. H., Waiter, G. D., Perra, O., Perrett, D. I., & Whiten, A. (2005). An fMRI study of joint attention experience. *Neuroimage, 25*(1), 133–140.

Wilms, M., Schilbach, L., Pfeiffer, U., Bente, G., Fink, G. R., & Vogeley, K. (2010). It's in your eyes – using gaze-contingent stimuli to create truly interactive paradigms for social cognitive and affective neuroscience. *Social and Cognitive Affective Neuroscience, 5*(1), 98–107.

CHAPTER 5

The social dimension as antecedent and effect of emotional mimicry

Ursula Hess, Isabell Hühnel, Job van der Schalk,
and Agneta H. Fischer

Emotional mimicry by definition requires two (or more) people who show congruent emotional expressions. Emotional mimicry further implies that the emotional display of the mimicker is dependent on the emotional display of the mimicked person. Although mimicry research to date has not always been conclusive with respect to the nature of this congruency, we follow Hess and Fischer's (2013) definition, arguing that the mimicked emotional display should reflect a *sharing* of the original emotional display, rather than a reaction to the original display. Specifically, Hess and Fischer (2013) have proposed a *Mimicry in Social Context* model holding that emotional mimicry depends on an understanding of the social meaning of the situation in which mimicry occurs. From this view, mimicry has an inherently communicative function and can be considered a social regulator. This view implies that whether we label an emotional reaction as mimicry depends on the nature of the relationship between expresser and the observer.

In this chapter, we will focus on the role and nature of this relationship and address two central issues. The first relates to the type of relationships in which mimicry occurs (see also Stel, Chapter 2, and Winkielman et al., Chapter 8). Research on behavioural mimicry – that is, on the mimicry of non-verbal behaviours that are not emotion displays (such as foot tapping) – presumes that mimicry *always* occurs, independent of the nature of the relationship. In fact, Chartrand and Bargh (1999) subsume mimicry as one of many automatic behaviours that are presumed to be preconscious and not goal dependent, that is, they are obligatory. With regard to mimicry, this means "the effect should occur among strangers when no affiliation goal is present" (p. 900).

Is this also true for emotional mimicry? Can emotional mimicry occur between strangers or even between antagonists, and if so, under which circumstances would this occur? In this context, we will discuss the role of social goals in an emotional exchange. Second, we will review evidence on the *effects* of emotional mimicry on social relationships. Does emotional mimicry improve social relations in all circumstances?

Affiliation and similarity

Can the nature of the relationship lead to an increase or decrease in emotional mimicry? Human relationships are characterized by two fundamental behavioural intentions: affiliation and dominance (Leary, 1957). Dominance relates to the position of an individual in a social hierarchy and the behaviours used to maintain that position, whereas affiliation relates to the sociability of the individual. Humans are most comfortable in interactions in which these are balanced between interaction partners, and mimicry is one behaviour of relevance in this context. In this vein, the *complementary contrast and assimilation theory* as formulated by Tiedens, Chow, and Unzueta (2007) can be used to outline the conditions under which mimicry can be expected. The theory is based on interpersonal theory (Kiesler, 1982; Leary, 1957; Wiggins, 1979). Interpersonal theory predicts that demonstrations of affiliative behaviour invite similar levels of affiliation on the part of the interaction partner. That is, affiliative behaviour is reciprocated. Mimicry is one important means of reciprocating affiliation, as reflected in the reference to "social glue" (Lakin, Jefferis, Cheng, & Chartrand, 2003). Yet, interpersonal contrast and assimilation theory also predicts that dominance-relevant behaviours invite contrasting behaviours. Thus, Tiedens and Fragale (2003) found that participants exposed to a dominant confederate decreased the dominance of their postural stance, whereas participants exposed to a submissive confederate increased their dominance. Hence, we would expect that in relationships that are characterized by liking and cooperation, mimicry should be the foremost response. By contrast, in relationships characterized by dislike or competition, no mimicry or even what has been termed counterempathy (Lanzetta & Englis, 1989) – incongruent facial reactions such as smiles to the pain of others – should be found. Similar considerations apply to the emotions mimicked. Happiness, sadness, and to some degree fear in response to an external event all signal affiliation (Hess, Blairy, & Kleck, 2000; Knutson, 1996) and hence should invite mimicry. By contrast, expressions such as anger and disgust signal dominance (Hess et al., 2000; Knutson, 1996). They should invite a contrasting submissive or ingratiating response. Behavioural mimicry can serve such a function (Lakin & Chartrand, 2005), but showing anger in response to the anger of others is a provocative act that challenges the dominance display of the other. As such, we would expect the response to depend on the nature of the relationship. For example, an angry face may elicit a neutral or fear response from an individual in a subordinate position, but an angry response from someone with an equal or higher power position. Neither of these would represent properly speaking mimicry. In what follows, we will consider mimicry in different types of relationships.

Most direct evidence for the role of observer–expresser relationship comes from studies in which friends and strangers have been compared. For example, in a study of mimicry of pride and disgust in a spontaneous interaction, Fischer, Becker, and Veenstra (2012) found that dyads composed of friends mimic each other's smiles more than do dyads of strangers. In this study, disgust was evoked by smelling a foul odour and pride by receiving a compliment. In dyads of friends, smiles were mimicked, both those that occurred in the disgust and those that occurred in the pride context. This was not the case for dyads of strangers, suggesting that the affiliative link between friends was required for smile mimicry. As can be expected from the above, mimicry of disgust was not found at all, whether among friends or strangers, as disgust – like anger – signals dominance and hence should not invite mimicry.

In fact, in lab-based research on facial mimicry, participants are typically not personally known to each other. However, observers may nonetheless have a basic favourable or unfavourable attitude towards an unknown expresser. This may be the case because they know something about the expresser. For example, studies by Bourgeois and Hess and McHugo and colleagues show that observers mimic politicians whose political orientation they share or of whom they approve of more, compared to those who hold a different political opinion or have a negative opinion of the politician (Bourgeois & Hess, 2008; McHugo, Lanzetta, & Bush, 1991; McHugo, Lanzetta, Sullivan, Masters, & Englis, 1985).

The relationship between expresser and observer can also be manipulated, for example by inducing a positive or negative evaluation or attitude towards this stranger. Thus, Stel and colleagues (2010) found more mimicry towards a liked person than a disliked one when manipulating the likeability of the target and measuring the amount of facial and postural mimicry in response to a woman in a video clip. A similar conclusion was reached by Likowski, Mühlberger, Seibt, Pauli, and Weyers (2008), who demonstrated that even when participants are presented with fictional characters shown as avatars, the mimicry of that character is affected by the likeability of the character based on narratives about them. The characters that were described as "good" were mimicked clearly, whereas those characters described as "bad" were not mimicked at all, irrespective of whether the emotional expression was positive (happy) or negative (sad).

This research on the effect of positive or negative attitudes on emotional mimicry can be extended to research on in-group and out-group members. Observers are more likely to mimic the emotional reactions of in-group members than those of out-group members. This effect was shown for facial mimicry, for example, by Bourgeois and Hess (Study 2, 2008) and by Van der Schalk and colleagues (2011). In these studies, the same targets showing emotions were presented as either in-group members or out-group members. The results show that observers mimic the negative expressions of in-group members more than the same expressions of out-group members. Interestingly, however, both studies independently did not find such an in-group effect for smiling. In both studies, smiling was mimicked to the same extent, independently of group membership. We will come back to this exception for happiness later. In another study, which extents findings based on the mimicry of facial expressions, Weisbuch and Ambady (2008) found that the anxious voice of an in-group member was imitated more than the anxious voice of an out-group member.

These and other studies that manipulated group membership of the emotion expresser (e.g. Yabar, Johnston, Miles, & Peace, 2006) seem to suggest that attitudes influences mimicry. In addition to attitude, similarity with the target may also affect affiliative stance. For example, Stel et al. (2010) found that similarity with the target increased mimicry, but only when the target was not liked. Guéguen and Martin (2009) examined the role of similarity on behavioural mimicry. They operationalized similarity as having similar names (Study 1) or having a similar field of studies (Study 2). The participants first watched a video of a woman who touched and rubbed her face very often during an interview and then read the CV of the woman, which contained the similarity/dissimilarity information. They were subsequently instructed to watch the video more closely and the amount of mimicry with the target was measured. As expected, participants in the similarity condition mimicked more than in the dissimilarity condition, in both studies. This effect was mediated by how much the respondents liked the target. Specifically, respondents who perceived themselves as similar mimicked the target more, because they liked the target more.

In sum, based on studies of both behavioural and emotional mimicry, there seems to be a tendency for friends, in-group members, and liked persons to be mimicked more than strangers, out-group members, and disliked persons. This supports the notion that mimicry is a means to reciprocate affiliation. Yet, in many studies, evidence for mimicry is observed even when no information about the other is provided, and the other does not seem overly similar either. A good example would be the classic studies by Dimberg (1982) using the PFA (Pictures of Facial Affect; Ekman & Friesen, 1976). Yet, for human beings as a social species, affiliative intent can be assumed to be the default stance for situations in which the other is a potential in-group member and no negative information is provided by the context. Thus, in cases where observers do not know the person, mimicry can be expected in most cases at least for affiliative emotions.

Yet, what can be expected in response to non-affiliative, dominant emotion expressions may depend on the nature of the relationship. Häfner and IJzermans (2011), for example, showed that individuals with a communal relationship smiled at the sight of a photo of their angry partner, but mimicked the angry expression of strangers by frowning. As reported earlier, other studies have found no mimicry of anger or disgust, whether in friends or strangers (Bourgeois & Hess, 2008, Study 2; Fischer et al., 2012) and in most contexts we do not expect displays involving non-affiliative emotions to invite mimicry. Showing anger in response to anger is generally seen as a provocative display. Smiling on the other hand may serve as a suitably submissive ingratiating display. For example, in a close relationship smiling should be predominantly an affiliative, appeasing, or accommodating response (Häfner & Ijzerman, 2011). Smiles can also signal dominance or superiority, however, and may hence be perceived as a provocation as well (Niedenthal, Mermillod, Maringer, & Hess, 2010). The question arises when strangers' anger expressions are mimicked, as was the case in the study by Häfner and Ijzerman (2011). This may not only depend on the nature of the relationship but also on the social interaction goals. One may mimic a stranger's anger when the anger expression is not perceived as directed to the self, and thus not as a signal to be acted upon (Bourgeois & Hess, 2008, Study 1). This may be often the case when viewing photos or videos, which create a passive stance, as there is no interaction goal in that situation. However, perceiving an angry face may also enhance a motive to signal dominance or superiority oneself, because it evokes a hostile motive. In this latter case, the expression would best be described as a reactive emotion display rather than mimicry (see also, Hess & Fischer, 2014).

Social goals and motives

The nature of an emotional exchange is not only dependent upon whether we have a positive or negative attitude towards a stranger, or whether we feel (dis)similar, but also on the goal of the emotional exchange and the interpretation and relevance of the other's motives (see also, Cesario, Plaks, & Higgins, 2006). For example, does a doctor mimic a patient's facial expressions when she tries to keep a distance? Or, does a poker player mimic his adversary's expressions? In most previous research on emotional mimicry, no information about the interactional or social goals of the target has been provided. This makes it impossible to know what the expression means and what impact it has on our relationship with the other person or the tasks we are engaged in. Thus, when another person expresses an emotion, we not only process information on whether we like the person or not but also on how we interpret this expression with regard to our own and the other's social goals. This interpretation can be based on a variety of contextual factors, such as the situation that may have elicited the emotion, the type of person expressing the emotion, the meaning of the emotional exchange for one's relationship with that person or the tasks we are engaged in.

The idea that social goals in an emotional exchange are relevant for the presence or attenuation of mimicry has been addressed in different contexts. Thus, Lakin, Chartrand, and Arkin (2008) manipulated affiliation goals in order to study their effects on mimicry. For this, they induced social inclusion or exclusion using an online Cyberball game (Williams & Jarvis, 2006) and instructed participants to describe a photo to a confederate in the second part of the experiment. The mimicry of the foot movement of the confederate was the dependent measure and the researchers found that participants in the exclusion condition mimicked the foot movement more than in the inclusion condition. The authors assumed that the motive to affiliate was stronger in the exclusion condition and that mimicry is one means to achieve this.

Another way to manipulate social goals is to place people in cooperative versus competitive conditions. In a classic study, Lanzetta and Englis (1989) told people that they would either cooperate or compete with a co-actor. They then saw the co-actor on a screen react to the game, which involved electroshocks when loosing. Participants mimicked both smiles and discomfort grimaces shown by the cooperating co-actor but not by the competing one. In fact, they showed counter-empathic expression to the grimaces of the competing other. These findings were replicated by Weyers and colleagues (2009) who used unconscious competition priming (versus neutral priming) and also found both an absence of mimicry and evidence for counter-empathy in the competition condition. Thus, participants in a competitive relationship are usually in an antagonistic rather than affiliative frame of mind and do *not* have the social goal to affiliate with the other and are therefore unlikely to mimic the facial displays of their opponent.

Still another line of research has argued that the perception of a specific social category not only evokes associated behaviours (e.g. elderly and walking slowly) but also prepares the perceiver's motivational system for an interaction with the specific target (Cesario et al., 2006). Following this line of argument, not merely perceiving a member from a social category would prime automatic behaviour, but a personal interaction goal could evoke a response that does not reflect the stereotype. Indeed in Study 2,

Cesario and colleagues showed that participants who were primed with gay (versus straight) targets reacted with a more hostile response, even though this is not part of the stereotype of gay men. Applying this to emotional mimicry, we could argue that the interaction goal of perceivers influences whether and which emotion displays are mimicked.

Two recent studies from our own laboratory (Hess, Blaison, & Semin, 2013; Hess, Dandeneau, & Blaison, 2015) explicitly addressed the effect of social goals on emotional mimicry. One specific goal in an interaction may be to ignore the other person's emotions, for example, when one does not want to be influenced by another person's emotions or tries to stay distant. In those cases, one would not expect mimicry to occur, because as in the antagonistic situations above, the social goal is precisely not to affiliate. We used a classical affective priming paradigm to examine what happens when participants are instructed to disregard the first of two sequentially presented facial expressions, thus making only the second expression meaningful. Participants first saw either a positive (happy), negative (angry), or neutral facial expression for 100 ms, which served as the prime and which the participants were told to ignore. Then a second facial expression was shown and remained on the screen for several seconds. This expression served as the target and was either congruent or incongruent with the prime. Participants were asked to decide whether the target showed either a positive or negative expression and to react as quickly as possible. Emotional mimicry towards the prime and the target was assessed using facial electromyography (EMG) at the *Corrugator Supercilii* (frown), *Orbicularis Oculi* (wrinkles around the eyes), and the *Zygomaticus Major* (lifting the corners of the mouth in a smile) sites.

Reaction time measures were in line with the classical affective priming effect, that is, reaction times to congruent targets were significantly shorter than reaction times to incongruent targets. This finding suggests that despite the instruction to ignore these faces, the facial primes were seen and processed by the participants. However, the facial EMG results for the prime and target faces revealed a different processing pattern. First, a short period of activation of the *Corrugator Supercilii* occurred, which was independent of the valence of the prime and seems to represent an orienting response towards the stimulus. Following this, at 300–500 ms after the presentation of the target face, muscle activation congruent with the target face was observed, such that for angry targets an increase of *Corrugator Supercilii* activity with a concurrent decrease of *Orbicularis Oculi* and *Zygomaticus Major* was found. The opposite pattern was found for happy primes.

This pattern of findings shows that even though they were clearly perceived and processed – as the primes were presented supraliminally and a classic affective priming effect had been obtained – the primes were not mimicked. By contrast, the targets were mimicked. These findings point to the importance of the observer's motivation and suggest that expressions that are to be disregarded are not perceived as meaningful to the current goals of the observer and are therefore not mimicked.

In a second study, we directly manipulated a social goal of understanding the other. Specifically, participants saw briefly (33 ms) presented expressions of sadness and anger and had to decide which emotion they saw. Some expressions were rewarded – that is, participants knew that they would receive a monetary reward if they were able to correctly decode these expressions, that is, demonstrate their understanding of the other's emotional expression. For half the participants, correctly decoded expressions on male faces were rewarded, for the other half correctly decoded expressions on female faces were rewarded. That is, participants were motivated to attend to the rewarded expressions and to understand their meaning so as to correctly decode them to receive the reward. The results showed that decoding accuracy for both emotions was higher in the reward condition. And as expected – at least for sadness – facial mimicry was also enhanced. That is, participants with the goal to understand the other better – so as to be more accurate in decoding and to receive the reward – showed more mimicry, and did indeed understand the expressions better. However, as noted above, increased mimicry was only found for sadness. As mentioned above, anger displays are non-affiliative and dominant and may not per se invite mimicry even when an external social goal was provided that can foster mimicry.

One limitation of most studies reported above is that sender and emotional message are confounded. That is, the social goal of the sender is directly signalled by the facial expression and hence mimicry can be seen as occurring in response to the sender but also in response to the expression. That is, what these studies can show is the importance of the interpretation of the social goal (which depends on the sender by emotion interaction) for mimicry to occur but they do not allow the reverse conclusion that the *sharing* of the emotion is a relevant dimension for mimicry.

Yet, the Mimicry in Social Context model by Hess and Fischer (2013) argues that the mimicked emotional display should reflect a *sharing* of the original emotional display rather than a reaction to the original display. Importantly, individuals are not understood to "blindly" mimic what they see, but rather they mimic what they understand about the others' feelings. This notion was first proposed by Bavelas (Bavelas, Black, Lemery, & Mullett, 1986) in an article appropriately titled "'I show how you feel': Motor mimicry as a communicative act." As such, all that would be required would be the knowledge about the emotional message – irrespective of its form. Evidence for this comes, for example, from cross-modal mimicry,

Figure 5.1 Example stick figure faces showing happiness, anger, sadness, and fear.

where individuals mimic facially emotions they hear (see Hawk and Fischer, Chapter 6).

When separating the content of the emotional message from the sender, it is possible to more directly investigate the emotional message while leaving the emotional display similar. Emotional messages may differ depending on who displays the emotion, eliciting different interaction goals. That is, we can vary the degree to which the emotional message has relevance for both sender and receiver and hence can be considered to represent a shared perspective. We conducted a study (Dietrich, Hühnel, Sangenstedt, & Hess, 2013) in which the message consisted of pictures that present minimal representations of human faces, namely stick figures (see Figure 5.1 for example).

Stick figures contain none of the context information such as age or social group that are inherently part of real human faces and hence on their own do not provide relationship-relevant information, and thereby unconfound sender relevance and message relevance. In addition, they quite clearly are not the sender, but rather a message composed by the sender. Hence the social goals of the sender and the meaningfulness of the message for the receiver are manipulated by identifying different senders. This was done by presenting the stick figures in three different contexts. One-third of the participants were told that the figures were created by stroke patients as part of an emotional training in their physical rehabilitation programme. Another third were told that a computer program had created the expressions based on a selection of facial features. The last third were told that the figures were created by children who had drawn a close person in different emotional states.

We expected that in the stroke patient condition the emotional message should be meaningful and relevant and thereby invite mimicry as the purported creator should not be perceived as either dominant or non-affiliative. Further, we would expect most observers to feel empathic towards the sender, as the sender is someone struggling to recover from a major health problem. Importantly, the emotional messages – the facial expressions shown by the stick figures – also should not signal dominance or affiliation intentions with regard to the observer as they are not directed at the observer and are not meant to signal dominance intent. Hence in this case, we would expect mimicry of all emotions, including anger. By contrast, stick figures created by a computer program should elicit the lowest level of mimicry because a computer cannot per se create an emotionally meaningful message or wish to affiliate. Hence the most obvious outcome would be an absence of mimicry in this condition. However, it is possible that this notion may not fully reflect the reality of human computer interaction. A recent study showed that the cortical processing of smiling emoticons, as indexed by the N170, resembled the processing of faces, but only when shown in the right direction (Churches, Nicholls, Thiessen, Kohler, & Keage, 2014). Further, when engaging in interactions, people have a strong urge to predict their inter-action partner's reaction to their own behaviour and to build mental models of the other person from which to predict the likely response of the other (Frith & Frith, 2006). However, humans create not only mental maps of other humans but also of their technological environment (Norman, 1987). As such, it is not impossible that especially young people who grew up interacting with computers mimic in this context if indeed reactions to emoticons generalize to reactions to stick figures. In this case, the mimicry might be most likely for happy and sad faces as happy and sad emoticons are very common, but not anger or fear emoticons. We expected the least motivation for mimicry for stick figures created by children. Naïve theories suggest that children's drawings do not represent clear messages as children frequently draw indiscriminately large numbers of images, making an individual image less meaningful.

One hundred and twenty female participants were recruited via an online participant database at Humboldt-Universität zu Berlin. Their mean age was 23.6 years, and they were either students or young profes-sionals. The participants were randomly assigned to one of the three conditions and first told about the supposed creator of the stick figures. Following this, we presented the stick figures with expressions of happi-ness, anger, sadness, or fear in random order, while we measured facial EMG at *Corrugator Supercilii, Orbicularis Oculi, Zygomaticus Major* and *Frontalis, pars medialis* sites to assess whether the expressions were mimicked.

Overall, emotional mimicry was present and varied meaningfully between the three conditions. As can be seen in Figure 5.2, and as pre-dicted, all emotion expressions were mimicked when the stroke patients were seen as the sender of the emotional message. This is in line with the notion that their emotional messages were seen as meaningful and affilia-tive. Also as expected, there was considerably less evidence for the mimicry of stick figures purportedly drawn by children. In this case, only happy expressions were mimicked. In fact, we had previously

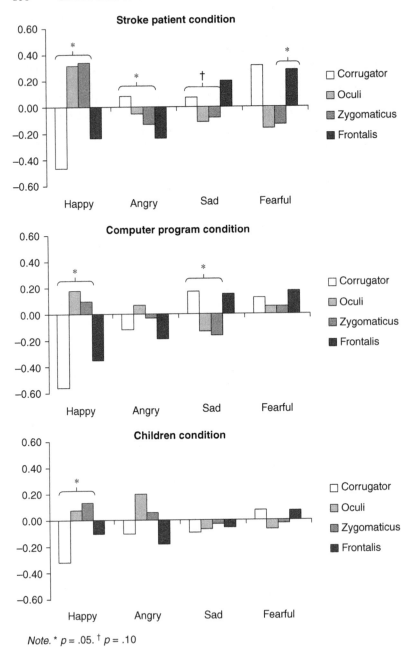

Note. * p = .05. † p = .10

Figure 5.2 Emotional mimicry to stick figures across conditions and emotions. Emotional mimicry was defined by patterns of muscle

noted that mimicry of happy expressions often occurs even when all other expressions are not mimicked.

This may lie in the nature of the emotional message of happy expressions. Mimicry is a means of affiliating. But, as noted in evolutionary psychology, affiliation has a positive side by providing us with sources of support, but also a negative side in that support may be demanded from us and this demand may exceed what we are willing to provide (Schaller, Park, & Kenrick, 2012). In that sense, sadness mimicry in particular can be understood as having a high social cost (Bourgeois & Hess, 2008). Happiness, however, signals that all is well and by its very nature therefore assures that no "expense" will accrue. As such, it may well be that happiness mimicry has a high likelihood to occur if there is no specfic reason why it should not (as would be the case if the happiness is attributed to a competitor who may feel glee over our loss, as in Lanzatta and Englis, 1989, above).

The most fascinating result stems from the condition where the stimuli were supposedly computer-generated faces, where mimicry was found for happy and sad expressions. This is suggestive of the notion that our participants did indeed share the perspective of computer-generated faces. It would be interesting to repeat this study with a group of participants who are not used to computers. In this case, we would expect no mimicry. In sum, this recent evidence from our laboratory suggests that the social goals that are active in an emotional interaction have an impact on emotional mimicry.

Effects of emotional mimicry on affiliation

Whereas existing relationships have an influence on the extent in which we mimic, mimicry in turn also has effects on this relationship. Especially studies on behavioural mimicry have shown that mimicry leads to increased liking and thus fosters affiliation (e.g. Chartrand & Bargh, 1999; Lakin et al., 2003). For example, research on mimicry in a real-life courtship context (Guéguen, 2009) supports this notion. Men and women were videotaped during a speed dating session, in which women talked for a short time with men, in rotating order. Three female confederates took part in the speed

Caption for Figure 5.2 (cont.)

activition. Happiness mimicry was defined as in increase in Zygomaticus and Oculi activation compared to Corrugator activation. Anger and sadness mimicry were defined by the reverse pattern of these muscles. Fear mimicry was defined as an increase in Frontalis, compared to Zygomaticus activation.

dating session and were instructed to either mimic some of the men or not. They did this by repeating five expressions or statements. After the speed dating, the men received questionnaires asking which women they liked most. The men evaluated the dating interaction more positively when the woman mimicked them, and mimicry was further associated with a higher evaluation score of the relation and the sexual attractiveness of the woman.

Similar effects have been shown for emotional mimicry as well. Thus, participants in a study by Yabar and Hess (2007) were either mimicked by a confederate or not, while recounting a sad event from their life. Participants rated the mimicking confederate as more warm, tender, and approving and overall more positive than the non-mimicking confederate. This was irrespective of whether the mimicking confederate was an in- or an out-group member.

Yet, mimicry affects not only whether the mimickee likes the mimicker but conversely can also affect whether the mimicker likes the mimickee. This was shown by Stel and colleagues (2010). The study first manipulated liking for a person who was then shown on video or in an immersive virtual environment with instructions to the participant to either mimic or not mimic the person. Results showed that when participants intentionally mimicked a disliked person, liking for that person was not enhanced, whereas when participants mimicked a liked person, liking for that person increased.

Van der Schalk and colleagues (2011) report a similar finding showing that the spontaneous mimicry of negative emotions of in-group members was positively related to likeability ratings. They first presented participants short video clips from the Amsterdam Dynamic Facial Emotion Expression Set (ADFES), consisting of different emotional expressions (anger, fear, happiness) posed by models. Half of the models were White (which represented an in-group to the White participants) and the other half of the models were non-White (representing an out-group to the White participants). Participants rated the likeability of the targets when showing a neutral face before they saw the emotional video clips and again after they had seen the different emotional video clips. The results showed that liking of the models had increased, but only when the model was an in-group member. In addition, the increase in liking was mediated by the mimicry of negative facial expressions.

Obviously, these studies are limited in that there was no real interaction and the models that were presented were strangers and thus not very socially relevant for the participants taking part of the study. We can only speculate about the effects of emotional mimicry on the relationship between mimickee and mimicker, but given the fact that mimicry only occurs in the presence of some affiliative intent from both sides, we may predict that emotional mimicry will further enhance these affiliative tendencies and improve the relationship.

That mimicry may play a larger role in social interactions is suggested by a study by Mauersberger, Blaison, Kafetsios, Kessler, and Hess (2015). Mauersberger et al. assessed the degree to which participants mimicked expressions of happiness, anger, sadness and disgust using facial EMG in a standard laboratory task. The participants also provided a ten-day diary on their daily interactions where they described any interaction of ten minutes or longer in terms of how positive versus negative they felt themselves, how positive versus negative they perceived the other person to feel, and how positive versus negative they rated the interaction as such. A clear pattern emerged which suggests that those who tend to mimic sadness in the laboratory reported the most positive interaction experiences whereas disgust mimicry had a negative effect. No direct effect of happiness and anger mimicry emerged. For these emotions, more complex interactions with personality emerged. This study, which analysed effects across all types of interactions within all types of relationships, is highly suggestive for the importance of mimicry in social interactions. Importantly, it also shows that mimicry in reaction to affiliative and non-affiliative emotion displays has different social consequences.

Conclusion

We have shown that whether individuals mimic the emotions of others strongly depends on their relationship with the other person (strangers, friends, intimates, positive, negative, similar, dissimilar), with the nature of this relationship (neutral, competitive, cooperative, etc.), and with the relevance of the emotional message in relation to potential social interaction goals (motivated to ignore, empathize, etc.). These studies suggest that emotional mimicry can help us to socially regulate interactions. The research presented here provides a tantalizing glimpse for the role of emotional mimicry in social interactions. This role is more complex but also more exciting than the simple function of "social glue." Rather, mimicry seems able to regulate social distance and mediate social meaning and does so in different ways depending on which emotion is – or is not – mimicked in a given context. In this sense of mimicry, the metaphor of a social bungee cord seems more adequate, as mimicry flexibly keeps social relations within bounds.

References

Bavelas, J. B., Black, A., Lemery, C. R., & Mullett, J. (1986). "I show how you feel": Motor mimicry as a communicative act. *Journal of Personality and Social Psychology, 50,* 322–329.

Bourgeois, P., & Hess, U. (2008). The impact of social context on mimicry. *Biological Psychology, 77*, 343–352.

Cesario, J., Plaks, J. E., & Higgins, E. T. (2006). Automatic social behavior as motivated preparation to interact. *Journal of Personality and Social Psychology, 90*, 893–910.

Chartrand, T. L., & Bargh, J. A. (1999). The chameleon effect: The perception-behavior link and social interaction. *Journal of Personality and Social Psychology, 76*, 893–910.

Churches, O., Nicholls, M., Thiessen, M., Kohler, M., & Keage, H. (2014). Emoticons in mind: An event-related potential study. *Social Neuroscience, 9*, 196–202.

Dietrich, J., Hühnel, I., Sangenstedt, S., & Hess, U. (2013). *Mimicry does not need to be social but social context influences mimicry.* Paper presented at the Society for Psychophysiological Research, Florence, Italy, October 2–6.

Dimberg, U. (1982). Facial reactions to facial expressions. *Psychophysiology, 19* (6), 643–647.

Ekman, P., & Friesen, W. V. (1976). *Pictures of facial affect.* Palo Alto: Consulting Psychologists Press.

Fischer, A. H., Becker, D., & Veenstra, L. (2012). Emotional mimicry in social context: The case of disgust and pride. *Frontiers in Psychology, 3*, Published online November 2.

Frith, C. D., & Frith, U. (2006). How we predict what other people are going to do. *Brain Research, 1079*, 36–46.

Guéguen, N. (2009). Mimicry and seduction: An evaluation in a courtship context. *Social Influence, 4*(4), 249.

Guéguen, N., & Martin, A. (2009). Incidental similarity facilitates behavioral mimicry. *Social Psychology, 40*(2), 88–92.

Häfner, M., & Ijzerman, H. (2011). The face of love: Spontaneous accommodation as social emotion regulation. *Personality and Social Psychological Bulletin, 37*, 1551–1563.

Hess, U., Blairy, S., & Kleck, R. E. (2000). The influence of expression intensity, gender, and ethnicity on judgments of dominance and affiliation. *Journal of Nonverbal Behavior, 24*, 265–283.

Hess, U., Blaison, C., & Semin, G. R. (2013). *Ignored emotions are processed but not mimicked.* Paper presented at the 53rd Annual Meeting of the Society for Psychophysiological Research, Florence, Italy, October 2–6.

Hess, U., Dandeneau, S., & Blaison, C. (2015). The impact of rewards on empathy. *Manuscript in preparation.*

Hess, U., & Fischer, A. (2013). Emotional mimicry as social regulation. *Personality and Social Psychology Review, 17*, 142–157.

Hess, U., & Fischer, A. (2014). Emotional mimicry: Why and when we mimic emotions. *Social and Personality Psychology Compass, 8*, 45–57.

Kiesler, D. J. (1982). Interpersonal theory for personality and psychotherapy. In A. J. J. C. Anchin & Kiesler, D. (Eds.), *Handbook of interpersonal psychotherapy*, (vol. 101, pp. 3–24). Oxford: Pergamon Press.

Knutson, B. (1996). Facial expressions of emotion influence interpersonal trait inferences. *Journal of Nonverbal Behavior, 20*, 165–182.

Lakin, J. L., & Chartrand, T. L. (2005). Exclusion and nonconscious behavioral mimicry. In K. D. Williams, J. P. Forgas, & W. von Hippel (Eds.), *The social outcast: Ostracism, social exclusion, rejection, and bullying* (pp. 279–295). New York: Psychology Press.

Lakin, J. L., Chartrand, T. L., & Arkin, R. M. (2008). I am too just like you: Nonconscious mimicry as an automatic behavioral response to social exclusion. *Psychological Science, 19,* 816–822.

Lakin, J. L., Jefferis, V. E., Cheng, C. M., & Chartrand, T. L. (2003). The chameleon effect as social glue: Evidence for the evolutionary significance of nonconscious mimicry. *Journal of Nonverbal Behavior, 27,* 145–162.

Lanzetta, J. T., & Englis, B. G. (1989). Expectations of cooperation and competition and their effects on observers' vicarious emotional responses. *Journal of Personality and Social Psychology, 56,* 543–554.

Leary, T. F. (1957). *Interpersonal diagnosis of personality:* New York: Ronald Press.

Likowski, K. U., Mühlberger, A., Seibt, B., Pauli, P., & Weyers, P. (2008). Modulation of facial mimicry by attitudes. *Journal of Experimental Social Psychology, 44,* 1065–1072.

Mauersberger, H., Blaison, C., Kafetsios, K., Kessler, C.-L., & Hess, U. (2015). The effects of individual differences in emotional mimicry on social interaction quality. *Manuscript under revision.*

McHugo, G. J., Lanzetta, J. T., & Bush, L. K. (1991). The effect of attitudes on emotional reactions to expressive displays of political leaders. *Journal of Nonverbal Behavior, 15,* 19–41.

McHugo, G. J., Lanzetta, J. T., Sullivan, D. G., Masters, R. D., & Englis, B. G. (1985). Emotional reactions to a political leader's expressive displays. *Journal of Personality and Social Psychology, 49,* 1513–1529.

Niedenthal, P. M., Mermillod, M., Maringer, M., & Hess, U. (2010). The Simulation of Smiles (SIMS) Model: Embodied simulation and the meaning of facial expression. *Behavioral and Brain Sciences, 33,* 417–433

Norman, D. A. (1987). Some observations on mental models. In R. M. Baecker (Ed.), *Human-computer interaction* (pp. 241–244). Burlington, MA: Morgan Kaufmann Publishers Inc.

Schaller, M., Park, J. H., & Kenrick, D. T. (2012). *Human evolution and social cognition.* Oxford Handbooks Online: Oxford University Press.

Stel, M., Blascovich, J., McCall, C., Mastop, J., van Baaren, R. B., & Vonk, R. (2010). Mimicking disliked others: Effects of a priori liking on the mimicry-liking link. *European Journal of Social Psychology, 40*(5), 867–880.

Stel, M., van Baaren, R. B., Blascovich, J., van Dijk, E., McCall, C., Pollmann, M. M. H., . . . Vonk, R. (2010). Effects of a priori liking on the elicitation of mimicry. *Experimental Psychology, 57*(6), 412.

Tiedens, L. Z., & Fragale, A. R. (2003). Power moves: Complementarity in dominant and submissive nonverbal behavior. *Journal of Personality and Social Psychology, 84,* 558–568.

Tiedens, L. Z., Chow, R. M., & Unzueta, M. M. (2007). Complementary contrast and assimilation: Interpersonal theory and the social functions of contrast and assimilation effects. In D. A. S. J. Suls (Ed.), *Assimilation and contrast in social psychology* (pp. 249–267). New York: Psychology Press.

Van der Schalk, J., Fischer, A. H., Doosje, B. J., Wigboldus, D., Hawk, S. T., Hess, U., & Rotteveel, M. (2011). Congruent and incongruent responses to emotional displays of ingroup and outgroup. *Emotion, 11,* 286–298.

Weisbuch, M., & Ambady, N. (2008). Affective divergence: Automatic responses to others' emotions depend on group membership. *Journal of Personality and Social Psychology, 95,* 1063–1079.

Weyers, P., Mühlberger, A., Kund, A., Hess, U., & Pauli, P. (2009). Modulation of facial reactions to avatar emotional faces by nonconscious competition priming. *Psychophysiology, 46,* 328–335.

Williams, K. D., & Jarvis, B. (2006). Cyberball: A program for use in research on interpersonal ostracism and acceptance. *Behavior Research Methods, 38*(1), 174–180.

Wiggins, J. S. (1979). A psychological taxonomy of trait-descriptive terms: The interpersonal domain. *Journal of Personality and Social Psychology, 37* (3), 395.

Yabar, Y., & Hess, U. (2007). Display of empathy and perception of out-group members. *New Zealand Journal of Psychology, 36,* 42–50.

Yabar, Y., Johnston, L., Miles, L., & Peace, V. (2006). Implicit behavioral mimicry: Investigating the impact of group membership. *Journal of Nonverbal Behavior, 30,* 97–113.

CHAPTER 6

More than just a mirror: examining the cross-channel mimicry of emotional expressions

Skyler Hawk and Agneta H. Fischer

One of the key elements in all forms of mimicry is that it is, in some way, an imitation of another's behaviour, whether in terms of gestures, posture, facial expressions, or other observable actions. We may mimic what we see or hear, but in order to define it as mimicry, there should be some match between the observed and mimicked behaviour. The issue that we will address in this chapter is the nature of this match. This issue is of particular importance because it tells us something about mimicry, and more importantly about the nature of emotional mimicry. We argue that the mimicry of an emotion can comprise the mimicry of expressions of that emotion in different channels, which is based on the representation of that specific emotion. This argument is in line with Bavelas et al.'s (1986, Study 1) original research on motor mimicry of pain, who adopted an extremely wide definition of mimicry by operationalizing it "as any expression of pain in the observer; it did not need to be literally what E1 had done, as long as it was appropriate to the other's situation" (Bavelas, Black, Lemery, & Mullett, 1986, p. 324). This study is widely cited in mimicry research, even though it does not fit the more narrow definition of mimicry in studies on automatic and unconscious behavioural imitation of others' gestural, postural, or facial expressions. In this latter research, mimicry is mostly defined in terms of exactly matching others' behaviours, such as foot tapping, body or face touching, or leg crossing (see, e.g., Ashton-James, van Baaren, Chartrand, Decety & Karremans, 2007), pen-playing (van Baaren, Fockenberg, Holland, Janssen, & van Knippenberg, 2006), or posture, body orientation, and position of arms and legs (van Baaren, Holland, Kawakami, & van Knippenberg, 2004). The match implied in the latter definition is more literal than the one implied by Bavelas and colleagues, and these different definitions also suggest different theoretical accounts of mimicry. We roughly distinguish two different theoretical perspectives that explain mimicry and its functions. The first can be categorized as the Motor Mimicry view (Chartrand & Bargh; 1999; Dijksterhuis & Bargh, 2001). In this perspective, mimicry is seen as the result of an automatic tendency to observe another person's acts and to subsequently perform the same act oneself. This account thus assumes a direct, one-to-one matching between others' motor behaviours and those that we display ourselves. The similarity between what one sees and what one does is crucial to this account.

A second theoretical perspective emphasizes more flexibility in the relation between what we observe and what we mimic and argues that mimicry requires the perception of an emotional action in its broader context. Bavelas and colleagues' previously mentioned definition of mimicry and related research fits in this account, as it suggests that the imitation of a broader category or construct, such as an emotional state, can in principle result in a different action than the one that is actually observed. The loose connection between the perception of an emotion and the mimicry of the emotion is also in line with an embodiment view (e.g., Niedenthal, Barsalou, Winkielman, Krauth-Gruber, & Ric, 2005), arguing that emotional representations are not abstract, but grounded in one's bodily experiences and thus modality specific. In this view, mimicry can be considered an embodied response to an emotion. A similar perspective is taken by a Contextual view of Emotional Mimicry (see Hess & Fischer, 2013), which emphasizes the interpretational nature of emotion perception. The Contextual view assumes that the mimicry of an emotional state implies the categorization and interpretation of a specific behaviour or expression as belonging to an emotional category. Central to the topic of this chapter, this raises the question of how we define "mimicry." If there is no literal, one-to-one match between perception and action, (how) can we still call this mimicry? One particular case in which this issue is clearly illustrated is "cross-channel mimicry," in which another's emotion is imitated through a different expressive (i.e., facial, vocal, or postural) behaviour than the one in which it was originally expressed. As one example of this phenomenon, individuals tend to reflexively show a smile on their faces when they hear another person laugh. Emotional mimicry thus may traverse a particular non-verbal channel in which an expression is initially perceived. Although there is no literal match between hearing laughter and displaying a smile, there is a clear match in emotional meaning. In other words, observers may mimic the emotional meaning of what they have observed, rather than the objective features of what they saw. We will argue that such instances of cross-channel transmission of emotions have the same features and functions as uni-channel, or "classic," mimicry. In this chapter, we will first review evidence on cross-channel mimicry and discuss its possible functions. We will subsequently discuss different mechanisms that might account for cross-channel mimicry, and the special position of facial expressions in this phenomenon.

Evidence for cross-channel mimicry and emotion processing

To date, mimicry research has overwhelmingly considered facial, vocal, and postural channels of expression in isolation from one another. However, there is broad evidence of an interrelation between the processing of emotion expressions through different channels. We can conclude this from the fact that the perception of emotion in facial, vocal/prosodic, and lexical channels is highly correlated (Borod et al., 2000). In addition, the processing of emotional stimuli in one channel, for example auditory, can produce reactions in another channel, for example facial. For example, Dimberg (1990) showed that participants produce more Corrugator Supercilii muscle activity (responsible for a frowning expression) than Zygomaticus Major muscle activity (responsible for smiling) in response to a highly aversive, that is a 95dB 1000-Hz, tone compared to a less aversive, that is 75dB 1000-Hz, tone.

The close association between emotion processing in different channels is also supported by research paradigms in which participants are presented with emotional stimuli in two different sensory modalities (De Gelder & Vroomen, 1996; 2000; Massaro & Egan, 1996). These studies have shown that emotion processing is facilitated when facial and vocal expressions signal the same emotion; visually presented emotional faces bias the selective processing of emotional tones of voice, and vice versa. For example, De Gelder and Vroomen (2000) showed that when participants are presented with a continuum of happy and sad faces and at the same time hear a sentence spoken in a happy, sad, or neutral tone, they are quicker to identify a face as belonging to one of the two emotion categories if this is congruent with the same emotional tone of voice. Pairings of facial and vocal expressions communicating the same emotion thus facilitate quick and accurate recognition of stimuli, whereas incongruent pairings reduce speed and accuracy, regardless of whether the target stimuli are facial or vocal (De Gelder, Pourtois, & Weiskrantz, 2002; De Gelder & Vroomen, 2000; De Gelder & Bertelson, 2003; Dolan, Morris, & De Gelder, 2001; Hietanen, Leppänen, Illi, & Surakka, 2004; Massaro & Egan, 1996; Pell, 2005). In addition, fMRI research has shown that similar parts of the somatosensory cortex are involved in the processing of both facial and acoustic stimuli (Banissy et al., 2010). These studies all suggest, at minimum, that the neural systems involved in processing emotional information communicated through different channels are interrelated and can therefore be seen as parts of a more integrative system (e.g., Warren et al., 2006). What evidence exists that we also mimic expressions across expressive channels? From a purely motor-resonance (non-emotional) view, auditory and visual yawning stimuli appear to activate facial motor responses in similar ways. While it has long been known that seeing another person yawn increases facial yawning in observers (Provine, 1986), neuroimaging research has also found that merely *hearing* yawning vocalizations activated brain regions involved in executing mouth actions and increased listeners' self-reported urges to yawn (Arnott, Singhal, & Goodale, 2009). Within the more relevant context of emotion expression, Verona and colleagues (Verona, Patrick, Curtin, Bradley, & Lang, 2004) examined prison inmates' facial electromyography (fEMG) responses to collections of non-verbal vocalizations with positive (e.g., baby laughter, erotic moans) or negative (e.g., attack sounds, baby cries) connotations. As predicted, activity in the Zygomaticus Major (smiling) and Corrugator Supercilii (frowning) facial muscles increased when hearing the positive and negative sounds, respectively. Similar facial responses have been reported when participants have listened to speech fragments with happy and angry (Hietanen, Surakka, & Linnankoski, 1998) or happy and fearful tones of voice (Magneé, Stekelenburg, Kemner, & De Gelder, 2007). These concordant frowning and smiling facial responses have additionally been observed when participants view images of fearful and happy body postures. Magnée and colleagues (2007) tested this multi-sensory integration of emotions by presenting participants happy and fearful face-voice pairs (Experiment 1) in an emotion-congruent or incongruent way. They found that participants who were presented with congruent fearful faces and voices showed more Corrugator Supercilii activity than participants presented with happy faces and fearful voices, or vice-versa. In addition, participants presented with happy faces and voices showed more Zygomaticus Major activity than participants presented with happy faces and fearful voices, or vice-versa. In a second experiment, participants saw happy or fearful bodies or happy or fearful faces. The results showed similar facial reactions to bodies as to faces, with Corrugator Supercilii responses being higher for bodies, and Zygomaticus Major activity higher in response to faces than bodies. Based on these findings, the authors suggested that there is no role for mimicry, but rather that the recognition of emotions, independently of the channel, elicits motor activity in the face. These preliminary studies demonstrating the cross-channel matching of emotion share one important caveat, in that none could make the case for *emotion-specific* mimicry between expressive channels. Instead, they only suggest that cross-channel mimicry extends to general distinctions between positive and negative emotions. Researchers have consistently relied on measuring the same facial muscles (Zygomaticus Major and Corrugator Supercilii) in order to make the case for concordant responding, even though different emotions have been examined between studies (see Hess & Fischer, 2013, for a more extensive examination of this issue). This point is especially pertinent with regard to negative emotions such as anger, disgust, sadness, and fear, because while all of these emotions might include activation of the Corrugator Supercilii muscle (Ekman & Friesen, 1978), each also incorporates facial movements that are relatively unique. A grimace of disgust prototypically features a wrinkled nose and a raised upper lip, for example, while a turned-down mouth is an iconic feature of sadness. A stronger case for emotion-specific mimicry across channels would be made if these additional movements also appeared on observers' faces when exposed to other forms of non-verbal expressions, such as in the voice or body. In order to examine whether individuals might also mimic these more emotion-specific actions across expressive channels, Hawk, Fischer, and Van Kleef (2012, Studies 1 and 2) presented participants with sound fragments of laughing, crying, disgust noises (e.g., "eeeww!"), and angry growls. A hidden camera recorded their facial expressions during these tasks. Using the Facial Action Coding System (FACS), the researchers were able to examine participants' emotion-specific facial actions. Results showed that participants' more specific facial expressions (e.g., wrinkled noses, downturned mouths) tended to conform to the discrete emotion sounds that they heard. These findings suggest that cross-channel responses to emotion expressions do not merely reflect the positive or negative valence of the signals. Instead, they might actually involve more specific actions involved in discrete emotional behaviour. Thus, ample evidence exists that observers' facial expressions register the emotional signals that others convey across a spectrum of non-verbal channels, eliciting the mimicry of these expressions. This evidence would seem to contradict a Motor Mimicry view. Instead, it appears that interaction partners match the particular emotional *meanings* of each other's expressions, supporting a contextual model. This implies that we mimic not only concrete actions but also more abstract categories that can be represented by a broader constellation of behaviours. Extending mimicry to these more abstract forms of emotional matching requires evidence that such mimicry would contain the same features and fulfils the same functions as "classical" mimicry.

Functions of emotional mimicry

1. Processing of Emotional Information. First, emotional mimicry has been proposed to facilitate accurate and fast recognition of others' emotions (see also Chapter 2). In other words, mimicry helps us to understand and process emotional information more fluently (Effron, Niedenthal, Gil, & Droit-Volet, 2006; Niedenthal, Brauer, Halberstadt, & Innes-Ker, 2001; Oberman, Winkielman, & Ramachandran, 2007; Stel & Van Knippenberg, 2008, but see Hess & Blairy, 2001). One line of research in uni-channel mimicry that has examined and found support for this idea is research in which mimicry has been blocked through some kind of physical interference, resulting in impaired emotional processing. For example, participants who were instructed to avoid making facial movements showed reduced recognition of positive and negative emotional displays (Stel & Van Knippenberg, 2008). Additionally, blocking the ability to smile by instructing participants to bite down on a pen with their teeth not only resulted in poorer recognition of happiness but also lowered recognition of disgust, when compared with a rest condition (Oberman et al., 2007). Across different studies, blocking the smile through a variety of manipulations (e.g., use of a mouth guard) has also resulted in poorer detection of authentic smiles compared to false smiles (Maringer et al., 2011; Rychlowska et al., 2014), or in slower detection of a happy face transitioning from a sad face (Niedenthal et al., 2001, see also Stel, Chapter 2, and Niedenthal et al., Chapter 3). The blocking of actual motor activity with different techniques not only has an effect on emotional processing in the same channel, however, and there is some evidence that blocking emotions in one channel may reduce recognition of the same emotion in another channel. For example, suppressing sensorimotor activity via transcranial magnetic stimulation seems to interfere with the discrimination of *auditory* emotions (Banissy et al., 2010). Further, studies of patients with brain lesions have investigated whether there is a common neuroanatomical basis for face and voice recognition, and evidence suggests that there is a relation between face and voice recognition impairments (Van Lancker, 1997). In a similar vein, Hawk and colleagues (2012, Study 3) blocked or allowed participants' facial mimicry of smiling during a task in which participants had to identify as quickly as possible a shift in volume prominence between two auditory emotion expressions (from laughter to crying or vice versa). The results showed that participants attended more to the expressions when they could freely mimic them, to the point of being less accurate in identifying the moment at which the other sound became more prominent. Individuals who were prevented from mimicking did not over-attend to the initial sound in this manner, and thus were more accurate in identifying the point of transition. Together, these studies suggest that blocking mimicry in one expressive channel affects the speed, accuracy, and level of attention involved in processing emotional information in other channels, just as has been found within single channels of expression.

2. Similarity and liking. Emotional mimicry has been suggested to serve at least three functions. The first is similar to behavioural mimicry, that is, to enhance social bonds or affiliation. Mimicry, at least appropriate mimicry (see Leander, Chartrand, & Bargh, 2012), and when there is no *a priori* disliking (Stel et al., 2010) can result in more liking of the mimicked person. There is ample evidence for this phenomenon in unimodal mimicry (Stel & Vonk, 2009; Stel et al., 2010). Signals of shared emotion facilitate social bonds and communicate appreciation of another's current circumstances (Batson, Turk, Shaw, & Klein, 1995; Bavelas et al., 1986). It also generates feelings of understanding, trust, and liking, thereby enhancing interpersonal rapport (Anderson & Keltner, 2002; Bavelas et al., 1986; Chartrand & Bargh, 1999; Fischer & Manstead, 2008; Keltner & Haidt, 1999; Van Kleef et al., 2008; Van der Schalk et al., 2011). Conversely, several studies have demonstrated that *a priori* liking and interpersonal/group similarity strengthens the mimicry of both non-emotional (Stel et al., 2010) and emotional behaviour (Van der Schalk et al., 2011). The links between mimicry and interpersonal rapport thus appear to be quite reciprocal in nature (see also Hess et al., Chapter 5). In a study on the relation between group membership and responses to "canned laughter" (Platow et al., 2005), researchers exposed participants to the same audio recordings of a stand-up comedy routine. The audience in these recordings was characterized as being students at participants' own university, or as members of a political party with very low membership at that particular college. Participants displayed heightened levels of smiling, as well as combined smiling and laughter, when they believed that the audience was composed of in-group members. Thus, at least one half of the bidirectional association between liking/ similarity and mimicry has been demonstrated in prior research. To date, there is less evidence that cross-channel mimicry results in greater liking or similarity perceptions towards the mimicker. Based on Bavelas' (1986) original research, however, we may speculate that the mimicry of emotions across channels would have a similar effect on similarity and liking, as long as the recipient both observes the response and interprets the behaviour as an expression of a similar emotion.

3. Facilitating emotion contagion. Third, emotional mimicry may result in emotional contagion, or experiencing feelings similar to those communicated by others in the environment. It is still unclear whether this contagion is the result of mimicry or is elicited directly by the emotional display of the other person. Within expressive channels, however, there is ample evidence that individuals often report feeling emotions similar to those that they observe. This has been supported not only by studies testing the facial feedback hypothesis (Duclos et al., 1989; Flack, Laird, & Cavallaro, 1999; Larsen, Kasimatis, & Frey, 1992; Strack, Martin, & Stepper,

1988) but also by studies examining the direct elicitation of emotion via exposure to affective signals. For example, Provine (1992) has shown that mere exposure to canned laughter is sufficient to elicit smiling, laughter, and positive mood. Further, Hawk et al. (2012) found that hearing discrete vocal expressions of anger, joy, disgust, and sadness increased participants' own subjective experiences of those emotions (Study 1). Indeed, interfering with participants' ability to make matching facial expressions when hearing such sounds also appeared to inhibit these stronger emotional experiences (Hawk et al., Study 4), implying that congruent emotional responses to expressions presented in one channel can be diminished by interfering with the mimicry of those emotions in other channels. Importantly, all three of these functions are crucial to physical and social survival. At the individual level, accurately recognizing emotions, sharing in others' feelings, and enhancing liking through mimicry (or alternatively, mimicking those we like) provides additional, intrapersonal cues about experiences that should be pursued or avoided (e.g., Fischer & Manstead, 2008; Keltner & Haidt, 1999; Klinnert, Emde, Butterfield, & Campos, 1986; Sorce, Emde, Campos, & Klinnert, 1985; Van Kleef, 2009) and prepares the mind and body to meet the same environmental challenges as our interaction partners. At the interpersonal level, emotion recognition, contagion, and mimicry-related bonding help individuals to synchronize social intentions and facilitate joint or group action (Anderson & Keltner, 2002; Fischer & Manstead, 2008; Keltner & Haidt, 1999; Preston & De Waal, 2002; Yabar & Hess, 2007). It stands to reason that these social functions of mimicry would be best served by a system that allows for more flexibility in the representation and re-enactment of an emotional expression, as opposed to a more strictly literal response. In conclusion, the unichannel evidence for these three functions of emotional mimicry seems to extend to cross-channel mimicry, at least on the basis of preliminary evidence. The evidence thus suggests that emotional mimicry does not merely reflect motor activity, but incorporates a broader network of affective systems (e.g., Duclos et al., 1989; Flack, 2006; Flack, et al., 1999; Niedenthal, 2007; Niedenthal, Winkielman, Mondillion, & Vermeulen, 2009). This brings us to the question how to explain cross-channel mimicry.

Theoretical accounts of cross-channel mimicry

There is still substantial debate over both the mechanisms governing mimicry responses, generally speaking, and the boundary conditions under which they operate. With regard to emotional mimicry, more specifically, evidence for the existence of cross-channel mimicry may bring us closer to a discussion on the pervasiveness of this phenomenon.

Motor Mimicry

The first broad theoretical account is Motor Mimicry, also referred to as the Perception–Behaviour link (e.g., Dijksterhuis & Bargh, 2001), which seems the least suitable to incorporate cross-channel mimicry. Particularly in stricter accounts of this perspective, the observation of an emotional expression is thought to directly and automatically activate a specific, one-to-one mental representation of the same behaviour in an observer. Interestingly, research advocating this stricter perception–behaviour link has often focused on non-emotional and concrete behaviours, such as foot-shaking (e.g., Chartrand & Bargh, 1999), that have no particular social meaning or corresponding representations in different modalities. In contrast, grounding mimicry in the direct perception of another's emotional display cannot account for the fact that we might mimic something we do not actually see. There are several other theoretical perspectives, however, that could explain cross-channel mimicry.

Perception Action Model

The Perception Action Model of empathy (PAM; Preston & De Waal, 2002) takes a somewhat broader perspective and situates the automatic imitation of emotional expressions within a wider framework of empathic responding, which also includes perspective-taking, identifying with others' experiences, and subjectively experiencing inner states. The PAM states that the "attended perception of the object's state automatically activates the subject's representations of the state, situation, and object, and that activation of these representations automatically primes or generates the associated autonomic and somatic responses, unless inhibited" (p. 4). In other words, perception of distress or other negative emotions would result in associated responses that might not necessarily be identical to the ones initially perceived. The link between perception and behaviour is not direct, but instead runs through a representation of the target's observed state. This also accounts for the fact that we can generally distinguish two types of responses to another's emotions: a response *with* and a response *to* the other (see Hess & Fischer, 2013). Whereas the PAM may explain that we mimic others' emotions when we feel empathic, it does not necessarily explain when and why we mimic, because empathic responding and mimicry are not inextricably linked (e.g., Hawk, Fischer, & Van Kleef, 2011).

Embodiment theory

A third account that could explain cross-channel mimicry argues that the multi-component representation of an emotion, and not the direct observation of its expression, serves as a basis for imitation. Embodiment theory argues that our representation of emotion concepts is not amodal, but instead is modality-specific (Barsalou, 2003), consisting of references to particular components that comprise our knowledge representation of a particular construct. Take the concept of anger, for example: Its representation not only consists of a semantic definition of what anger is, and when it takes place, but is also strongly based on recollections of anger experiences, including how we express such feelings. Anger representations are thus partial *simulations* or reenactments in perceptual, motoric, and affective modalities. When thinking of anger, our muscles become tense, our voices become louder and harsher, and we have piercing eyes and a frown on our face. These modality-specific representations are embodied recollections of our own experiences, as well as the recollections of others' displays. In other words, we construct the meaning of anger as a concept at least partially from our own prior bodily and subjective experiences of anger (see Niedenthal et al., 2005, and Niedenthal et al., Chapter 3). The crucial issue here is that these different sensory modalities are closely connected, and thus may be activated as part of the modality system. Hearing someone talking in a very angry tone may automatically activate both facial expressions of anger and tightening of the muscles in preparation for aggression. Moreover, the subjective feeling of anger can be considered as just another sensory modality, meaning that expressive behaviours and introspective states can activate one another in a dynamic fashion (Keysers & Gazzola, 2009; Niedenthal, 2007; Van der Gaag, Minderaa, & Keysers, 2007). Exposure to an emotional stimulus in any particular modality can initiate cascading simulations of other components, in order to "fill in" unperceived aspects of an original experience (Barsalou, Niedenthal, Barbey, & Ruppert, 2003). Individuals thus draw upon their own personal history of emotion expressions, subjective experiences, and eliciting contexts in order to make sense of others' emotional circumstances and to share in their joy, pain, revulsion, or anger. The "cross-talk" between modalities implies that an observer's internal and outward simulation of another's expression may extend to behaviour across several non-verbal channels.

In line with the notion of re-enacting multiple components of an emotion expression when exposed to a stimulus in a single channel, Hawk and colleagues (2012, Study 1) instructed participants to first listen to, and then repeat, vocal expressions of anger, sadness, joy, and disgust. The Facial Action Coding System was used to examine hidden camera footage of participants' expressions during both tasks. Results showed that participants performed emotion-specific facial movements when making each respective set of vocalizations, but also showed the same muscle activations when merely *listening* to the sounds. More importantly for a simulation account, facial activity between the listening and vocalizing tasks was significantly correlated; this indicated that the stronger these actions were when participants made the sounds themselves, the more strongly they reacted with the same movements upon mere exposure to the auditory stimuli. Across studies in this research, concordant facial responses when listening to the recordings also appeared to be more frequent when participants intended to repeat the sounds (Study 1), as compared to when no vocalizing goal was present (Study 2). Thus, not only did this cross-channel mimicry appear to be based on participants' own associations between facial and vocal expressions of the same emotion, but overt intent to imitate the expression in the original channel appeared to increase the frequency of mimicry in another related modality.

Contextual view

A fourth perspective that could explain these cross-channel effects is a contextual account of emotional mimicry (Hess & Fischer, 2013), which argues that the mimicry of emotional signals depends on how the signal is interpreted and understood within a specific context. Individuals do not see a frown, or hear a sigh, but perceive "anger," or "relief," depending on how the circumstances dictate their expectations. This perspective is in line with what Soussignan and colleagues have termed the "emotional appraisal view" (Soussignan et al., 2013), also underlining the idea that we try to make sense of our emotional environment and interpret facial or other non-verbal signals as relevant for our own concerns. Soussignan and colleagues found an effect for gaze direction in interaction with the type of emotion, showing that participants only mimicked angry and happy faces when the gaze was directed towards them, reflecting self-relevant appraisals, whereas gaze direction did not have an effect on the mimicry of fearful and sad faces. The authors conclude that mimicry is an emotional and not a motor response (Soussignan et al., 2013), which is in agreement with a contextual view, because individuals interpreted anger and happiness differently depending on whether they were directed at them, and thus, an attack or an affiliative signal, or at others. A contextual view can incorporate cross-channel mimicry because it assumes that mimicry results from the interpretation of multiple expressive and situational emotional cues – whether joy is communicated through a smile or a laugh, an observer will interpret and respond to this signal in a similar way because both expressions have similar potential social consequences for him/her. Indeed, a contextual view allows for flexibility in the representation and mimicry of an emotional expression, so long as expressions in different channels are interpreted in a similar manner.

There is to date no research that explicitly examines contextual cues as a basis of cross-channel emotional mimicry, and thus we can only speculate based on some examples. For instance, hearing someone laugh may lead to smiling, as much as smiling itself evokes smiling. The question is whether contextual cues that would suggest an appropriate or inappropriate reason for smiling would have a different impact on cross-channel mimicry versus uni-channel mimicry. For example, would individuals mimic smiling or laughing behaviour more strongly if they thought a target was responding to an amusing film, as opposed to enjoying watching another person being physically harmed? And, would this facial mimicry interact with whether individuals see or hear this laughter? If mimicry would be equally strong in both contexts, a contextual view would not have additional explanatory value to an embodiment view as outlined above. However, the aforementioned finding that individuals show increased smiling in response to in-group laughter compared to out-group laughter (Platow et al., 2005) raises intriguing questions about how social context may serve to strengthen or weaken cross-channel mimicry responses. Similar questions could be asked in relation to the cross-channel mimicry of negative emotions, although in these cases it may crucially depend on the type of negative emotions. For example, we reported evidence that hearing vomit sounds makes people look disgusted. However, would contextual cues, such as disgust from eating cockroaches versus eating tomatoes, also result in different amounts of mimicry? And, additionally, would this be different in cross-channel versus uni-channel mimicry? These are questions that could be answered in future research and would shed more light on the nature of context effects upon emotional mimicry, more generally.

The special role of the face

Special attention needs to be paid to the role of the face in cross-channel mimicry. Almost all related research focuses on facial mimicry as a response to postural or acoustic cues. Indeed, we may suggest that the fact that we find facial reactions to emotional cues from various non-verbal channels indicates that any recognition of emotions, in whatever channel, elicits motor activity in the face. This suggestion, first of all, raises the question of whether the reverse can also be found: is there evidence of postural or vocal mimicry when we see emotional faces? To our knowledge, there is no evidence of such mimicry effects, but a confirmatory answer to this question would be in line with other findings from embodiment research, such as showing that posture aligns with the activation of specific emotion concepts (Oosterwijk, Rotteveel, Fischer, & Hess, 2009). Whether we find cross-channel mimicry effects other than on the face may also depend on the role of the face as part of embodied emotion representations. Because faces are the most visible and explicit element in most emotions, at least in Western culture, faces may be more prominent than other modalities, such as posture, voice, gestures, or physiology. Further, vocalizations have an on/off quality that typically requires conscious and effortful activation, and usually attracts considerable attention from others. In contrast, the face and body operate in a continuous flow, to which neither the expresser nor the observer might not always consciously attend (Scherer, 1980, 1988). Additionally, the face appears capable of expressing a range of discrete emotional states than can be successfully communicated by either tone of voice (Hawk, Van Kleef, Fischer, & Van der Schalk, 2009) or bodily postures (cf. Coulson, 2004). The more subtle, emotion-specific, and analogue nature of the facial channel might make it especially suited for the rapid, moment-to-moment matching of others' states (e.g., Niedenthal, Mermillod, Maringer, & Hess, 2010), which in turn may facilitate observers' ability to process and respond to a variety of emotion signals. This could mean that the face is the most central channel in emotional mimicry and maybe the "central processor" of affective information, including (but not limited to) emotion expressions in various channels (Niedenthal et al., 2010). In other words, the facial imitation of emotion signals from other expressive channels might have adaptive value; the attention-eliciting and on/off nature of vocalization may not be as advantageous for continuous emotion processing as compared to the relatively covert, analogue, and emotion-specific facial channel. In addition, eye contact seems a crucial factor for increasing mimicry, as initially demonstrated by the work of Bavelas and colleagues (1986), and replicated for other behavioural acts (e.g., hand movements, Wang et al., 2011). However, eye contact is not a necessary condition for mimicry, as is shown in research where gaze direction, and thus eye contact, is manipulated (see also Niedenthal et al., Chapter 3).

Conclusion

We have reviewed and discussed evidence for cross-channel mimicry of emotions in this chapter. The crucial question with which we started our review regarded the boundary conditions under which emotional mimicry operates. Can we stretch the definition of mimicry to encompass actions that are similar, but not identical, to what we have perceived? Or, should we abandon the term "mimicry" altogether, and just refer to an emotional response that can either be similar or dissimilar to an observed expression? We have discussed different theoretical perspectives that give different answers to these questions, and most theories seem to agree that we should not restrict the term "emotional mimicry" to the exact copying of emotional expressive cues. Across several theories, there appears to be consensus that individuals process emotional information on the basis of more abstract representations, and thus the mimicry of an emotional expression should be based on such representations. This would explain the phenomenon of cross-channel mimicry. How exactly the perception of different modal cues is integrated, how this leads to the production of a mimicry response, and whether the role of the face is special in comparison with that of the voice or the body is still unclear. These questions should provide ample inspiration for future studies on the nature, ubiquity, and functions of emotional mimicry.

References

Anderson, C., & Keltner, D. (2002). The role of empathy in the formation and maintenance of social bonds. *Behavioral and Brain Sciences, 25,* 21–22.

Arnott, S. R., Singhal, A., & Goodale, M. A. (2009). An investigation of auditory contagious yawning. *Cognitive, Affective, & Behavioral Neuroscience, 9,* 335–342.

Ashton-James, C., van Baaren, R. B., Chartrand, T. L., Decety J., & Karremans, J. (2007). Mimicry and me: The impact of mimicry on self-construal. *Social Cognition, 25,* 518–535.

Banissy, M. J., Sauter, D. A., Ward, J., Warren, J. E., Walsh, V., Scott, S. K. (2010). Suppressing sensorimotor activity modulates the discrimination of auditory emotions but not speaker identity. *Journal of Neuroscience, 30,* 13552–13557.

Barsalou, L.W. (2003). Situated simulation in the human conceptual system. *Language and Cognitive Processes, 18,* 513–562.

Barsalou, L. W., Niedenthal, P. M., Barbey, A. K., & Ruppert, J. A. (2003). Social embodiment. In B. H. Ross (Ed.), *The psychology of learning and motivation: Advances in research and theory* (pp. 43–92). Elsevier: Academic Press.

Batson, C. D., Turk, C. L., Shaw, L. L., & Klein, T. R. (1995). Information function of empathy: Learning that we value the other's welfare. *Journal of Personality and Social Psychology, 68,* 300–313.

Bavelas, J. B., Black, A., Lemery, C. R., & Mullett, J. (1986). "I show how you feel": Motor mimicry as a communicative act. *Journal of Personality and Social Psychology, 50,* 322–329.

Borod, J. C., Pick, L. H., Hall, S., Sliwinski, M., Madigan, N., Obler, L. K., . . . Tabert, M. (2000). Relationships among facial, prosodic, and lexical channels of emotional perceptual processing. *Cognition and Emotion, 14,* 193-211.

Chartrand, T. L., & Bargh, J. A. (1999). The chameleon effect: The perception-behavior link and social interaction. *Journal of Personality and Social Psychology, 76,* 893–910.

Coulson, M. (2004). Attributing emotion to static body postures: Recognition accuracy, confusions, and viewpoint dependence. *Journal of Nonverbal Behavior, 28*, 117–139.

De Gelder, B., & Bertelson, P. (2003). Multisensory integration, perception and ecological validity. *Trends in Cognitive Sciences, 7*, 460–467.

De Gelder, B., & Vroomen, J. (1996). Auditory illusions as evidence for a role of the syllable in adult developmental dyslexics. *Brain Language, 52*, 373–385.

De Gelder, B., & Vroomen, J. (2000). Bimodal emotion perception: Integration across separate modalities, cross-modal perceptual grouping or perception of multimodal events? *Cognition and Emotion, 14*, 321–324.

De Gelder, B., Pourtois, G., & Weiskrantz, L. (2002). Fear recognition in the voice is modulated by unconsciously recognized facial expressions but not by unconsciously recognized affective pictures. *Proceedings of the National Academy of Sciences, 99*, 4121–4126.

Dijksterhuis, A., & Bargh, J. A. (2001). The perception-behavior expressway: Automatic effects of social perception on social behavior. In M. P. Zanna (Ed.), *Advances in experimental social psychology* (pp. 1–40). Elsevier: Academic Press.

Dimberg, U. (1990). Facial electromyography reactions and automatic activity to auditory stimuli. *Biological Psychology, 31*, 137–147.

Dolan, R.J., Morris, J.S., & de Gelder, B. (2001). Crossmodal binding of fear in voice and face. *Proceedings of the National Academy of Sciences, 98*, 10006–10010.

Duclos, S. E., Laird, J. D., Schneider, E., Sexter, M., Stern, L., & Van Lighten, O. (1989). Emotion-specific effects of facial expressions and postures on emotional experience. *Journal of Personality and Social Psychology, 57*, 100–108.

Effron, D., Niedenthal, P.M., Gil, S., & Droit-Volet, S., (2006). Embodied temporal perception of emotion. *Emotion, 6*, 1–9.

Ekman, P., & Friesen, W.V. (1978). *The facial action coding system: A technique for the measurement of facial movement.* Palo Alto, CA: Consulting Psychologists Press.

Fischer, A. H., & Manstead, A. S. R. (2008). Social functions of emotion. In M. Lewis, J. Haviland-Jones, & L. F. Barrett (Eds.), *Handbook of emotions,* 3rd ed. New York: Guilford Press.

Flack, W. F. (2006). Peripheral feedback effects of facial expressions, bodily postures, and vocal expressions on emotional feelings. *Cognition and Emotion, 20*, 177–195.

Flack, W. F., Laird, J. D., & Cavallaro, L. A. (1999). Separate and combined effects of facial expressions and bodily postures on emotional feelings. *European Journal of Social Psychology, 29*, 203–217.

Hawk, S. T., Fischer, A. H., & Van Kleef, G. A. (2011). Taking your place or matching your face: Two paths to empathic embarrassment. *Emotion, 11*, 502–513.

Hawk, S. T., Fischer, A. H., & Van Kleef, G. A. (2012). Face the noise: Embodied responses to nonverbal vocalizations of discrete emotions. *Journal of Personality and Social Psychology, 102*, 796–814.

Hawk, S. T., Van Kleef, G. A., Fischer, A. H., & Van der Schalk, J. (2009). "Worth a thousand words": Absolute and relative decoding of nonlinguistic affect vocalizations. *Emotion, 9*, 293–305.

Hess, U., & Blairy, S. (2001). Facial mimicry and emotional contagion to dynamic emotional facial expressions and their influence on decoding accuracy. *International Journal of Psychophysiology, 40*, 129–141.

Hess, U. & Fischer, A. (2013). Emotional mimicry as social regulation. *Personality and Social Psychology Review, 17*, 142–157.

Hietanen, J. K., Surakka, V., & Linnankoski, I. (1998). Facial electromyographic responses to vocal affect expressions. *Psychophysiology, 35*, 530–536.

Hietanen, J.K., Leppänen, J.M., Illi, M., and Surakka, V. (2004). Evidence for the integration of audiovisual emotional information at the perceptual level of processing. *European Journal of Cognitive Psychology, 16*, 769–790.

Keltner, D., & Haidt, J. (1999). Social functions of emotions at four levels of analysis. *Cognition and Emotion, 13*, 505–521.

Keysers, C., & Gazzola, V. (2009). Expanding the mirror: Vicarious activity for actions, emotions and sensations. *Current Opinions in Neurobiology, 19*, 1–6.

Klinnert, M. D., Emde, R. N., Butterfield, P., & Campos, J. J. (1986). Social referencing: The infant's use of emotional signals from a friendly adult with mother present. *Developmental Psychology, 22*, 427–432.

Larsen, R. J., Kasimatis, M., & Frey, K. (1992). Facilitating the furrowed brow: An unobtrusive test of the facial feedback hypothesis applied to unpleasant affect. *Cognition & Emotion, 6*, 321–338.

Leander, N. P., Chartrand, T. L., & Bargh, J. A. (2012). You give me the chills: Embodied reactions to inappropriate amounts of behavioral mimicry. *Psychological Science, 23*, 772–779.

Magnée, M. J. C. M., Stekelenburg, J. J., Kemner, C., & De Gelder, B. (2007). Similar facial electromyographic responses to faces, voices, and body expressions. *Cognitive Neuroscience and Neuropsychology, 18*, 369–372.

Maringer, M., Fischer, A.H., Krumhuber, E.G., & Niedenthal, P.M. (2011). Beyond smile dynamics: Mimicry and beliefs in judgments of smiles. *Emotion, 11*, 181–187.

Massaro, D.W. & Egan, P.B. (1996). Perceiving affect from the voice and the face. *Psychonomic Bulletin and Review, 3*, 215–221.

Niedenthal, P. M. (2007). Embodying emotion. *Science, 316*, 1002–1005.

Niedenthal, P. M., Mermillod, Maringer, M., & Hess, U. (2010). The Simulation of Smiles (SIMS) Model: A window to general principles in processing facial expression. *Brain and Behavioural Sciences, 33*, 417–433.

Niedenthal, P. M., Brauer, M., Halberstadt, J. B., & Innes-Ker, Å. (2001). When did her smile drop? Facial mimicry and the influence of emotional state on the detection of change in emotional expression. *Cognition and Emotion, 15*, 853–864.

Niedenthal, P. M., Winkielman, P. Mondillon, L., & Vermeulen, N. (2009). Embodiment of emotional concepts. *Journal of Personality and Social Psychology, 96*, 1120–1136.

Niedenthal, P.M., Barsalou, L.W., Winkielman, P., Krauth-Gruber, S., & Ric, F. (2005). Embodiment in attitudes, social perception, and emotion. *Personality and Social Psychology Review, 9*, 184–211.

Oberman, L., Winkielman, P., & Ramachandran, V. S. (2007). Face to face: Blocking facial mimicry can selectively impair recognition of emotional expressions. *Social Neuroscience, 2*, 167–178.

Oosterwijk, S., Rotteveel, M., Fischer, A. H., & Hess, U. (2009). Embodied emotion concepts: How generating words about pride and disappointment influences posture. *Euroean Journal of Social Psychology, 39*, 457–466.

Pell, M. D. (2005). Prosody-face interactions in emotional processing as revealed by the facial affect decision task. *Journal of Nonverbal Behavior, 29*, 193–215.

Platow, M. J., Haslam, S. A., Both, A., Chew, I., Cuddon, M., & Goharpey, N., et al. (2005). "It's not funny if they're laughing": Self-categorization, social influence, and responses to canned laughter. *Journal of Experimental Social Psychology, 41*, 542–550.

Preston, S. D., & De Waal, F. B. M. (2002). Empathy: Its ultimate and proximate bases. *Behavioral and Brain Sciences, 25*, 1–72.

Provine, R. R. (1986). Yawning as a stereotyped action pattern and releasing stimulus. *Ethology, 72*, 109–122.

Provine, R. R. (1992). Contagious laughter: Laughter is a sufficient stimulus for laughter and smiles. *Bulletin of the Psychonomic Society, 30*, 1–4.

Rychlowska, M., Cañadas, E., Wood, A., Krumhuber, E. G., Fischer, A. H., & Niedenthal, P. M. (2014). Blocking mimicry makes true and false smiles look the same. *PLoS one, 9* (3).

Scherer, K. R. (1980). The functions of nonverbal signs in conversation. In R. N. St Clair & H. Giles (Eds.), *The social and psychological contexts of language* (pp. 225–244). Hillsdale, NJ: Lawrence Erlbaum.

Scherer, K. R. (1988). On the symbolic functions of vocal affect expression. *Journal of Language and Social Psychology, 7*, 79–100.

Sorce, J. F., Emde, R. N., Campos, J., & Klinnert, M. D. (1985). Maternal emotional signaling: Its effects on the visual cliff behavior of 1-year-olds. *Developmental Psychology, 21*, 195–200.

Soussignan, R., Chadwick, M., Philip, L., Conty, L., Dezecache, G., & Grezes, J. (2013). Self-relevance appraisal of gaze direction and dynamic facial expressions: Effects on facial electromyographic and autonomic reactions. *Emotion, 13*, 330–337.

Stel, M., & van Knippenberg, A. (2008). The role of facial mimicry in the recognition of affect. *Psychological Science, 19*, 984–985.

Stel, M. & Vonk, R. (2009). Empathizing via mimicry depends on whether emotional expressions are seen as real. *European Psychologist, 14*, 342–350.

Stel, M., Blascovich, J., McCall, C., Mastop, J., Van Baaren, R.B., & Vonk, R. (2010). Mimicking disliked others: Effects of a priori liking on the mimicry–liking link. *European Journal of Social Psychology, 40*, 876–880.

Strack, F., Martin, L. & Stepper, S. (1988). Inhibiting and facilitating conditions of the human smile: A nonobtrusive test of the facial feedback hypothesis. *Journal of Personality and Social Psychology, 54*, 768–777.

van Baaren, R. B., Holland, R. W., Kawakami, K., & van Knippenberg, A. (2004). Mimicry and prosocial behavior. *Psychological Science, 15*, 71–74.

van Baaren, R. B., Fockenberg, D. A., Holland, R. A., Janssen, L., & van Knippenberg, A. (2006). The moody chameleon: The effect of mood on non-conscious mimicry. *Social Cognition, 24*, 426–437.

Van der Gaag, C. Minderaa, R. B., & Keysers, C. (2007). Facial expressions: What the mirror neuron system can and cannot tell us. *Social Neuroscience, 2*, 179–222.

Van der Schalk, J., Fischer, A. H., Doosje, B. J., Wigboldus, D. H. J., Hawk, S. T., Rotteveel, M., & Hess, U. (2011). Convergent and divergent responses to emotional displays of ingroup and outgroup. *Emotion, 11*, 286–298.

Van Kleef, G. A. (2009). How emotions regulate social life: The emotions as social information (EASI) model. *Current Directions in Psychological Science, 18*, 184–188.

Van Kleef, G. A., Oveis, C., Van der Löwe, I., LuoKogan, A., Goetz, J., & Keltner, D. (2008). Power, distress, and compassion: Turning a blind eye to the suffering of others. *Psychological Science, 19*, 1315–1322.

Van Lanker, D. (1997). Rags to riches: Our increasing appreciation of cognitive and communicative abilities of the human right cerebral hemisphere. *Brain and Language, 57*, 1–11.

Verona, E., Patrick, C. J., Curtin, J. J., Bradley, M. M., & Lang, P. J. (2004). Psychopathy and physiological response to emotionally evocative sounds. *Journal of Abnormal Psychology, 113*, 99–108.

Wang, Y., Ramsey, R., & Hamilton, A. F. D. C. (2011). The control of mimicry by eye contact is mediated by medial prefrontal cortex. *The Journal of Neuroscience, 31*(33), 12001–12010.

Warren, J. E., Sauter, D. A., Eisner, F., Wiland, J., Dresner, M. A., Wise, R. J., et al. (2006) Positive emotions preferentially engage an auditory-motor "mirror" system. *Journal of Neuroscience, 26*, 13067–13075.

Yabar, Y., & Hess, U. (2007). Display of empathy and perception of out-group members. *New Zealand Journal of Psychology, 36*, 42–49.

CHAPTER 7

Emotional mimicry: underlying mechanisms and individual differences

Marianne Sonnby-Borgström

In human interactions, individuals frequently become affected by each other's emotions. For example, when a friend shows signs of being upset and sad, you will probably feel distressed yourself. On the other hand, when a friend smiles and laughs, your own mood will most likely be modified in a positive direction. One mechanism behind such transfers of emotions in social interactions has been proposed to be the imitation or mimicry of facial expressions.

Imitation or mimicry refers to a behaviour whereby we observe another individual and replicate what we observe, and it appears in many different forms, as for example in mimicry of facial expressions, of postures, hand movements, or verbal mimicry (Chartrand & van Baaren, 2009). When talking about imitation or mimicry in everyday language we usually refer to imitation that we are aware of. However, we tend to mimic each other automatically without cognitive effort, and the imitator/mimicker is seldom aware of his imitative/mimicking behaviour (Dimberg, Thunberg, & Grunedal, 2002; Sonnby-Borgström, 2002a; Sonnby-Borgström, Jönsson, & Svensson, 2008b). The nature of facial expressions can either be overt and visible or consist of weak muscle activations that are covert and unvisible to an observer (Tassinary & Cacioppo, 1992; Tassinary & Cacioppo, 2000).

The present chapter focuses on automatic facial mimicry in face-to-face interaction and on the relationship between automatic facial mimicry and the emotional experience of the observer of the facial expression. It also includes aspects of more controlled and cognitively modulated facial and emotional responses to facial expressions. Further, it describes individual differences in the tendency to imitate or mimic others.

Some of the presented evidence refers to studies on other forms of imitation than facial mimicry, for example, imitation of movements of fingers, arms, or feet (Chartrand & Bargh, 1999; Heyes, 2011), since they have much in common with facial expression mimicking. Other forms of motoric mirroring movements are assumed to have similar functions as the imitation of facial expressions. They are automatically evoked, and like all forms of imitations, they have their neurological base in the mirror neuron system (Carr, Iacoboni, Dubeau, Mazziotta, & Lenzi, 2003; Chartrand & Bargh, 1999; Oberman & Ramachandran, 2007, but see also Schilbach, Chapter 4, and Schuler et al., Chapter 9). On the other hand, facial imitation and the imitation of other movements differ concerning the closer and faster neural conections between the facial expressions and the affect system, a connection that is not assumed to exist to the same extent for other muscle groups (Tomkins, 1962).

Imitation serves many purposes in social interaction, for the imitator as well as for the person who is imitated, including the strengthening of social bonds and liking between interaction partners (Chartrand & van Baaren, 2009; Lakin, Jefferis, Cheng, & Chartrand, 2003; Stel & Vonk, 2010). Exposure to facial expressions at a subliminal level also affects the motivational state and the observer's consumption behaviour, which is assumed to be influenced by covert facial mimicry (Winkielman, Berrige, & Wilberger, 2005). Mimicry of facial expressions facilitates the recognition memory for emotional pictures (Ravaja, Kallinen, Saari, & Keltikangas-Jarvinen, 2004). Further, mimicry of facial expressions is involved in our ability to spontaneously catch the emotions of others in face-to-face interaction situations and in empathic under-standing (Gallese, 2001; Sonnby-Borgström, 2002b). The latter emotional communication functions of facial mimicry are emphasized in the present chapter.

The present model and underlying mechanisms

The mechanisms behind the catching of others' feelings in face-to-face interactions are under debate and one model is elaborated in the present chapter. Alternative models and explanations are discussed in other chapters of this book.

The present model

The model emphasized in the present chapter perceives facial mimicry as biologically prewired and elaborated in early life through learning processes. This dynamic developmental model of emotional communication assumes that facial and emotional responses to facial expressions are the result of automatic mimicry tendencies and facial feedback, of learnt expectations (internal schemas), as well as of attentionally loaded infor-mation processes related to the social context.

This perspective is the theoretical basis for the design of several experiments that are described in the present chapter (Sonnby-Borgström, 2002a, 2002b, 2009; Sonnby-Borgström & Jönsson, 2003; Sonnby-Borgström & Jönsson, 2004; Sonnby-Borgström, Jönsson, & Svensson, 2003; Sonnby-Borgström, Jönsson, & Svensson, 2008a; Sonnby-Borgström et al., 2008b). The designs are based on percept-genetic theory (Brown, 1985; Smith, 1991), which proposes that perceptual processing of emotional information is hierarchically organized from more primitive, unconscious, and automatic information processing levels to more elaborated and emotionally controlled processing levels. The end product of the process is assumed to be a result of a micro process in time evolving from a few milliseconds to a couple of seconds. In the described experiments the facial stimuli were shown initially at very short exposure times (subliminally) with backward masking to interrupt more elaborated cognitively loaded information processing. Subsequently, the facial stimuli were presented at longer exposure times to allow more advanced emotional information processing and emotional regulation. This experimental set-up was hypothesized to result in modulation of the first automatic, spontaneous facial mimicry responses, which in turn via feedback from facial responses and more elaborated information processing may change the emotional experience. The model is illustrated in Figure 7.1 and elaborated and explained in the following sections.

Shortcomings and advantages of the model and the experimental design

The described experimental design, based on exposures of facial stimuli (representing the sender in a face-to-face interaction) and recordings of emotional responses in the observer (facial muscle responses and reported emotional experiences), is a simplified and momentary picture of a complicated social interaction situation. In authentic face-to-face emotional communication, the interaction between the sender and the observer is a reciprocal emotional exchange, in which the sender and observer continuously change roles.

The experimental set-up with short exposures of facial expressions and electromyographical (EMG) recordings of facial muscle movements has the advantage that it makes it possible to catch automatic responses to facial stimuli, which are fast, unconscious, and often too weak to be conveyed by an observer (Dimberg et al., 2002; Sonnby-Borgström, 2002a; Tassinary & Cacioppo, 1992; Tassinary & Cacioppo, 2000). Successively prolonged exposures make it possible to catch modulations of facial responses and emotional experiences from more primitive and unconscious information processing level to more cognitively controlled

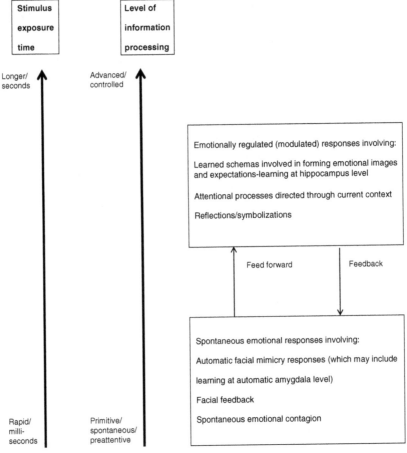

Figure 7.1   A potential model illustrating the process involved in emotional responding in a face-to-face interaction situation, an interaction situation that does not include special generated expectations. The experimental design based on percept genetic theory used successively prolonged exposure times of facial emotional stimulus from milliseconds to seconds, a design which is assumed to simulate the hierarchically organized emotional information process from spontaneous to regulated responses. The concepts illustrated in the figure are further elaborated in the following section of the chapter.

and advanced levels. However, no measures of brain activity were included in the experiments, and measures of brain activity at different temporal stages would have improved the possibilities to draw conclusions about information processing levels.

Facial expressions and emotions

Communication via facial expressions is assumed to be crucial for emotional communication in the described model, in which facial responses to facial expressions are used in the experimental set-ups.

According to Silvan Tomkins' theory (Tomkins, 1962, 1963) facial expressions are essential components of different evolutionary-based affect programmes, which are evoked in evolutionary-relevant situations. The programmes activate the facial expressive muscles as well as other somatic and visceral responses and prepare the body for adaptive actions relevant to the situational demands. The body will prepare us for running away or to fight the danger in a situation that is threatening; when meeting an attractive potential partner our body will prepare us for approaching the attractive object; when losing a close and beloved relative we tend to go into a state of withdrawal, and our body will physically adjust us to a low level of activity. Thus, an activated affect programme consists of a motivational state that includes both somatic and visceral responding. The facial expressions and visceral responses correspond to motivational states that may or may not result in emotional subjective experiences, which we become aware of. These motivational/emotional states are often modulated by more controlled and emotionally regulated processes and may not result in overt behaviour.

According to Tomkins, each basic motivational/emotional state corresponds to a certain basic facial expression. Happiness is expressed as a smile and anger is displayed as a frown. Through these facial expressions our motivational state is non-verbally and automatically communicated to our social environment. We are also assumed to be biologically prepared to respond to others' facial expressions with facial emotional expressions. Studies in both Western and other cultures have found support for Tomkins' affect theory, in which the biologically based affect programmes are assumed to be expressed as different facial expressions. The basic facial expressions, evoked in specific emotional situations, were found to be similar in different cultures and the basic emotional displays (showing, for example, happiness, anger, fear, sadness, and disgust) were by observers in these cultures decoded as expressions of the same underlying emotion. Thus, the basic facial expressions appear to be independent of cultural context and can be seen as results of biologically prepared affect programmes (Ekman, Friesen, & Ancoli, 1980; Ekman, Friesen, & Ellsworth, 1972; Izard, 1994; Keltner & Ekman, 2000), and these signals are essential in all social communication situations. Facial expressions are, however, also influenced by learning processes through social interactions in the childhood and by culturally influenced display rules (Buck, 1984; Eisenberg, Spinrad, & Cumberland, 1998; Elfenbein, Beaupré, Lévesque, & Hess, 2007).

The emotional contagion hypothesis

The model described earlier assumes that the emotional transfer process in a face-to-face interaction is initiated by emotional responses at an automatic and primitive information-processing level. The emotional contagion hypothesis fits well into this model since it assumes that we catch the emotion of others in face-to-face interactions through our tendency to automatically mimic others' facial expressions. The emotional experience of the other person is according to the emotional contagion hypothesis assumed to be transferred to the observer through feedback from the observer's mimicry. Thus, mimicking creates in the observer an experience that corresponds to the emotion of the observed person, a process called emotional contagion (Hatfield, Cacioppo, & Rapson, 1992; Hatfield, Rapson, & Le, 2011).

Evidence for congruent responses to facial expressions and for emotional contagion

The initial component in the aforementioned emotional contagion hypothesis predicts mimicry of others' facial expressions. This part of the hypothesis has been examined in several studies, in which facial responses towards facial expressions have been recorded. Static pictures of facial expressions, dynamic facial expressions, and finally also live models' expressions have been used as stimuli, and the facial responses have often been recorded with EMG, which assesses the electric activity in the facial muscles. Robust evidence supports that observers of facial expressions tend to respond with activity in the same facial muscles as in the expression they observe, thus they mimic the facial expression (Dimberg, 1982; Dimberg, 1989; Hess & Blairy, 2001; Hess, Philippot, & Blairy, 1998; McIntosh, 2006; Weyers, Mühlberger, Hefele, & Pauli, 2006). Mimicry tends to be a fast, automatic response that occurs without the mimicker's intention (Dimberg et al., 2002, 482; Heyes, 2011; Sonnby-Borgström, 2002a), and can, in addition, be evoked by subliminally exposed facial expressions without the receiver's awareness of the facial stimuli (Dimberg et al., 2002; Sonnby-Borgström et al., 2008b). Responses evoked at subliminal exposures of facial expressions cannot be dependent on cognitively loaded interpretations of the other person's internal state. According to these results, when exposed to another's facial expression, we tend to respond with a congruent facial expression, although not always a visible one.

Furthermore, a positive relationship has been suggested between the degree of mimicking and the tendency to experience the same emotions as conveyed by the facial expression (Dimberg, 1988; Hsee, Hatfield, Carlsson, & Chetomb, 1990; Lundqvist, 1995; McIntosh, 2006; Neumann & Strack, 2000; Sonnby-Borgström et al., 2008b; Wild, Erb, & Bartels,

2001). It is, however, still unclear exactly how the positive relationship between mimicry and the tendency to experience emotional contagion can be explained.

The facial feedback hypothesis

The facial feedback hypothesis (FFH) (Tomkins, 1962) provides one possible explanation for the positive relationship between mimicry and emotional contagion. According to the FFH, neural feedback from the mimicking of facial muscles affects the imitator's emotional experience, a hypothesis in line with the theory that feedback from somatic and visceral responses are considered to be crucial in shaping emotional "knowledge" (Damasio, 1994; Gallese, 2001, 2003; Niedenthal, Winkielman, Mondillon, & Vermeulen, 2009). Facial mimicry is a very fast, automatic response that occurs about 300 milliseconds after stimulus onset (Dimberg, 1997). The visceral responses, which also are involved in the imitator's emotional experience, are evoked later than the facial responses. The convergence of the facial nerve and visceral projections may account for the suggestion that somatic feedback from the face is involved in modulating autonomic activity (Schore, 1994). Facial expressions are, thus, essential as tools in interpersonal as well as in intra-individual communication.

There are several alternative explanations emanating from the FFH concerning the relationship between facial expressions and the expresser's subjective experience. One of these proposes that feedback from facial expression muscle movements is nessecary for the emotional experience (the necessity hypothesis), another that facial feedback from facial muscles may be sufficient (suffiency hypothesis) for the initiation of the expresser's subjective experience of emotion, and a third variant proposes that feedback from facial expressions may modulate (monotonicity hypothesis) the expresser's subjective experience (Ekman et al., 1980). The necessity hypothesis has not been supported by experimental results (Davis, Senghas, Brandt, & Ochsner, 2010; Keillor, Barett, Crucian, Kortenkkamp, & Heilman, 2002), whereas there is mounting experimental evidence in favour of the monotonicity hypothesis (Soussignan, 2002). The sufficiency hypothesis has not been rejected, but the evidence in favour of it is rather infrequent (McIntosh, 1996; Soussignan, 2002).

Some studies are, however, supportive of the sufficiency hypothesis. Ekman, Levenson, and Friesen (1983) have found that posing facial expressions influences the emotional experience of the expresser, and that posing of different facial expressions results in distinctive physiological responses. The participants in Ekman's experiment (Ekman, Levenson, & Friesen, 1983) were instructed to produce facial expressions and report their emotional experiences. In addition, their autonomic physiological responses were assessed. When the participants produced expressions, for example, anger, disgust, fear, happiness, and surprise, they reported different emotional experiences, and characteristic physiological outcomes were also identified. In another experiment (Hess, Kappas, McHugo, Lanzetta, & Klerk, 1992) participants were instructed to feel certain emotions (feeling condition), to pose (without feeling) facial expressions corresponding to these emotions, or to simultaneously feel and express these emotions (feeling and expressing condition). The investigators found that instructions to pose an expression and simultaneously feel it had a facilitative effect on the self-generation of emotion in comparison to the feeling condition, a result in support of the monotonicity hypothesis. The study also found that simply posing an emotional expression resulted in autonomic changes and in self-reported affect consistent with the posed expression, a partial support of the sufficiency hypothesis. Flack (2006) examined the effects of voluntarily posed facial expressions, posed bodily postures, and voluntarily produced emotional vocalizations of anger, sadness, and fear on subjective emotional experience. The aim of the study was disguised to the participants. The outcome indicated that specific facial expressions and bodily postures tended to produce the corresponding categorical affects. The magnitude of the effects of posed facial expressions exceeded those of the bodily postures, which in turn exceeded the magnitude of the effect of vocalizations. Lewis (2012) found that self-reported mood was negatively affected after participants were instructed to lower their eyebrows. Contracting of corrugator muscles are used in frowns involved in negative emotions. These results demonstrate that posing a facial expression, without any external emotional stimuli present, tends to influence the expresser's emotional experience, and are thus in favour of the sufficiency hypothesis.

Several studies (Dimberg & Söderkvist, 2011; Kleinke, Peterson, & Rutledge, 1998; Soussignan, 2002) show evidence in support of the monotonicity hypothesis. In Strack et al.'s classical experiment (Strack, Martin, & Stepper, 1988) some participants were instructed to hold a pen between their teeth, an activity that stimulates the Zygomaticus Major muscles, used when smiling. Other participants were instructed to hold a pencil between their lips. Pressing the lips together inhibits the same muscles. The participants were exposed to comic cartoons and asked to report the amount of amusement during exposure. Those who had activated the Zygomaticus Major (a posed smile) reported more amusement than those with inhibited Zygomaticus Major (an inhibited smile). A similar effect on the evaluative judgement of cartoons was obtained in a recent study (Foroni & Gun, 2011), where different facial expressions were shown subliminally before the judgement process. In one condition, the Zygomaticus Major was blocked by holding a pen between the lips and in another condition the Zygomaticus Major was unblocked. The evaluations of the cartoons were affected only when positive emotional mimicry was not blocked. In some studies of the facial feedback hypothesis, Botox-injections have been used, a toxin that induces a temporary muscle denervation and blocks the impulses from the facial expressive muscles. These studies show that blocking of impulses from facial expressive muscles affects the subjective emotional experiences in experimental situations (Davis et al., 2010; Neal & Chartrand, 2011) as well as in longer-lasting mood states (Finzi & Wassermann, 2006; Lewis & Bowler, 2009). In summary, experimental results favour the monotonicity hypothesis that feedback from somatic motoric responses influences the expressor's experience. The question of whether facial feedback is sufficient to initiate an emotional experience is, however, still debated.

Mirror neurons, mimicry, and emotional contagion

Our tendency to imitate or mimic others has also been a focus for neurological research. In brain-imaging studies it has been shown that when a monkey observes another monkey performing an act, the same neurons will fire in pre-motor cortex of the observing monkey, as if the monkey prepared for the action himself. The result is a mirror pre-motor activation in the observer (Perrett & Emergy, 2000; Rizzolatti, Gallese, & Fongassi, 1995; Williams, Whiten, Suddendorf, & Perrett, 2001). The neural system that fires when the monkey observes another performing an action, as well as when it performs the action itself, has been called the mirror neuron system (MNS). The evidence of mirroring came initially from research on monkeys. Neural simulation has, however, also been found in humans (Carr et al., 2003; Fadiga, Fogassi, Pavesi, & Rizolatti, 1995; Iacoboni et al., 1999). In one study, human participants (Carr et al., 2003) were asked to either observe or imitate facial expressions. Passive observation as well as imitation activated the same neural areas: the ventro-lateral frontal cortex and the inferior frontal gyrus (IFG) (see also Schilbach, Chapter 4, and Schuler et al., Chapter 9).

The IFG region has been called the area of "cold" motor simulation, reflecting mere motor mimicry. It has been demonstrated that not only the motor area but also emotional brain regions are activated when observing a facial expression as well as during the experience of the corresponding emotion. A transition zone between insula and frontal operculum (IFO) is activated both during the observation of disgusted facial expressions and during the experience of disgust (Jabbi, Swart, & Keysers, 2007; Wicker et al., 2003). This area, IFO, has been called the "hot" simulation area, because it is activated by an individual's subjective emotional experience, and may be involved in empathic simulation. The activity in the simulating pre-motor brain region (IFG) has been found to precede the activation of the hot empathic brain area (IFO), which suggests a causal relationship (Jabbi & Keysers, 2008).

In summary, if the results regarding IFG and IFO are translated into responses on facial expressions, it could be hypothesized that the observation of facial expressions initially results in the activation of cold (motor) mirror neurons (IFG) involved in facial mimicry (muscle activation), which then via facial feedback activates the hot emotional brain regions (IFO), and as a consequence leads to the observer's emotional experience (emotional contagion).

In addition, a study has found a positive relationship between facial imitation and MNS activity and between MNS activity and empathic ability as well (Pfeifer, Iacoboni, Mazziotta, & Dapretto, 2008). Thus, there are reasons to assume a positive relationship between the MNS activation, mimicry, and empathy (Iacoboni, 2009). Further research is, however, needed to be able to allow conclusions about the causal relationship between these variables.

Emotional communication: a dynamic developmental process on different levels of information processing

According to the dynamic developmental model described earlier, more advanced processes than mere emotional contagion participate in a face-to-face emotional communication situation. The impact of learnt cognitive schemas and attentional processes on facial responses to facial expression are hypothesized to play an essential role in communication as well, especially at more advanced levels of information processing.

The development of emotional communication and emotional regulation

The elaboration of the emotional communication process from primitive and biologically prewired to more advanced forms may be elucidated by a description of the early development of children's responses to facial expressions.

During the child's early preverbal period the emotional communication between the parent and the neonate is a non-verbal process. The parent's tone of voice and emotional facial expressions are essential non-verbal emotional signals for the child (Stern, 1985). According to Meltzoff and Moore (1977) and Field, Woodson, and Greenberg (1982) neonates tend to respond with imitation to their parent's facial expressions. Their conclusions about neonates' biologically prepared ability to imitate have been questioned, since many researchers have failed to replicate their results (Anisfeld, 1991; Jones, 2009). A recent supportive study (Nagy, Pilling, Orvos, & Molnar, 2012) included 115 newborns who were tested for imitation of tongue protrusion within their first five days of life. Support was obtained for neonates' tendency to imitate in this early period of life, a result which cannot be explained as mimicry based on previous learning. Early imitation also appears to exist across species. Suomi (2006) has observed imitation of facial gestures, such as lip smacking, tongue protrusion, and mouth opening, in neonatal rhesus macaques. Thus, neonates appear to be prewired to react to certain facial expressions with imitation, and furthermore their imitation skill rapidly increases (Field et al., 1983). The child's emotional communication develops through social interactions; especially crucial is the initial, early non-verbal communication between the caretaker and the child. It has been observed that adults imitate infants once every minute during face-to-face interactions in the first two years of life (Pawlby, 1977). Further, if mothers imitate their child frequently, the child's tendency to imitate others is influenced in a positive direction (Masur, 1987). Children only show perfect imitation of facial expressions during their first three months. After three months they rather favour natural interactions, in which emotionally well-attuned parents match the infant's internal state, a matching called "affect attunement" (Jonsson, Clinton, Fahrman, & Mazzaglia, 2001; Markova & Legerstee, 2006). Through social learning processes new sets of schemas and expectations will influence the child's social awareness as well as the child's tendency to imitate. Synchronization between the caretaker's and the child's emotional states through non-verbal communication is assumed to regulate the infant's emotions to a comfortable state and as a consequence affect the child's ability to regulate emotional distress in future social relationships (Field, 2012; Schore & Schore, 2008). In a review article, Eisenberg et al. (1998) discuss evidence that argues for the important role that parental emotional socialization practices have for the development of children's social competence and well-being. Parents' negative responses to children's emotion expressions have been associated with the development of a disposition towards negative emotions and low social competence (Eisenberg et al., 1998). Positive emotional expressivity has been associated with children's development of high social competence and adaptive emotion regulation (Valiente et al., 2004). Accordingly, the early emotional communication between parent and child is fundamental in shaping the child's future development of strategies for expressing and regulating emotions. Recent findings support the idea that the biologically based mirror neuron system is subject to change through learning processes as well (Catmur, Walsh, & Heyes, 2007; Del Giudice, Manera, & Kaysers, 2009).

Bottom-up and top-down processes

The neonate's early imitative responses may be characterized as bottom-up responses to facial expressions. Internal schemas or expectations shaped by experiences have no impact on neonates' responses to the emotional stimulus. This form of primitive, prewired communication is elaborated through social interactions as described in the previous section. Emotional imaging and emotional expectations as well as attentional processes become successively, via learning in social interactions, involved in our responses to other's facial expressions. Information processing, influenced by more elaborated schemas, is called top-down processing.

Facial muscle activation is not only caused by the observation of external facial stimuli but facial expressive muscle movements may also be elicited by top-down processes, for example, when participants were instructed to imagine an emotional interaction situation (Tassinary & Cacioppo, 2000). The facial muscle responses, recorded by EMG, were found to reflect the imagined emotional interaction. Such top-down processes may in a face-to-face interaction situation modulate automatically evoked facial responses. Thoughts about what to expect in a special situation, formed by either the situational context or by our life history, may influence our emotional facial responses and the emotions evoked in social situations. Emotional-cognitive schemas, which participate in emotional memories and expectations, are assumed to activate similar responses in the perceptual and somatic brain regions as those evoked in the original situations related to the memories (called embodied simulation) (Gallese, 2003; Hawk, Fischer, & Van Kleef, 2011; Likowski, Muhlberger, & Seibt, 2011; Likowski, Muhlberger, Seibt, Pauli, & Weyers, 2007; Niedenthal et al., 2009).

According to the model described here, the facial responses in a social face-to-face interaction are assumed to initially occur automatically (within milliseconds) as a response to the other's facial expression, as bottom-up process. At later processing levels (within seconds) this spontaneous facial and emotional response may be modified by top-down processes, which in turn may influence the subjective experience. The communication may be seen as an internal dynamic process between information processing levels as well as a dynamic interaction between individuals.

Intra-individual information processing levels

Percept-genetic theory, presented in the model earlier, proposes that the processing of emotional information is hierarchically organized, and that the end product of the process is a result of a micro process in time evolving from a few milliseconds to a couple of seconds (Brown, 1985;

Smith, 1991). The response to a facial stimulus at the initial, primitive processing level, in a neutral situation, can be supposed to be fast and automatically evoked, without influences of previous learning (Leventhal, 1984; Öhman, 1993). This form of information processing level is probably present only in an infant without previous experience of emotional communication. The response at the second information processing level involves a separate memory system, which is based on amygdala activation, which may include activation of learning processes and memories at the classical conditioning level. This level operates without access to conscious awareness and is also automatic (Heyes, 2011; Leventhal, 1984; Öhman, 1993; Pally, 1998). Automatic imitation takes place without intentional effort and cannot be voluntarily controlled (Dimberg et al., 2002). Rapid modulations of facial expressions, including amygdala-based memories, may also take place without cognitive effort, as suggested by Achaibou, Pourtois, and Schwartz (2008), in a study using combined EMG and EEG (electroencephalography) recordings. The third step in information processing activates the conscious perception channels and the input is interpreted in interaction with secondary memory systems. This controlled and more emotionally regulated level is supposed to be based on memories involving hippocampus activation (LeDoux, 1996; Leventhal, 1984; Öhman, 1993; Pally, 1998).

This dynamic developmental perspective on facial imitation and emotional contagion views our responses to facial expressions as the result of phylogenetically prepared mimicry tendencies, of learnt expectations (internal schemas), which modulate the expressions at more or less conscious information processing levels, as well as of more controlled and attentionally loaded processes (Achaibou et al., 2008; Bourgeois & Hess, 2008; Niedenthal & Halberstadt, 2003; Sonnby-Borgström, 2002b; Yan & Shihui, 2008). Modulation of automatic facial responses by more controlled top-down processes may in turn regulate the emotional experience through facial feedback and serve as a component in our emotion regulation system (Izard, 1990; Sonnby-Borgström, 2002b).

Individual differences in facial mimicry

Even though there is wide support of the hypothesis that we commonly tend to respond to others' facial expressions with mimicry or imitation, individual differences in this phenomenon have also been demonstrated. The differences may be explained by variations in the infant's genetically prepared imitation tendencies as well as by the individual's emotional interaction experiences during development (Chartrand & van Baaren, 2009). The social context around interacting persons also influences facial responses to expressions (Bourgeois & Hess, 2008). The impact of social context is addressed in Chapter 9 of this book. The following sections of the present chapter focus on individual differences in facial mimicry responses related to more durable personality traits associated with empathic ability.

Facial mimicry as related to empathic ability

Our ability to understand other's emotions and internal states is of crucial importance in all social interactions. Individuals who have an impaired empathic ability may have severe difficulties in closer social relationships as well as in daily social interactions. Empathy has been defined as "An emotional response that stems from another's emotional state or condition, and involves at least a minimal degree of differentiation between self and other" (Eisenberg & Fabes, 1990, p. 132). This definition of empathy is intimately linked to the emotional contagion concept, which according to the emotional contagion hypothesis is supposed to be a result of the mimicry of facial expression in interaction situations. It could, hence, be assumed that individuals who are good empathizers, would have stronger tendencies to mimic others than those who are less empathic.

The assumption of a positive relationship between individual's tendencies to mimic or imitate others and their empathic ability has been supported. For example, in one study small children watched movies that showed persons who express distress (Eisenberg, Losoya, & Spinrad, 2003). Children who had stronger tendencies to imitate the expressed feelings of the distressed person, also expressed more motivation to help the person in trouble. It could be assumed that the children's mimicking of the distressed persons influenced the children's emotional experience and as a consequence they were more willing to help them. A positive relationship between imitation of gestures and empathy has also been found in experimentally created interaction situations (Chartrand & Bargh, 1999). Some participants were instructed to execute special postures and mannerisms, when they were involved in a conversation with other "naive" participants. Those who scored high on a self-report questionnaire assessing cognitive empathy were more prone to imitate their confederates' postures than participants scoring low on cognitive empathy.

Other studies, using electromyography (EMG) to measure facial responses, have demonstrated that more empathic individuals differed from less empathic individuals in their tendency to imitate pictures of emotional expressions (Sonnby-Borgström, 2002a; Sonnby-Borgström et al., 2003). The experimental designs used in these studies were based on percept-genetic theory proposing different levels of information processing (Brown, 1985; Smith, 1991). Pictures of angry and happy expressions were shown with successively prolonged exposure times ranging from milliseconds (subliminally) to more than 1,000 milliseconds, a design that was assumed to evoke responses at different levels of information processing, from spontaneous/automatic to more emotionally controlled and attentionally loaded levels (Leventhal, 1984; Öhman, 1993). Backward masking was used to interrupt information processing. Empathic ability was assessed with the self-report Questionnaire Measurement of Emotional Empathy (QMEE) (Mehrabian & Epstein, 1972). The participants reported their emotional experiences during the exposures on a Likert scale including alternatives from positive to negative emotional experience. At the first subliminal exposure time no differences in facial responding were found between high- and low-empathic participants. At "medium" exposure times (17–75 milliseconds), called the automatic level, significant differences in muscle responses were found between high- and low-empathy participants, whereas at the longer exposure times (more than 1,000 milliseconds), assumed to be more cognitively controlled, no such differences were found. The high-empathy participants responded with the expected mimicry at the "automatic" exposure times, whereas the low-empathy participants did not (Sonnby-Borgström, 2002a; Sonnby-Borgström et al., 2003). Further, a positive relationship was observed between facial muscle responses and the reported emotional experiences only for the high-empathy participants (Sonnby-Borgström, 2002a). In a mimicry study with a similar design (Sonnby-Borgström, 2009) the participants' degree of alexithymia was assessed with a self-report questionnaire, the Toronto Alexithymia Scale (TAS-20) (Bagby, Taylor, & Parker, 1994). Individuals scoring high on alexithymia are characterized by impairments in the ability to represent emotions mentally (Taylor, Bagby, & Parker, 1997). The low-alexithymia participants scored higher on a questionnaire measuring empathy than did the high-alexithymia individuals. The participants classified as low in alexithymia and thus more empathic showed stronger tendencies to mimic facial expressions and further they showed a positive relationship between their verbally reported emotional contagion and their facial responses at the cognitively controlled level of responses, whereas high-alexithymia participants did not. It has also been demonstrated in another mimicry study, using facial expressions as stimuli and EMG to assess facial responses (Andréasson & Dimberg, 2008), that individuals high in trait empathy tend to be more sensitive to facial feedback than individuals low in empathic ability.

The results from the studies by Sonnby-Borgström and colleagues (Sonnby-Borgström, 2002a; Sonnby-Borgström et al., 2003), showing a positive relationship between empathic ability and facial responses to facial expressions, have been confirmed by other researchers also assessing mimicry responses with EMG (Dimberg, Andréasson, & Thunberg, 2011). In the study by Dimberg et al. (2011) pictures of facial expressions were shown for 5 seconds. The results confirmed that more empathic individuals responded with stronger Zygomaticus Major responses to happy faces and with stronger Corrugator Supercilii responses to angry faces compared to less empathic individuals. Harrison, Morgan, and Critchley (2010) used the "Balanced Emotional Empathy Scale" to measure trait empathy in a mimicry study and found support for a positive relationship only for trait empathy and Corrugator Supercilii mimicry. The results were explained as reflecting the closer neural connectivity between Corrugator Supercilii and the amygdala as well as the cingulate motor cortex, which are involved in mimicry.

The effect of state empathy, rather than trait empathy, was investigated by Likowski et al. (2011) in a study in which the context was manipulated to be either competitive or cooperative. Present empathy state was found to influence the facial responses of the other's facial expressions. Inverse facial responses (contra empathic) were evoked in situations involving competition; the participants increased Corrugator Supercilii activity (frowned) when "the other" showed a positive expression (won) and increased Zygomaticus Major responses (smiled), when the other showed a negative expression (lost). In the cooperative condition the participants showed regular mimicry responses.

Some individuals have specific disabilities in empathy and social competent behaviour. Such disabilities are frequent in boys with social disruptive behaviour disorder (DBD), who score lower on self-report questionnaires of empathy than normal controls. In a mimicry study their Corrugator Supercilii activity was found to be lower in response to angry and sad faces (De Wied, Van Boxtel, Posthumus, Goudena, & Mattys, 2009; De Wied, van Boxtel, Zaalberg, Goudena, & Mattys, 2006). Further, individuals diagnosed with autistic spectrum disorder (ASD) are characterized by impairment in social communication and have severe problems in sharing and understanding others' emotions (Hill & Frith, 2003). Individuals with ASD show less imitation and mimicry than controls (McIntosh, Reichmann-Decker, Winkelman, & Wilbarger, 2006; Oberman & Ramachandran, 2007; Oberman, Winkielman, & Ramachandran, 2009; Williams, Whiten, & Singh, 2004). Additionally, individuals with ASD have been observed to have deficits in the cortical areas subserving the mirror neuron system (Hadjikhani, Joseph, Snyder, & Tager-Flusberg, 2006). The relationship between mimicking, emotional communication, and ASD is further elaborated in Chapter 8 (Winkielman et al.) in this book.

The experiments described earlier have related trait empathy to facial imitation or facial mimicry, which is assumed to result in emotional contagion. Empathic understanding in a face-to-face interaction situation is, however, presumed to include more elaborated processes than mere mimicking and emotional contagion (Davis, 1983). Empathy may be seen as a dynamic process evolving through different levels of information processing, in which automatic perceptual responses that result in emotional contagion are involved as well as more sophisticated forms of mind-reading, including fantasies and perspective taking (Coricelli, 2005; Davis, 1983; Decety & Lamm, 2006). Mere emotional contagion is seldom enough to result in helping behaviour that is assumed to be a result of empathy. For example, if an observer of a distressed person becomes too distressed himself, this often results in the observer's self-focused anxiety-related behaviour and not in actions to help the other person (Eisenberg et al., 2003). A high level of anxiety may interfere with the crucial other-directed response. A mother, who responds with a high degree of distress to threatening situations, may have difficulties in soothing her distressed child. Effective and adaptive emotion regulation strategies are often a prerequisite to be able to elaborate the automatic emotional distress response into an empathic and prosocial response directed towards the other (Eisenberg et al., 2003). This perspective on empathy as involving different processing levels is in line with recent results of a study that proposes two routes to empathic embarrassment, one route dependent on more primitive non-verbal mimicry and emotional contagion and another route involving more cognitively loaded components such as perspective taking (Hawk et al., 2011). Research on the temporal neural dynamics involved in empathic responses has also found support for a model involving different processing levels in empathic responding (Yan & Shihui, 2008). In a study on neurological processing when observing pain, it was found that the activation of a neural component underlying emotional sharing preceded a later neural component underlying top-down related cognitive evaluation.

The relationship between mimicry and empathic ability as a durable state is doubtless multidimensional and complex. The positive relationship between facial responding and empathic ability is probably bidirectional. Mimicry may result in emotional contagion, which automatically activates internal schemas (involving personality traits) and situational expectancies, which in turn, via top-down processes, may influence the facial responses and the regulation or modulation of the facial responding. The modulation of facial expressions may also, via feedback, influence the observer's vicarious emotional experience.

Facial mimicry and attachment orientation

Individuals can be categorized according to their attachment orientations, that is, their strategies for handling emotions in relation to the self
(model-of-self) and towards others (model-of-others) (Bartholomew,
1993; Bartholomew & Horowitz, 1991). Attachment orientations and
empathic ability have been found to be positively associated (Joireman,
Needham, & Cummings, 2002; Kestenbaum, Farber, & Sroufe, 1989;
Mikulincer et al., 2001), and as a consequence attachment orientations
can be expected to be associated with differences in facial mimicry.
Further, since individuals with different attachment orientations are
characterized by special strategies for handling negative emotions in
relation to the self and towards others, it can be suggested that they will
respond in specific ways to social emotional information (Ainsworth &
Bowlby, 1991; Bretherton & Munholland, 1999; Niedentahl &
Halberstadt, 2003; Sonnby-Borgström, 2002b). A facial expression com-
municates the emotional state of the sender in an interaction and this
might challenge the perceiver of the facial expression in different ways
depending on attachment orientation. Further, it has been found that
children with secure versus insecure attachment show differences in
their facial expressions during the separation episodes in the strange-
situation procedure (SSP), in which children are separated from their
caregiver for a short time in an unfamiliar context. In this situation the
insecurely attached children more rarely displayed facial expressions of
the positive emotion of interest and more often the facial expressions of
sadness than the securely attached children (Shiller, Izard, & Hembree,
1986). Thus, there are strong reasons to expect attachment orientation to
have an impact on facial mimicry.

Adult attachment orientation is often assessed with Bartholomew's
self-report scale (Relationship Scale Questionnaire, RSQ), in which individuals can be scored on two dimensions going from positive to negative,
which represent the internal schemas model-of-self and model-of-others
(Bartholomew, 1993; Bartholomew & Horowitz, 1991). Based on the inter-
section between these two dimensions, individuals can be characterized
as belonging to one of four different attachment orientations. Individuals
with a *secure attachment* orientation have a positive self-evaluation
(model-of-self) and a positive evaluation of others (model-of-others).
Secure individuals do not erect defences against negative affect
(Anderson & Guerrero, 1998). *Preoccupied* individuals have a positive
evaluation of others but a negative self-evaluation. They try to regulate
their high level of anxiety through dependency on their relational partner; they dwell on negative affect and anxiety and seek support and
comfort from others in a "hyper vigilant" manner (Anderson &

Guerrero, 1998; Mikulincer & Shaver, 2003). Individuals in the *fearful-avoidant* category have a negative self-evaluation and they do not trust others. They fear rejection and worry about being hurt if they get too close to others, they have no effective strategy to regulate their negative emotions, and they experience constantly a high level of anxiety (Anderson & Guerrero, 1998; Mikulincer & Shaver, 2003). Individuals with a *dismissing-avoidant* attachment orientation see themselves as worth caring for and have on a verbally reportable information processing level a positive self-evaluation (positive model-of-self), but see others as unavailable for them (negative model-of-others). On the conscious and more cognitively controlled information processing level, the dismissing-avoidant individuals report a low level of distress and consider relationships as unimportant (Anderson & Guerrero, 1998). Negative external information is avoided and they deny their internal experience of negative affect and anxiety (Anderson & Guerrero, 1998; Brennan, Clark, & Shaver, 1998; Mikulincer & Florian, 1998; Mikulincer & Shaver, 2003). As a consequence of the defensive exclusion of negative information, dismissing-avoidant individuals may be described as having two incompatible sets of internal working models, one consciously accessible and one inaccessible or only intermittently accessible to consciousness. They are supposed to have one positive model-of-self operating at a conscious level and another model of a fragile self, which is related to negative emotions, operating outside of awareness (Bartholomew, 1990; Bretherton & Munholland, 1999; Klohnen & John, 1998). The models can be assumed to operate at different temporal stages in the processing of information.

The relationship between attachment orientation and facial mimicry has been studied in an investigation based on the percept-genetic model using the design decribed earlier. Attachment orientation was assessed by the previously described self-evaluative scale RSQ (Bartholomew & Horowitz, 1991; Bäckström & Holmes, 1999; Griffin & Bartholomew, 1994). Facial mimicry responses towards angry faces were compared between individuals with different attachment orientations, including a negative model-of-self and high levels of anxiety (preoccupied and fear-avoidant), and those with a positive model-of-self and lower levels of anxiety (secure and dismissing-avoidant). Participants with negative models-of-self amplified their Corrugator Supercilii response towards angry faces from the shortest to the longest, more cognitively controlled exposure times, whereas individuals with a positive model-of-self did not show such tendencies. The Corrugator Supercilii responses towards angry faces showed significant differences at the longest exposure time (Sonnby-Borgström & Jönsson, 2003). The result may be interpreted as a consequence of the preoccupied and the fear-avoidant individuals' difficulties to regulate their negative emotional responses to threatening social information. Individuals with negative internal models-of-self can be hypothesized to lack comforting internal schemas that may serve as modulaters of negative expressions and emotions. Internal emotion regulating schemas are assumed to be developed in childhood through social interaction between child and parents (Eisenberg et al., 1998). The results showing augmented negative facial responses for the anxious-attached participants are in line with results in a study in which participants with different attachment orientations were exposed to emotional pictures (Zilber, Goldstein, & Mikulincer, 2007). Electroencephalography (EEG) was used to measure the late positive potential (LPP), which has been found to be stronger when watching emotionally arousing pictures than neutral pictures. Participants scoring high on attachment anxiety elicited greater LPP than participants scoring low, when watching negative emotional pictures. The findings of Niedenthal and colleagues (Niedenthal & Halberstadt, 2003; Niedenthal, Brauer, Robin, & Innes-Ker, 2002) may also be seen as consistent with the results of the Sonnby-Borgström study (Sonnby-Borgström & Jönsson, 2003). Niedenthal et al. examined the relationship between attchment orientation and the perception of facial expressions. Movies of "morphed" facial expressions were used as stimuli. Morphed facial expressions consist of pictures of an expressor, which gradually change from one facial expression to another. The participants observed films showing these gradually changing facial expressions and they were instructed to stop the film when the initial expression no longer appeared to be on the face. In one of the experiments (Niedenthal et al., 2002) participants with different attachment orientations were manipulated to experience a high level of distress assumed to arouse the activation of the attachment system. Participants with insecure attachment orientations (preoccupied, dismissing-avoidant, and fearful-avoidant) were predicted to perceive the off-set of the negative facial expression later than the secure group. The results supported the hypothesized relations and the participants with an insecure attachment orientation saw the negative facial expressions lasting longer than did the secure individuals; the effect was especially strong for fearful individuals, who have no organized strategy to manage their anxiety. The longer-lasting perception of negative facial expression for the insecure individuals may, according to Niedenthal et al., be explained by the assumption that facial perception relies on feedback from facial mimicry muscles (cf. Niedenthal & Halberstadt, 2003). This assumtion is in line with the result showing incresed facial Corrugator Supercilii mimicry responses towards angry faces for individuals with attachment orientations associated with a higher level of anxiety/distress (Sonnby-Borgström & Jönsson, 2003).

As a result of facial feedback from amplified Corrugator Supercilii mimicry the insecurely attached participants could be expected to perceive the negative facial expressions as lasting longer than secure individuals (Niedenthal et al., 2002).

In another study by Sonnby-Borgström, using the same experimental design as in the previously described study with successively prolonged exposures of facial expressions (Sonnby-Borgström & Jönsson, 2004), comparisons were made between participants with dismissing-avoidant attachment orientation and participants with other attachment orientations (secure, preoccupied and fear-avoidant; non-dismissing). Individuals with dismissing-avoidant attchment orientation are characterized by denial of anxiety (supression) at the consious, verbal level, but they are assumed to have an unconscious level of high anxiety beneath the surface (Bretherton & Munholland, 1999; Milkulincer & Orbach, 1995), whereas suppression of anxiety does not characterize individuals with other attachment orientations (non-dismissing). The dismissing-avoidant participants in the Sonnby-Borgström et al. study responded at the automatic exposure time (56 milliseconds) with a Corrugator Supercilii imitative response towards angry faces, as expected, indicating negative emotions, but their facial responses changed to an inverted response at longer exposure times (2,350 milliseconds). They responded at longer exposure times with stronger Zygomaticus Major activity (indicating positive emotions) and no Corrugator Supercilii mimicry towards angry faces, wheras the non-dismissing participants increased their mimicry responses at the longer exposure times. The change from an expected negative response to an inverted facial response might be interpreted as a mechanism underlying the supression of negative emotions. Emotional feedback from the Zygomaticus Major responses at longer exposures, indicating more emotionally controlled information processing levels, may participate in the suppression of the automatically evoked distressing negative emotion. This interpretation is consistent with the results of an interview study, in which Adult Attachment Interviews (AAI) were conducted and the participants' physiological responses were measured during the interview (Roisman, Tsai, & Chiang, 2004). An increase in electrodermal responses, which are a sign of emotion suppression, were found for individuals with dismissing-avoidant attachment orientation. Further, the results of a brain-imaging study (Suslow et al., 2009) are consistent with the results showing inverted facial responses for individuals with dismissing-avoidant attachment orientation. Brain activity was assessed during the participants' exposure to pictures of sad faces. Attachment avoidance was found to be negatively related to activity in the somatosensory cortex, a cortical region, which is known to be critically involved in emotional mimicry.

Additionally, the participants with dismissing-avoidant attachment orientation in the study by Sonnby-Borgström and Jönsson (2004) scored significantly lower on an empathy scale than did non-dismissing participants. It has been shown that masking/suppression of facial mimicry results in difficulties to read the facial expressions of others (Schneider, Hempel, & Lynch, 2013). Thus, it may be suggested that the dismissing-avoidant participants' emotion regulation strategy, consisting of suppression of facial expression and mimicry, may result in less emotional contagion and further in deficits in empathic ability (Carr et al., 2003).

Conclusions regarding the relationship between attachment orientation and facial responses to facial expression are so far based on few studies and further investigations are needed to confirm the results. The suggestion that facial muscle movements are a mechanism underlying emotion regulation and suppression is tentative, and the hypothesis is an interesting area for future research.

Gender differences and facial mimicry

Gender is one factor that has been associated with individual differences in trait empathy, and gender thus could be assumed to be related to differences in facial mimicry. Women have been found to be more empathic than men in a large number of studies using self-report questionnaires to measure empathy (Baron-Cohen & Wheelwright, 2004; Davis, 1983; Eisenberg et al., 1988; Hardy, 2001; Gilet, Mella, Studer, Gruhn, & Labouvie-Vief, 2013; Tobari, 2003), and women are more emotionally expressive than men as well (Ashmore, 1990; Brody & Hall, 1993; Buck, William, & Miller, 1974; Hall, 1984; Kring & Gordon, 1998). Research using EMG recordings to measure facial responding has also provided support for women as superior in emotional expressiveness (Bradley, Codispoti, Sabatinelli, & Lang, 2001; Greenwald, Cook, & Lang, 1989; Schwartz, Brown, & Ahern, 1980; Schwartz, Fair, Salt, Mandel, & Klerman, 1976; Thunberg & Dimberg, 2000). Women are, further, found to be more sensitive to and more accurate at labelling the emotional facial expression (Biel & Grabowska, 2006; Hall & Matsumo, 2004; Montagne, Kessels, Frigerio, & de Haan, 2005; Wakabayashi, Sasaki, & Ogawa, 2012), but see also Hutchison and Gerstein (2012), who did not find any differences between men and women in decoding accuracy.

Few studies, though, have examined gender differences in mimicking behaviour. In one study, men's and women's mimicry responses were compared and women showed stronger congruent EMG responses to the facial stimuli than men did (Dimberg, 1990). This study did, however, not assess EMG responses at different information processing levels.

Another, similar, mimicking study, examined gender differences in facial EMG responses to facial expressions, but included exposure times and information processing levels as additional experimental factors. The experiment was based on percept-genetic theory and pictures of facial expressions were shown at successively longer exposure times from 23 milliseconds (subliminal) to 2,500 milliseconds with backward masking to interrupt information processing (Sonnby-Borgström et al., 2008a). Women amplified their mimicry responses at longer exposure times, and at the longest exposure time the gender differences were significant. In addition, women reported increased emotional contagion from shorter to longer exposure times, whereas men did not (Sonnby-Borgström et al., 2008a). At the longer exposure times the participants' responses can be supposed to be more influenced by cognitively controlled processes and the automatic, spontaneous responses may be modified. The results of another study (Knyazev, Slobodsy-Plusnin, & Bocharov, 2010) may be considered as in line with the results of the study just described. Gender differences in emotional facial processing were studied at different processing levels, which used event-related EEG theta synchronization (ERSP) as a marker of the processing of emotional faces. Different instructions were used to induce either implicit (corresponding to more automatic processing and responding) or explicit (corresponding to more controlled processing and responding) modes of processing in participants when observing facial expressions. Men reacted with stronger ERSP responding during the early implicit condition (unconscious and automatic), whereas women responded with more ERSP during the later explicit (more conscious and cognitively controlled) condition. Thus, later and more elaborated processing levels (explicit) showed stronger activation in women, whereas implicit processing levels were more activated in men. These findings are in line with the results of the study described earlier (Sonnby-Borgström et al., 2008a), in which women responded with stronger facial responses and increased emotional contagion from less elaborated information processing levels to more elaborated levels, whereas men did not.

Differences in emotional expressiveness and facial mimicry between men and women may be hypothesized to be influenced by biologically prepared gender differences as well as by differences in social learning and culturally determined gender rules for how to control emotions and facial displays (Bradley et al., 2001; Buck, 1984; Ekman & Friesen, 1982; Hall, Carter, & Horgan, 2000). Cultural norms that prescribe different emotional behaviours for men and women may also influence men's and women's facial responses to facial expressions. Display rules are social and cultural standards of how and when to express emotions (Buck, 1984). The influence of display rules and emotion socialization can be built into the emotional response and be an integrated part of facial expressions and imitation (Buck, 1984). At more elaborated levels of processing (longer exposure times) displays may be more influenced by learnt display rules and by emotional control. The contemporary Western culture is based on certain norms for being a "real man." Traditional Western masculine identity prescribes autonomy, achievement, aggression, and stoicism (Harris, 1995; Pleck, 1981). Men's way of coping with emotions has been called "restrictive emotionality" (Levant, 1995). Thus, the social norms regarding masculine identity, internalized through the emotion socialization process, may influence men's emotional expressiveness. It has been claimed that boys, during their development, increasingly learn to inhibit their emotional expressions of most emotions, especially those expressing vulnerability (Brody, 1985). In a review by Brody (2000) she refers back to studies that argue for different parental practices in the emotion socialization of boys and girls. In these studies it was found that mothers smile more often at their daughters and engage in more positive interactions with their daughters than with their sons (Brody, 2000). Parents encouraged their daughters' expressions of sadness and fear, but not in their sons. On the other hand, their sons were allowed to express anger, but not their daughters. Mothers of boys reported that they told their boys to control their feelings, whereas mothers of girls did not. Both mothers and fathers reported that they expressed affection by holding, hugging, and kissing their daughters more often than their sons. These gender differences in the parental control or modulation of their children's spontaneously evoked emotions and emotional displays may influence the emotional experience via feedback, which in turn may influence empathy responses towards others (Hall et al., 2000; Levenson, Ekman, & Friesen, 1990; Strack et al., 1988; Tomkins, 1962).

Gender differences in empathy and facial responses to facial expressions may additionally rely on biological factors. The amount of the hormone testosterone is higher in men than in women, and it has been found that a high level of testosterone is positively associated with aggressive behaviour and negatively to prosocial behaviour (Harris, Rushton, Hampson, & Jackson, 1996). A negative relationship has also been found between foetal testosterone hormone level and results on empathy tests (Chapman et al., 2006). Experimentally manipulated testosterone exposure has been demonstrated to influence mimicry. In a study including only women, some of the women received testosterone. Those who received testosterone decreased their facial mimicry (Hermans, Putman, & van Honk, 2006). Thus, elevated testosterone levels appear to decrease the tendency to mimic, which in turn may result in less emotional contagion as well as inferior empathic understanding.

Other studies of gender differences have compared men's and women's brain activity while processing facial expressions and emotional stimuli. A brain-imaging study (Schulte-Ruther, Markowitsch, Shah, Fink, & Piefke, 2008) found that women recruited areas containing mirror neurons in the inferior frontal cortex in the right hemisphere to a greater extent than men, whereas men relied more on activation of the left temporal parietal region assumed to mediate the distinction between the self and the other. Corresponding gender differences in the mirror neuron system have also been shown in an experimental study using EEG recordings to detect mu rhythm suppression, which indicates MNS activity (Yawei, Lee, Yang, Lin, & Decety, 2008). When women observed hand actions of others, they showed stronger indication of MNS activity than did men. The aforementioned empirical evidence favours the hypothesis that gender differences in imitation and empathy to a certain extent may be explained by biologically related gender differences in testosterone levels as well as in MNS activity. According to these results, referring to parents' differential socialization practices for boys and girls as well as to sex differences in hormone levels and in the mirror neuron system (MNS), gender differences in mimicking and in empathic responding may be assumed to be explained as a dynamic interaction between biological and social factors.

Summary and reflections

Different explanations of the origins of mind-reading and empathy have existed for a long time. The significance of cognitively loaded top-down processes to reach empathic understanding have been claimed by some researchers while others have argued for a more spontaneous, emotional simulation approach to explain empathic understanding. These contrasting views can be contained in the model described in the present chapter. The model is tentative and more research is still needed to give further support.

The dynamic process perspective on information processing as evolving through different stages includes automatic, spontaneous processes, such as mimicry and emotional contagion, as well as more cognitively loaded top-down processes, such as expectations, imaginations, and attention. The mirror neuron system and automatic mimicry can be seen as the biologically prewired base for emotion transfer and mind-reading. The prewired mirror system, resulting in facial mimicry, develops and is modulated via social interactions. Internal schemas created in social interactions become associated with the mirror neuron system and are as well supposed to be activated in the process leading to empathy. Individual differences in empathy are thus assumed to be influenced by genetic factors as well as by social interactions. Children who are being imitated and emotionally well attuned with their caretakers tend to develop adaptive emotion regulation strategies and a secure attachment orientation, which is positively related to empathic understanding. Cultural rules may also, via social learning, result in different emotion regulation strategies and as a consequence influence our mimicry tendencies and our tendencies to catch others' emotions.

A further implication of recent research on mirror neurons and mimicry is that evolution has prewired us for abilities such as mind-reading and empathy. Human biology has often been associated with self-serving individualism, whereas culture enables us to be more altruistic and rise above our primitive, selfish human nature. The evolution of the mirror neurons system (MNS) and automatic imitation show that we are biologically prewired to be social, empathic, and cooperative as well. On the other hand, we can frequently observe that humans tend to treat each other in ways that are both heartless and cruel. Such behaviour might instead be explained by heightened activity in our fight-and-flight system. Thus, we typically tend to catch each other's emotions and respond with empathic behaviour, but cultural influences, the individual's social learning history, as well as situational factors may result in less empathic behaviour. Accordingly, research aiming at exploring factors in our culture and social environment that influence our tendency to mimic others, catch others' emotions, and behave empathically are of crucial importance. The creation of social circumstances that promote human empathic responding is, however, a political issue rather than a scientific question.

References

Achaibou, A., Pourtois, G., Schwartz, S., & Vuillement, P. (2008). Simultaneously recording of EEG and facial muscles reactions during spontaneous emotional mimicry. *Neuropsychologia, 46*, 1104–1113.

Ainsworth, M. D., & Bowlby, J. (1991). An ethological approach to personality development. *American Psychologist, 46*, 333–341.

Anderson, P. A., & Guerrero, L. K. (1998). Principles of communication and emotion in social interaction. In P. A. Anderson & L. K. Guerrero (Eds.), *Handbook of communication and emotion* (pp. 49–88). London: Academic Press.

Andréasson, P., & Dimberg, U. (2008). Emotional empathy and facial feedback. *Journal of Nonverbal Behaviour, 32*, 215–224.

Anger Elfenbein, H., Beaupré, M., Lévesque, M., & Hess, U. (2007). Toward a dialectic theory: Cultural differences in the expression and recognition of posed facial expressions. *Emotion, 7*, 131–146.

Anisfeld, M. (1991). Neonatal imitation. *Developmental Review, 11*, 60–97.

Ashmore, R. D. (1990). Sex, gender and the individual. In L. A. Pervin (Ed.), *Handbook of personality: The research and method.* New York: Guilford Press.

Bäckström, M., & Holmes, B. (1999). Measuring adult attachment: A construct validation of two self-report instruments. *Scandinavian Journal of Psychology, 42,* 79–86.

Bagby, R. M., Taylor, G. J., & Parker, J. D. A. (1994). The twenty-item Toronto Alexithymia Scale II. Convergent, discriminant and concurrent validity. *Journal of Psychosomatic Research, 38,* 33–40.

Baron-Cohen, S., & Wheelwright, S. (2004). The empathy quotient: An investigation of adults with Asperger's syndrome or high functioning Autism, and normal sex differences. *Journal of Autism and Developmental Disorders, 34,* 163–165.

Bartholomew, K. (1990). Avoidance of intimacy: An attachment perspective. *Journal of Social and Personal Relationships, 7,* 147–178.

Bartholomew, K. (1993). From childhood to adult relationships: Attachment theory and research. In S. Duck (Ed.), *Learning about social relationships* (pp. 30–62). Newsbury Park, CA: Sage.

Bartholomew, K., & Horowitz, L. M. (1991). Attachment styles among young adults: A test of a four-category model. *Journal of Personality and Social Psychology, 61,* 226–244.

Biel, C., & Grabowska, A. (2006). Sex differences in perception of emotion intensity in dynamic and static facial expressions. *Experimental Brain Research, 171,* 1–6.

Blairy, S., Herrera, P., & Hess, U. (1999). Mimicry and the judgement of emotional facial expressions. *Journal of Nonverbal Behaviour, 23,* 5–41.

Bourgeois, P., & Hess, U. (2008). The impact of social context on mimicry. *Biological Psychology, 77,* 343–352.

Bradley, M., Codispoti, M., Sabatinelli, D., & Lang, P. (2001). Emotion and motivation II: Sex differences in picture processing. *Emotion, 1,* 300–319.

Bretherton, I., & Munholland, K. A. (1999). Internal working models in attachment relationships. In J. Cassidy & P. R. Shaver (Eds.), *Handbook of attachment* (pp. 89–111). New York: Guilford Press.

Brennan, K. A., Clark, L. C., & Shaver, R. P. (1998). Self-report measurement of adult attachment: An integrative overview. In J. A. Simpson & S. W. Rholes (Eds.), *Attachment theory and close relationships* (pp. 46–76). New York: The Guilford Press.

Brody, L. (1985). Gender differences in emotional development. *Journal of Personality, 53,* 102–149.

Brody, L.R. (2000). The socialization of gender differences in emotional expressions: Display rules, infant temperament, and differentiation. In A. Fischer (Ed.), *Gender and Emotion.* Cambridge: Cambridge University Press.

Brody, L. R., & Hall, J. A. (1993). Gender and emotion. In M. Lewis & J. M. Haviland (Eds.), *Handbook of emotions* (pp. 447–460). New York: Gulford Press.

Brown, J. W. (1985). Clinical evidence for the concept of levels of action and perception. *Journal of Neurolinguistics, 1,* 89–141.

Buck, R. (1984). *The communication of emotion.* New York: Guilford.

Buck, R., William, F. C., & Miller, E. M. (1974). Sex, personality, and physiological variables in the communication of affect via facial expression. *Journal of Personality and Social Psychology, 30,* 587–596.

Carr, L., Iacoboni, M., Dubeau, M. C., Mazziotta, J. C., & Lenzi, G. L. (2003). Neural mechanisms of empathy in humans: a relay from neural system for imitation to limbic areas. *Proceedings in National Academic Science, 100,* 5497–5502.

Catmur, C., Walsh, V., & Heyes, C. (2007). Sensimotor learning configures the human mirror neuron system. *Current Biology, 17,* 1527–1531.

Chapman, E., Baron-Cohen, S., Auyeung, B., Knickmeyer, R., Taylor, K., & Hackett, G. (2006). Fetal testosterone and empathy: Evidence from empathy Quotient (EQ) and the "Reading the Mind in the Eyes" test. *Social Neuroscience, 1,* 135–148.

Chartrand, T. L., & Bargh, J. A. (1999). The chameleon effect: The perception-behavior link and social interaction. *Journal of Personality and Social Psychology, 76,* 893–910.

Chartrand, T. L., & van Baaren, R. (2009). Human mimicry. In M. P. Zanna (Ed.), *Advances in experimental social psychology* (Vol. 41, pp. 219–274). Burlington: Academic Press.

Coricelli, G. (2005). Two-levels of mental states attribution: from automaticity to voluntariness. *Neuropsychologica, 43,* 294–300.

Damasio, A. R. (1994). *Decartes' Error.* New York: Grosset/Putnam Book.

Davis, J. I., Senghas, A., Brandt, F., & Ochsner, K. N. (2010). The effects of BOTOX injections on emotional experience. *Emotion, 10,* 433–440.

Davis, M. H. (1983). Measuring individual differences in empathy: Evidence for a multidimensional approach. *Journal of Personality and Social Psychology, 44,* 113–126.

De Wied, M., van Boxtel, A., Posthumus, J. A., Goudena, P. P., & Mattys, W. (2009). Facial EMG and heart rate response to emotion-inducing film clips in boys with disruptive behaviour disorders. *Psychophysiology, 46,* 996–1004.

De Wied, M., van Boxtel, A., Zaalberg, R., Goudena, P. P., & Mattys, W. (2006). Facial EMG responses to dynamic emotional facial expressions in boys with disruptive behavior disorders. *Journal of Psychiatric Research, 40,* 112–121.

Decety, J., & Lamm, C. (2006). Human empathy through the lens of social neuroscience. *The Scientific World Journal, 6,* 1146–1163.

Del Giudice, M., Manera, V., & Kaysers, C. (2009). Programmed or learned? The ontogeny of mirror neurons. *Developmental Science, 12,* 350–363.

Dimberg, U. (1982). Facial reactions to facial expressions. *Psychophysiology, 19,* 643–647.

Dimberg, U. (1988). Facial electromyography and the experience of emotion. *Journal of Psychophysiology, 2,* 277–282.

Dimberg, U. (1989). Facial expressions and emotional reactions: A psychobiological analysis of human social behaviour. In H. L. Wagner (Ed.), *Social psychophysiology and emotion: Theory and clinical applications* (Vol. 36, pp. 132–149). London: John Wiley & Sons Ltd.

Dimberg, U. (1990). Gender differences in facial reactions to facial expressions. *Biological Psychology, 30,* 151–159.

Dimberg, U. (1997). Rapidly evoked emotional responses. *Journal of Psychophysiology, 11,* 115–123.

Dimberg, U., Andréasson, P., & Thunberg, M. (2011). Emotional empathy and facial reactions to facial expressions. *Journal of Psychophysiology, 25,* 26–31.

Dimberg, U., & Söderkvist, S. (2011). The voluntary facial action technique: A method to test the facial feedback hypothesis. *Journal of Nonverbal Behaviour, 35,* 17–33.

Dimberg, U., Thunberg, M., & Grunedal, S. (2002). Facial reactions to emotional stimuli: Automatically controlled emotional responses. *Cognition and Emotion, 16,* 449–471.

Eisenberg, N., & Fabes, R. (1990). Empathy: Conceptualization, measurement, and relation to prosocial behaviour. *Motivation and Emotion, 14,* 131–150.

Eisenberg, N., Losoya, S., & Spinrad, T. (2003). Affect and Prosocial Responding. In R. J. Davidson, K. R. Scherer & H. H. Goldsmith (Eds.), *Handbook of Affective Science* (pp. 787–803). New York: Oxford University Press.

Eisenberg, N., Schaller, M., Fabes, R. A., Bustamantes, D., Mathy, R. M., Shell, R., et al. (1988). Differentiation of personal distress and sympathy in children and adults. *Developmental Psychology, 24,* 766–775.

Eisenberg, N., Spinrad, T. L., & Cumberland, A. (1998). Parental socialization of emotion. *Psychological Inquiry, 9,* 317–333.

Ekman, P., & Friesen, W. V. (1982). Felt, false, and miserable smiles. *Journal of Nonverbal Behaviour, 6,* 638–252.

Ekman, P., Friesen, W. V., & Ancoli, S. (1980). Facial signs of emotional experience. *Journal of Personality and Social Psychology, 39,* 1125–1134.

Ekman, P., Friesen, W. V., & Ellsworth, P. C. (1972). *Emotion in the human face: Guidelines for research and integration of findings.* New York: Pergamon.

Ekman, P., Levenson, R., & Friesen, W. V. (1983). Autonomic nervous system activity distinguishes among emotions. *Science, 221,* 1208–1210.

Fadiga, L., Fogassi, G., Pavesi, G., & Rizolatti, G. (1995). Motor facilitation during action observation: a magnetic stimulation study. *Journal of Neuropsychology, 73,* 2608–2611.

Field, T. (2012). Relationships as regulators. *Psychology, 3,* 467–479.

Field, T. M., Woodson, R., Cohen, D., Greenberg, R., Garcia, R., & Collins, K. (1983). Discrimination and imitation of facial expressions by preterm and neonates. *Infant Behavior & Development, 6,* 485–489.

Field, T. M., Woodson, R., & Greenberg, R. (1982). Discrimination and imitation of facial expressions by neonates. *Science, 218,* 179–181.

Finzi, E., & Wassermann, E. (2006). Treatment of depression with botulinum toxin A: A case series. *Dermatological Surgery, 32,* 645–649.

Flack, W. (2006). Peripheral feedback effects of facial expressions, bodily postures, and vocal expressions on emotional feelings. *Cognition and Emotion, 20,* 177–195.

Foroni, F., & Gun, R. S. (2011). When does mimicry affect evaluative judgement? *Emotion, 11,* 687–690.

Gallese, V. (2001). The "shared manifold" hypothesis: From mirror neurons to empathy. *Journal of Consciousness Studies, 8,* 33–50.

Gallese, V. (2003). The manifold nature of interpersonal relations: The quest for a common mechanism. In C. Frith & D. Wolpert (Eds.), *The neuroscience of social interaction. Decoding, imitating, and influencing the actions of others* (pp. 159–183). Oxford: Oxford University Press.

Gilet, A-L., Mella, N., Studer, J., Gruhn, D., & Labouvie-Vief, G. (2013). Assessing dispositional empathy in adults: A French validation of the interpersonal reactivity index (IRI). *Canadian Journal of Behaviour Research, 45,* 42–48.

Greenwald, M. K., Cook, E. W., & Lang, P. J. (1989). Affective judgement and psychophysiology. *Journal of Psychophysiology, 3*(1), 51–64.

Griffin, D., & Bartholomew, K. (1994). The metaphysics of measurement: The case of adult attachment. *Advances in Personal Relationships, 5,* 17–52.

Hadjikhani, N., Joseph, R. M., Snyder, J., & Tager-Flusberg, H. (2006). Abnormal differences in the mirror neuron system and social cognition network in autism. *Cerebral Cortex, 16,* 1276–1282.

Hall, J. A. (1984). *Nonverbal sex differences: Communication accuracy and expressive style.* Baltimore, MD: John Hopkins University Press.

Hall, J. A., Carter, J. D., & Horgan, T. G. (2000). Gender differences in nonverbal communication. In A. H. Fischer (Ed.), *Gender and emotion. Social and psychological perspectives* (pp. 97–117). Cambridge: Cambridge University Press.

Hall, J. A., & Matsumo, D. (2004). Gender differences in judgement of multiple emotions from facial expressions. *Emotion, 4,* 201–206.

Hardy, K. (2001). *Influence of gender and emotion on children's pattern of vicarious emotional responding and social functioning.* Doctoral dissertation abstract, Duke University.

Harris, I. A. (1995). *Messages men hear. Constructing masculinities.* London: Taylor & Francis.

Harris, J. A., Rushton, J., Hampson, E., & Jackson, D. N. (1996). Salivary testosterone and self-reported aggressive and prosocial personality characteristics in men and women. *Aggressive Behaviour, 22,* 321–331.

Harrison, N. A., Morgan, R., & Critchley, H. D. (2010). From facial mimicry to emotional empathy: A role for norephinedrine? *Social Neuroscience, 5,* 393–400.

Hatfield, E., Cacioppo, J., & Rapson, R. L. (1992). Emotional contagion. In M. S. Clark (Ed.), *Review of personality and social psychology: Emotion and Social Behaviour* (Vol. 14, pp. 151–177). Newbury Park, CA: Sage.

Hatfield, E., Rapson, R. L., & Le, Y.-C. L. (2011). Emotional contagion and empathy. In J. Decety & W. Ickes (Eds.), *The social neuroscience of empathy* (pp. 19–30). London: The MIT Press.

Hawk, S. H., Fischer, A. H., & Van Kleef, G. (2011). Taking your place or matching your face: Two paths to empathic embarrassment. *Emotion, 11,* 502–513.

Hermans, E. J., Putman, P., & van Honk, J. (2006). Testosterone administration reduces empathic behaviour: A facial mimicry study. *Psychoneuroendocrinoly, 31,* 859–866.

Hess, U., & Blairy, S. (2001). Facial mimicry and emotional contagion to dynamic emotional facial expressions and their influence on decoding accuracy.International. *Journal of Psychophysiology, 40,* 129–141.

Hess, U., Kappas, A., McHugo, G. J., Lanzetta, J. T., & Kleck, R. E. (1992). The facilitative effects of facial expressions on the self-generation of emotion. *International Journal of Psychophysiology, 12,* 251–265.

Hess, U., Philippot, P., & Blairy, S. (1998). Facial reactions to emotional facial expressions: Affect or cognition? *Cognition and Emotion, 12,* 509–531.

Heyes, C. (2011). Automatic imitation. *Psychological Bulletin, 137,* 463–483.

Hill, E., & Frith, U. (2003). Understanding autism: Insights from mind and brain. In U. Frith & E. Hill (Eds.), *Autism: Mind and brain* (pp. 1–19). New York: Oxford University Press.

Hsee, C. K., Hatfield, E., Carlsson, J., & Chetomb, C. (1990). The effect of power on susceptibility to emotional contagion. *Cognition and Emotion, 4,* 327–340.

Hutchison, A.N. & Gerstein,L.H. (2012) What's in face? Counselings trainees' ability to read emotions. *Training and Education in Professional Psychology, 6,* 100–112.

Iacoboni, M. (2009). Imitation, empathy and mirror neurons. *Annual Review of Psychology, 60,* 653–670.

Iacoboni, M., Woods, R. P., Brass, M., Bekkering, H., Mazziotta, J. C., & Rizzolatti, G. (1999). Cortical mechanisms of human imitation. *Science, 286,* 2526–2528.

Izard, C. E. (1990). Facial expressions and the regulation of emotions. *Journal of Personality and Social Psychology, 58,* 487–498.

Izard, C. E. (1994). Intersystem connection. In P. Ekman & R. J. Davidson (Eds.), *The nature of emotion: Fundamental questions* (pp. 356–361). New York: Oxford University Press.

Jabbi, M., & Keysers, C. (2008). Inferior frontal gyros activity triggers anterior insula response to emotional facial expressions. *Emotion, 8,* 775–780.

Jabbi, M., Swart, M., & Keysers, C. (2007). Empathy for positive and negative emotions in the gustatory cortex. *NeuroImage, 34,* 1744–1753.

Joireman, J. A., Needham, T. L., & Cummings, A.-L. (2002). Relationships between dimensions of attachment and empathy. *North American Journal of Psychology, 4,* 63–80.

Jones, S. S. (2009). The development of imitation in infancy. *Philosophical Transactions of the Royal Society. Series B: Biological Sciences, 364,* 2325–2335.

Jonsson, C-O., Clinton, D., Fahrman, M., & Mazzaglia, G. (2001). How do mothers signal shared feelings to their infants? An investigation of affect attunement and imitation during the first year of life. *Scandinavian Journal of Psychology, 42,* 377–381.

Keillor, J., Barett, A., Crucian, G. P., Kortenkkamp, S., & Heilman, K., M. (2002). Emotional experience and perception in the absence of facial feedback. *Journal of the International Neuropsychology Society, 8,* 130–135.

Keltner, D., & Ekman, P. (2000). Facial expression of emotion. In M. Lewis & J. M. Haviland-Jones (Eds.), *Handbook of emotions* (pp. 236–249). New York: The Guilford Press.

Kestenbaum, R., Farber, E. A., & Sroufe, A. L. (1989). Individual differences in empathy among preschoolers: Relation to attachment history. *New Directions for Child and Adolescent Development,* 51–64.

Kleinke, C. L., Peterson, T. R., & Rutledge, T. R. (1998). Effects of self-generated facial expressions on mood. *Journal of Personality and Social Psychology, 74,* 272–279.

Klohnen, E. C., & John, O. P. (1998). Working models of attachment: A theory-based prototype approach. In J. A. Simpson & W. S. Rholes (Eds.), *Attachment theory and close relationships* (pp. 115–138). New York: The Guilford Press.

Knyazev, G. G., Slobodsy-Plusnin, J. Y., & Bocharov, A. V. (2010). Gender differences in implicit and explicit processing of emotional facial processing as revealed by event-related theta synchronization. *Emotion, 10,* 678–687.

Kring, A. M., & Gordon, A. H. (1998). Sex differences in emotion: Expression, experience and physiology. *Journal of Personality and Social Psychology, 74,* 686–703.

Lakin, J. L., Jefferis, V. E., Cheng, C. M., & Chartrand, T. L. (2003). The chameleon effect as social glue: Evidence for the evolutionary significance of non-conscious mimicry. *Journal of Nonverbal Behaviour, 27,* 145–162.

LeDoux, J. (1996). *The emotional brain: The mysterious underpinnings of emotional life.* New York: Simon & Schuster.

Levant, R. F. (1995). Towards the reconstruction of masculinity. In R. F. Levant & W. S. Pollack (Eds.), *A new psychology of men* (pp. 229–252). New York: HarperCollins.

Levenson, R. W., Ekman, P., & Friesen, W. V. (1990). Voluntary facial action generates emotion specific nervous system activity. *Psychophysiology, 27,* 363–384.

Leventhal, H. (1984). A perceptual motor theory of emotion. In L. Berkowitz (Ed.), *Advances in experimental social psychology* (Vol. 17, pp. 117–182). Madison, Wisconsin: Academic Press, Inc.

Lewis, M. B. (2012). Exploring the positive and negative implications of facial feedback. *Emotion, 12,* 852–859.

Lewis, M. B., & Bowler, P. J. (2009). Botulinum toxin cosmetic therapy correlates with a more positive mood. *Journal of Cosmetic Dermatology, 8,* 24–26.

Likowski, K. U., Muhlberger, A., & Seibt, B. (2011). Processes underlying congruent and incongruent facial reactions to emotional facial expressions. *Emotion, 11,* 457–467.

Likowski, K. U., Muhlberger, A., Seibt, B., Pauli, P., & Weyers, P. (2007). Modulation of facial mimicry by attitudes. *Journal of Experimental Psychology, 44,* 1065–1072.

Lundqvist, L.-O. (1995). Facial EMG reactions to facial expressions: A case of emotional contagion? *Scandinavian Journal of Psychology, 36,* 130–141.

Markova, G., & Legerstee, M. (2006). Contingency, imitation and affect sharing: Foundations of infants' social awareness. *Developmental Psychology, 42,* 132–141.

Masur, E. F. (1987). Imitative interchanges in a social context: Mother infant matching behaviour at the beginning of the second year. *Merrill-Palmer Quarterly, 33,* 453–473.

McIntosh, D. N. (1996). Facial feedback hypothesis: Evidence, implications, and directions. *Motivation and Emotion, 20,* 121–147.

McIntosh, D. N. (2006). Spontaneous facial mimicry, liking, and emotional contagion. *Polish Psychological Bulletin, 37,* 31–42.

McIntosh, D. N., Reichmann-Decker, A., Winkelman, P., & Wilbarger, J. L. (2006). When the social mirror breaks: Deficits in automatic, but not voluntary, mimicry of emotional facial expression in autism. *Developmental Science, 9,* 295–302.

Mehrabian, A., & Epstein, N. (1972). A measure of emotional empathy. *Journal of Personality, 40,* 525–543.

Meltzofff, A. N., & Moore, M. K. (1977). Imitation of facial and manual gestures by human neonates. *Science, 205,* 702–709.

Mikulincer, M., & Florian, V. (1998). The relationship between adult attachment style and emotional and cognitive reactions to stressful events. In J. A. Simpson & S. W. Rholes (Eds.), *Attachment theory and close relationships* (pp. 144–165). New York: Guilford Press Publications, Inc.

Mikulincer, M., Gillath, O., Halevy, V., Avihou, N., Avidan, S., & Eshkoli, N. (2001). Attachment theory and reactions to others' needs: Evidence that activate the sense of attachment security promotes empathic responding. *Journal of Personality and Social Psychology, 81,* 1205–1224.

Milkulincer, M., & Orbach, I. (1995). Attachment styles and repressive defensiveness: The accessibility and architecture of affective memories. *Journal of Personality and Social Psychology, 68,* 917–925.

Mikulincer, M., & Shaver, P. R. (2003). The attachment behavioral system and repressive defensiveness: Activation, psychodynamics and interpersonal process. In M. Zanna (Ed.), *Advances in experimental social psychology* (Vol. XXXV, pp. 56–152). New York: Academic Press.

Montagne, B., Kessels, P. C. R., Frigerio, E., & de Haan, E. H. F. (2005). Sex differences in the perception of affective facial expressions: Do men really lack emotional reactivity? *Cognitive Processing, 6,* 136–141.

Nagy, E., Pilling, K., Orvos, H., & Molnar, P. (2012). Imitation of tongue protrusion in human neonates: Specificity of the response in a large sample. *Developmental Psychology,* online publication.

Neal, D., & Chartrand, T. L. (2011). Embodied emotion perception. *Social Psychological and Personality Science, 2,* 673–678.

Neumann, R. & Strack, F. (2000). "Mood contagion": The automatic transfer of mood between persons. *Journal of Personality and Social Psychology, 79,* 211–223.

Niedenthal, P. M, Brauer, M., Robin, L., & Innes-Ker, Å. H. (2002). Adult attachment and the perception of facial expression of emotion. *Journal of Personality and Social Psychology, 82,* 419–433.

Niedenthal, P. M., & Halberstadt, J., B. (2003). Top-down influences in social perception. *European Review of Social Psychology, 14,* 49–76.

Niedenthal, P. M, Winkielman, P., Mondillon, L., & Vermeulen, N. (2009). Embodiment of emotion concepts. *Journal of Personality and Social Psychology, 96,* 1120–1136.

Oberman, L. M., & Ramachandran, V. S. (2007). The simulating social mind: The role of mirror neuron system and simulation in the social communicative deficits of autism spectrum disorders. *Psychological Bulletin, 133,* 310–327.

Oberman, L. M., Winkielman, P., & Ramachandran, V. S. (2009). Slow echo: facial EMG evidence for the delay of spontaneous, but not voluntary, emotional mimicry in children with autism spectrum disorder. *Developmental Science, 12*(4), 510–520.

Öhman, A. (1993). Fear and anxiety as emotional phenomena: Clinical phenomenology, evolutionary perspectives and information processing mechanisms. In M. Lewis & J. M. Haviland (Eds.), *Handbook of emotion* (pp. 511–536). New York: The Guilford Press.

Pally, R. (1998). Emotional processing: The mind-body connection. *Journal of Psychoanalysis, 79,* 349–362.

Pawlby, S. J. (1977). Imitative interaction. In H. Schaffer (Ed.), *Studies in mother-infant interaction* (pp. 203–224). New York: Academic Press.

Perrett, D. I., & Emergy, N. J. (2000). How can studies of the monkey brain help us understand "theory of mind" and autism in humans. In S. Baron-Cohen, H. Tager-Flusberg & D. J. Cohen (Eds.), *Understanding other minds – perspectives from developmental cognitive neuroscience.* Oxford: Oxford University Press.

Pfeifer, J. H., Iacoboni, M., Mazziotta, J. C., & Dapretto, M. (2008). Mirroring others' emotions relates to empathy and interpersonal competence in children. *NeuroImage, 39,* 2076–2085.

Pleck, J. H. (1981). *The myth of masculinity.* Cambridge, MA: MIT Press.

Ravaja, N., Kallinen, K., Saari, T., & Keltikangas-Jarvinen, L. (2004). Suboptimal exposure to facial expressions when viewing video-messages from a small screen: Effects on emotions, attention and memory. *Journal of Experimental Psychology, 10,* 120–137.

Rizzolatti, G., Gallese, V., & Fongassi, L. (1995). Premotor cortex and the recognition of motor actions. *Cognitive Brain Research, 3,* 131–141.

Roisman, G., Tsai, J. L., & Chiang, S. K.-H. (2004). The emotional integration of childhood experience: Physiological, facial expressive, and self-reported emotional response during the Adult Attachment Interview. *Developmental Psychology, 40,* 776–789.

Schneider, K. G., Hempel, R. J., & Lynch, T. R. (2013). That "poker face" just might lose you the game! The impact of expressive suppression and mimicry on sensitivity to facial expressions of emotions. *Emotion, 13,* 852–866.

Schore, A. N. (1994). *Affect regulation and the origin of the self.* Hillsdale, New Jersey: Lawrence Erlbaum Associates Publisher.

Schore, J. R., & Schore, A. N. (2008). Modern attachment theory: The central role of affect regulation in development and treatment. *Clinical Social Work Journal, 36,* 9–20.

Schulte-Ruther, M., Markowitsch, H. J., Shah, N. J., Fink, G., & Piefke, M. (2008). Gender differences in brain networks supporting empathy. *NeuroImage, 42,* 393–403.

Schwartz, G., Brown, S. L., & Ahern, G. L. (1980). Facial muscle patterning and subjective experience during affective imagery: Sex differences. *Psychophysiology, 17,* 75–82.

Schwartz, G. E., Fair, P. I., Salt, P., Mandel, M. R., & Klerman, G. R. (1976). Facial muscle pattering to affective imagery in depressed and non-depressed individuals. *Science, 19,* 489.

Shiller, V. M., Izard, C. E., & Hembree, E. A. (1986). Patterns of emotion expressions during separation in the strange-situation procedure. *Developmental Psychology, 22,* 378–382.

Smith, G. J. W. (1991). Percept-genesis: A frame of reference for neuropsychological research. In R. E. Hanlon (Ed.), *Cognitive microgenesis. A neuropsychological perspective.* New York: Springer Verlag.

Sonnby-Borgström, M. (2002a). Automatic mimicry reactions as related to differences in emotional empathy. *Scandinavian Journal of Psychology, 43,* 433–443.

Sonnby-Borgström, M. (2002b). *Between Ourselves: Automatic mimicry as related to empathic ability and patterns of attachment.* Doctoral thesis, Lund University, Lund.

Sonnby-Borgström, M. (2009). Alexithymia as related to facial imitation, mentalization, empathy, and internal working models-of-self and -others. *Neuropsychoanalysis, 11,* 107–123.

Sonnby-Borgström, M., & Jönsson, P. (2003). Model-of-self and others as related to mimicry reactions at different levels of cognitive control. *Scandinavian Journal of Psychology, 44,* 153–163.

Sonnby-Borgström, M., & Jönsson, P. (2004). Dismissing-avoidant pattern of attachment and mimicry reactions at different levels of information processing. *Scandinavian Journal of Psychology, 45,* 103–113.

Sonnby-Borgström, M., Jönsson, P., & Svensson, O. (2003). Emotional empathy as related to mimicry reactions at different levels of information processing. *Journal of Nonverbal Behaviour, 27,* 3–23.

Sonnby-Borgström, M., Jönsson, P., & Svensson, O. (2008a). Gender differences in facial imitation and verbally reported emotional contagion from spontaneous to emotionally regulated levels. *Scandinavian Journal of Psychology, 49,* 111–122.

Sonnby-Borgström, M., Jönsson, P., & Svensson, O. (2008b). Imitative responses and verbally reported emotional contagion from spontaneous, unconscious to emotionally regulated, conscious information-processing levels. *Neuropsychoanalysis, 10,* 81–85.

Soussignan, R. (2002). Duchenne smile, emotional experience and autonomic reactivity: A test of the facial feedback hypothesis. *Emotion, 2*, 52–74.

Stel, M., & Vonk, R. (2010). Mimicry in social interaction: Benefits for mimickers, mimickees, and their interaction. *British Journal of Psychology, 101*, 311–323.

Stern, D. N. (1985). *The interpersonal world of the infant: A view from psychoanalysis and developmental psychology*. New York: Basic Books.

Strack, F., Martin, L. L., & Stepper, S. (1988). Inhibiting and facilitating conditions of human smile: A non-obtrusive test of the facial feedback hypothesis. *Journal of Personality and Social Psychology, 54*, 768–777.

Suomi, S. J. (2006). Risk, resilience and gene X environment interactions in rhesus monkeys. *Annals of the New York Sciences, 1094*, 52–62.

Suslow, T., Kugel, H., Rauch, A. V., Dannlowski, U., Bauer, J., Konrad, C., et al. (2009). Attachment avoidance modulates neural response to masked facial emotion. *Human Brain Mapping, 30*, 3553–3562.

Tassinary, L. G., & Cacioppo, J. T. (1992). Unobservable facial actions and emotion. *Psychological Science, 3*, 28–33.

Tassinary, L. G., & Cacioppo, J. T. (2000). The skeletomotor system: Surface electromyography. In J. T. Cacioppo, L. G. Tassinary & G. G. Berntsson (Eds.), *Handbook of psychophysiology* (pp. 163–199). Cambridge: Cambridge University Press.

Taylor, G. J., Bagby, R. M., & Parker, J. D. A. (1997). *Disorders of affect regulation: Alexithymia in medical and psychiatric illness*. Cambridge: Cambridge University Press.

Thunberg, M., & Dimberg, U. (2000). Gender differences in facial reactions to fear-relevant stimuli. *Journal of Nonverbal Behaviour, 24*, 45–51.

Tobari, M. (2003). The development of empathy in adolescence: A multidimensional view. *Japanese Journal of Developmental Psychology, 14*, 136–148.

Tomkins, S. (1962). *Affect, imagery and consciousness. Volume I: The positive affects*. New York: Springer Verlag.

Tomkins, S. (1963). *Affect, imagery and consciousness: Volume II: The negative affects*. New York: Springer Verlag.

Valiente, C., Eisenberg, N., Fabes, R. A., Shepard, S. A., Cumberland, A., & Losoya, A. (2004). Prediction of children's empathy-related responding from their effortful control and parent's expressivity. *Developmental Psychology, 40*, 911–926.

Wakabayashi, A., Sasaki, J., & Ogawa, Y. (2012). Sex differences in two fundamental cognitive domains: Empathizing and systemizing in children and adults. *Journal of Individual Differences, 33*, 24–34.

Weyers, P., Muhlberger, A., Hefele, C., & Pauli, P. (2006). Electromyographic responses to static and dynamic avatar emotional expressions. *Psychophysiology, 43*, 450–453.

Wicker, B., Keysers, C., Plailly, J., Royet, J. P., Gallese, V., & Rizzolatti, G. (2003). Both of us disgusted in my insula: the common neural basis of seeing and feeling disgust. *Neuron, 40*, 655–664.

Wild, B., Erb, M., & Bartels, M. (2001). Are emotions contagious? Evoked emotions while viewing emotionally expressive faces: Quality, quantity time course and gender differences. *Psychiatry Research, 102,* 109–124.

Williams, J. H.G., Whiten, A., & Singh, T. (2004). A systematic review of action imitation in autistic spectrum disorder. *Journal of Autism and Developmental Disorders, 34,* 285–299.

Williams, J. H. G., Whiten, A., Suddendorf, T., & Perrett, D. I. (2001). Imitation, mirror neurons and autism. *Neuroscience and Biobehavioural Reviews, 25,* 287–295.

Winkielman, P., Berrige, K. C., & Wilberger, J. L. (2005). Unconscious affective reactions to masked versus angry faces influence consumption behaviour and judgements of value. *Personal and Social Psychology Bulletin, 31,* 121–135.

Yan, F., & Shihui, H. (2008). Temporal dynamics of neural mechanisms involved in empathy for pain: An event-related brain potential study. *Neuropsychologia, 46,* 160–173.

Yawei, C., Lee, P.-L., Yang, C.-Y., Lin, D. H., & Decety, J. (2008). Gender differences in mu rhythm of the mirror neuron system. *PLoS ONE 3*(5): e2113.

Zilber, A., Goldstein, A., & Mikulincer, M. (2007). Adult attachment and the processing of emotional pictures. *Personality and Individual Differences, 43,* 1898–1907.

CHAPTER 8

Mimicry, emotion, and social context: insights from typical and atypical humans, robots, and androids

Piotr Winkielman, Evan W. Carr, Bhismadev Chakrabarti, Galit Hofree, and Liam C. Kavanagh

A key task for the field of psychology (and related disciplines) is to identify mechanisms that allow individuals to perceive, understand, influence, and coordinate with others. Within the last decade, *imitation* has been the focus of many empirical and theoretical discussions, since it is thought to be one such social mechanism. Much of this discussion surrounds *intentional imitation* – a phenomenon where an individual deliberately replicates similar movements or performs an action with a similar goal (i.e., *emulation*). Intentional imitation is essential to sociality, given that it constitutes an important source of *social learning*, which involves the transmission of skills, norms, traditions, and rituals. These imitative behaviours are also important in *social communication*, such as signalling group membership (e.g., dressing alike), admiration (e.g., adopting "superior" accents) but also derision (e.g., parodying and parroting). Critically though, intentional imitative behaviours are often exquisitely complex, revealing sophisticated considerations about the rationality and usefulness of the copied behaviours (see the following for excellent reviews on this topic – Csibra & Gergely, 2009; Mesoudi, 2009; Tomasello, Kruger, & Ratner, 1993). We will not focus on intentional imitation here, though we should note at the outset that some of our insights into spontaneous imitation were inspired by the just-mentioned literatures.

Here, our focus is on a more basic (and perhaps simpler) form of imitation: *spontaneous mimicry*. This is a phenomenon where merely observing another individual's behaviour elicits a corresponding action in the observer, without instruction to initiate such a response. Many have argued that mimicry appears to have phylogenetic roots, since these behaviours can appear in non-human primates (e.g., contagious yawning and smiling; Anderson, Myowa-Yamakoshi, & Matsuzawa, 2004). Such uninstructed mimicry occurs across a variety of modalities and effectors

162

(e.g., face, voice, body, etc.), and it can arise anywhere from fractions of a second (e.g., finger mimicry; Leighton, Bird, Orsini, & Heyes, 2010), around a half-second (e.g., facial mimicry; Dimberg, 1982), to several seconds (e.g., yawning, pronunciation, and postural mimicry; Tiedens & Fragale, 2003) after the stimulus onset. Spontaneous mimicry clearly occurs in many different real-world social situations and can be used by both producers and perceivers in a non-conscious, dynamic, and adaptive fashion (as we discuss later). In turn, research on mimicry may help to elucidate some basic mechanisms of the mind, informing questions about the way perception and action are connected, the nature of action- and emotion-recognition, and so forth. While many results are based within social and cognitive psychology, they easily extend to more broad and applied domains with clinical relevance (e.g., we will later discuss mimicry's involvement in emotion-recognition within typical and atypical populations). Moreover, as we also elaborate on later, spontaneous imitation also influences some core social judgements and behaviours, including feelings associated with rapport, trust, competence, and interpersonal similarity. In short, spontaneous mimicry is of interest to a wide variety of researchers from all areas of psychology, cognitive science, and neuroscience.

In this chapter, we hope to advance the understanding of spontaneous mimicry by focusing on three central questions. The first question concerns the role of spontaneous mimicry in the debates about the embodied nature of the mind: More concretely, what does spontaneous mimicry tell us about the relation between perception and action, along with the role of somatosensory processes in higher-order conceptual information? The second question concerns the "simple" versus "complex" – or to say it more dramatically, "dumb" versus "smart" – nature of spontaneous mimicry. Specifically, when is mimicry driven by direct-matching processes, which ensure that perceivers motorically reproduce what they observe? And when does it reflect goals, intentions, and social-emotional context, which results in more complex input–output relations? Finally, the third (and most practically important) question addresses the implications of these debates for understanding atypical individuals. Specifically, what can research on spontaneous mimicry tell us, for example, about autism, and can such research offer any insights into practical interventions?

With these questions in mind, the structure of this chapter is as follows: We begin by introducing the framework of embodiment, as it helps to focus both ours and related research on spontaneous mimicry within the larger intellectual environment. Next, we evaluate the occurrence of motor reaction during stimulus perception, outline the role of sensori-motor feedback in recognition of emotional expressions, and consider how higher-order concepts contribute to mimicry phenomena. Following this, we move to the discussion of "smart" versus "dumb" processes of mimicry – to do this, we highlight spontaneous imitation in the context of higher-order social variables, including a transformational role of social power, and also within the context of robotics, which demonstrates both its reflexive and reflective aspects. We then extend these findings to the larger context of real-life social interactions. And finally, we discuss the implications of all this work for investigations of developmental disorders (such as autism) by showing the basic atypicality of mimicry, possibilities for some mimicry-based interventions, and highlighting recent research on contextual and affective modulation of mimicry.

Embodiment vs. traditional theories

Research on spontaneous mimicry is often situated within broader debates about the relation between perception and action. As such, before we go into specifics of mimicry, it is worth highlighting a few points about the larger contextual framework of embodiment, which guides much of recent research (including our own) and serves as a major conceptual model for understanding the mind (Niedenthal, Barsalou, Winkielman, Krauth-Gruber, & Ric, 2005; Schubert & Semin, 2009; Winkielman, Niedenthal, Wielgosz, Eelen, & Kavanagh, 2015).

One way to appreciate the importance of embodied theories is to contrast them with the traditional, amodal view of processing according to which cognitive processes operate on abstract, non-perceptual symbols. According to those theories, in order to become subjects of "thought," information initially encoded in the perceptual system (e.g., vision and audition) must be re-described and stored in a way that is amodal – that is modality-free, or at least modality independent (Fodor, 1975; Pylyshyn, 1984). This traditional view proposes that when perceiving a stimulus (such as a face or a body), information is initially encoded in the brain's modality systems (such as the visual, auditory, and probably affective systems) and then is extracted into an abstract language-like symbol (a "proposition") and stored as a *node* of a larger propositional network. In the associative network view (e.g., Anderson, 1983; Collins & Loftus, 1975), the node might be the word "SMILE" or the concept of "MIDDLE FINGER." This symbol or node is stored in some relation to other information that represents features such as "FUNNY" or "RUDE." Later, when thinking about FUNNY or RUDE, what is extracted from memory and used to make inferences are (at least) these pieces of information in their language-like form, which serve as a label for the concept and a list of its features. Thus, in *associative network models*, nodes arbitrarily stand for units of information, and those units provide the primary vehicle for processes such as inference, categorization, memory, and other cognitive operations. Any involvement of somatosensory processes in perception and cognition is therefore perceived as primarily incidental.

In contrast, the basic idea of embodiment theories is that higher-level processing is grounded in the organism's sensory and motor experiences – such frameworks are often called *grounded cognition theories* (Barsalou, 1999; 2008; Clark, 1999; Wilson, 2002). According to embodiment theories, processing of information about (for example) emotional faces, gestures, tools, flavours, melodies, driving directions, social personality characteristics, and even abstract social, moral, emotional, or motivational concepts, along with many other kinds of information, is influenced, informed, associated with, and sometimes dependent on perceptual, somatosensory, and motor resources. An important assumption of this perspective is that thinking involves partial reproduction or "simulation" of experiential and motor states that occur when the perceiver has actually encountered the object. For example, when thinking about whether a concept (e.g., a lemon) includes the property "sour," the perceiver actually recreates the sensory experience (e.g., tasting the lemon). Similarly, when perceivers try to recognize a facial expression or a bodily gesture, they construct a simulation using their own actions to reproduce the hypothesized face or gesture. Critically, embodiment theories hold that, far from being incidental, such re-enactment can be crucial to recognition and reasoning. Further, this re-enactment – called *embodied simulation* – does not have to be a conscious, full-blown physical episode. It also does not need to have any peripheral or behavioural manifestations, as it presumably can run solely on the brain's modality systems. Instead, simulation involves re-instantiating enough of the original experience to be useful in further processing. As we will see shortly, these assumptions of embodiment theories are reasonably supported by empirical research, including research on spontaneous mimicry, though mimicry may not always represent an embodied simulation (e.g., when mimicry is simple reflexive process) and that not all embodied simulation will lead to mimicry (e.g., when simulation is run purely centrally, or on modalities that do not manifest externally).

Spontaneous mimicry and the processing of facial emotions

Empirical studies in the field of emotional facial expressions serve as central demonstrations that somatosensory processes are involved in perception, cognition, and emotion. This point goes back to the original interest in motor processes in cognition and emotion and facial feedback mechanisms (Buck, 1980; Zajonc & Markus, 1984). In fact, a lively debate went on for years about the relative importance of such processes for emotional perception, experience, and behaviour and about the mechanisms by which such resources work (for a sampling of different views, see McIntosh, 1996).

Critically, note that according to traditional amodal models, expression recognition is primarily a matter of detecting features (e.g., curves at the corners of the mouth, lines in the corners of the eyes, etc.) that are probabilistically associated with an expression (e.g., smile). In other words, the recognition of a smile is very much like the recognition of any other stimulus (e.g., recognizing that an analogue clock is showing 2:45). Of course, the processing of the face itself may involve some unique and dedicated circuitry, but the essence of the process is basically described by the feature extraction models (e.g., Kanwisher, McDermott, & Chun, 1997). In contrast, embodied accounts of expression recognition emphasize that we not only see faces, but that we also have our own faces. As a result, we can employ somatosensory and motor representations of our own faces in the recognition process (Barsalou, 1999; Damasio, 1999; Niedenthal et al., 2005). From the embodied perspective, one can think of the act of smiling, for example, as a partial simulation of happiness when one is thinking about such an affective state, which can verify (via facial feedback) a match between one's own state and the mood of the person we are imitating (while in other cases, a "smile" could merely be an expression of an experienced positive emotional state). Note also that while mimicry often refers to the rote reproduction of a *motor* state (i.e., perceived action or behaviour), embodied simulation posits the reenactment of the underlying mental state itself (which then has downstream consequences on motor behaviour). Given this, many have argued that spontaneous imitation can, at least occasionally, play a useful role in this process.

Motor processes and facial processing

Multiple studies offer evidence that perception of emotional expression is accompanied by spontaneous activation of relevant motor processes. Studies using functional magnetic resonance imaging (fMRI) show that merely observing facial expressions enhances activity in the relevant somatosensory areas of brain (e.g., Carr, Iacoboni, Dubeau, Mazziotta, & Lenzi, 2003; Keysers, Kaas, & Gazzola, 2010; Molenberghs, Cunnington, & Mattingley, 2012). Further, the mere observation of a facial expression leads to activation of actual facial movements, which tend to match the perceived stimulus. This match can be driven by physical appearance but often also by valence – suggesting that both imitative and evaluative processes play a role (for more, see Moody,

McIntosh, Mann, & Weisser, 2007; Neumann, Schulz, Lozo, & Alpers, 2014). Thus, when people see smiles, they produce incipient smiles, and when they see frowns, they produce incipient frowns. We will describe some complications to this simple matching pattern shortly, but under "default" conditions, such facial reactions appear relatively straightforward and relatively automatic. Thus, they occur very quickly – within a half- to full-second after seeing an expression (e.g., Dimberg, 1982; Lundqvist & Dimberg, 1995). They occur even when participants are asked not to let a facial response occur or when they are asked to respond to the perceived facial stimulus in the opposite way (Dimberg, Thunberg, & Grunedal, 2002). Further, facial reactions can occur after minimal stimulus input, even with sub-threshold presentations for expressions of happiness or anger (Dimberg, Thunberg, & Elmehed, 2000). Finally, the facial reactions themselves may not be available to conscious awareness. For example, in a recent study, participants were briefly flashed happy, neutral, or angry faces and were asked to identify their valence (Bornemann, Winkielman, & van der Meer, 2012). As in earlier studies, we monitored participants' physiological activity using facial electromyography (EMG) and found that angry and happy faces produced different (and congruent) patterns of EMG activity. But were these reactions consciously available? To test this, we asked one group of participants to do the valence detection task while focusing on their feelings, including "subtle twitches in their faces." Another group was instructed to use a visual focus strategy. The last group received no strategy instructions. Our results revealed no benefit of the feeling-focused strategy on valence detection rates, suggesting that responses to facial stimuli were consciously unavailable. Given all the aforementioned evidence that perceivers often simply match what they observe, some theories (but not others) propose that facial reactions to facial expressions are mere byproducts of perception-action links or visuomotor priming, at least under some conditions. However, we will discuss later that these simple modifications can transition to being subtly complex, suggesting that direct-matching theories often cannot fully explain "smart" imitation, particularly when it is socially and contextually grounded (see also Hess & Fischer, 2013).

Nevertheless, this evidence is also perfectly compatible with the idea that motor activations are there "only for the ride" and result from frequent associative pairing of perception and action (e.g., when we see a smile, we usually smile). Note that the same concern holds regarding the evidence showing that seeing a gesture (e.g., finger or hand moment) is correlated with activation of peripheral and central motor processes (Cook, Bird, Catmur, Press, & Heyes, 2014). This, of course, raises an important question of whether these motor processes actually *contribute* to perception. Fortunately, some research provides evidence for the causal, constitutive role of such spontaneous mimicry in emotion recognition. For example, preventing participants from engaging expression-relevant facial muscles sometimes impairs their ability to detect briefly presented or relatively ambiguous facial expressions that involve that specific muscle – though one should note that this evidence is much stronger for smiles than other emotions, and for expressions that are weak, ambiguous, or brief (Niedenthal, Brauer, Halberstadt, & Innes-Ker, 2001; Oberman, Winkielman, & Ramachandran, 2007; Stel & Knippenberg, 2008). Further support for the causal contribution of motor representations to recognition of facial emotion comes from natural and experimental (temporary) lesion studies that examined the effects of (*a*) damage to sensory-motor areas and (*b*) transitional inactivation of the fusiform face area (FFA) with repetitive transcranial magnetic stimulation (TMS) (Adolphs et al., 2000; Pitcher et al., 2008).

Having said that, it is clear that more work needs to be done to fully understand the *boundary conditions* for causal mechanisms of facial mimicry in emotion-recognition. In fact, we are far from proposing that mimicry is always involved in the processing of facial expressions (or that it is always causally necessary). For instance, in some studies, observers mimicked emotional faces, but the degree of mimicry was not correlated with decoding accuracy (Blairy, Herrera, & Hess, 1999). Further, Calder, Keane, Cole, Campbell, & Young (2000) found that three patients with Möbius syndrome (a congenital condition that causes facial paralysis, thus preventing mimicry) were able to appropriately categorize standard emotional faces, with impairments noticeable only at high levels of recognition difficulty. Another study found that individuals with Möbius syndrome do not differ in facial emotion-recognition accuracy compared to controls (Rives-Bogart & Matsumoto, 2010), though such individuals also had a life to learn alternative recognition strategies. Additionally, as discussed below, autistic participants, who show reductions or delays in mimicry, may also develop alternative routes to recognition. Here, the critical point is that typical perceivers may activate the somatosensory networks, when appropriate, in the course of everyday processing. Further, such activations can be useful for recognition, especially when the recognition cannot be achieved via a simple, highly automated pattern-recognition strategy. Just to illustrate this point, motor feedback is probably not important to recognize a huge, simple smile, but could be quite useful in more subtle recognition tasks with weak, ambiguous or brief expressions, as mentioned above. In addition, the inhibition of smiles results in poorer differentiation between "true" and "false" smiles – a task that relies on processing of very subtle facial distinctions (Maringer, Krumhuber, Fischer, & Niedenthal, 2011; Rychlowska et al., 2014).

Faces and concepts: the sensorimotor bridge

Spontaneous mimicry may not only facilitate online processing but it also links sensorimotor representations with higher-order concepts (Zajonc & Markus, 1984). This notion was explored in a study testing whether people's own facial reactions to other individuals' emotional faces interact with conceptual information about those faces (Halberstadt, Winkielman, Niedenthal, & Dalle, 2009). In these studies, participants were first asked to look at the faces of several different individuals with ambiguous facial expressions. For each face, they were asked to consider the possibility that each of these individuals might feel "happy" or "angry" (i.e., concept label was randomly paired with the ambiguous face). EMG responses were monitored and showed that the faces paired with the "happy" concept label elicited more smiling than faces paired with the "angry" label. This already shows the influence of higher-order concepts of "happiness" or "anger" on participants' own facial responses (see also Niedenthal, et al., 2005). Critically though, in the second phase of the experiment, participants were also asked to recall the exact expression presented by each individual. The data showed that participants' memory of expression was biased in the direction of the earlier concept (e.g., remembering a face as happier when it was earlier associated with a "happy" label). In this second phase, participants were also asked to merely view the faces, and EMG data showed that they spontaneously smiled more to "happy" faces than "angry" faces. Importantly, the memory distortion effect was correlated with spontaneous facial EMG response during mere viewing. One interpretation of this effect suggests that *concept*-driven motor representations get tied to the *perception*-driven motor representations of the face. As a result, later spontaneous "mimicry" reflects a combination of both perceptual and conceptual influences. Indeed, mimicry could be said to represent a bridge between the sensorimotor and cognitive system.

Social variables

As mentioned earlier, spontaneous mimicry can reflect simple, direct-matching effects (e.g., yawn-to-yawn, smile-to-smile, finger-to-finger, etc.). However, it is also clear that individuals' imitative behaviors are profoundly impacted by the social context in which the interaction occurs (see also Hess et al., Chapter 5). This is also true for spontaneous mimicry, which is sensitive to interpersonal cues such as prosociality (Leighton et al., 2010), group membership (Bourgeois & Hess, 2008), attitudes (Likowski, Mühlberger, Seibt, Pauli, & Weyers, 2008), and competition (Weyers, Mühlberger, Kund, Hess, & Pauli, 2009). As a result, recent theories of facial mimicry suggest that imitation is substantially dependent on higher-level processes such as goals, appraisals, and meaning-construction (Hess & Fischer, 2013). Importantly, these social theories serve as a contrast to more traditional direct-matching theories – for example, the Associative Sequence-Learning account (ASL; Cook, Johnston, & Heyes, 2013) and Perception-Action Model (PAM; Preston & de Waal, 2002), among others – which, for the most part, predict stimulus-congruent responses (e.g., smile-to-smile).

One stark demonstration of the role of social flexibility comes from research on power (i.e., how much objective or subjective control and authority someone possesses in an interaction; see Keltner, Gruenfeld, & Anderson, 2003). This research has found that spontaneous facial mimicry of emotional expressions dynamically adjusts to cues of social hierarchy and to the relative relationship between the perceiver and target (Carr, Winkielman, & Oveis, 2014). More specifically, in this study, participants were primed with either a high-power, low-power, or neutral writing task (Galinsky, Gruenfeld, & Magee, 2003) to manipulate the perceivers' feelings of subjective power. They were then exposed to happy and angry videos of four different targets that were paired with either a high-power profession (i.e., physician or CEO) or low-power profession (i.e., fast-food worker or grocery store stocker) in order to manipulate the targets' status levels. While the participants viewed the videos, facial EMG was recorded over two muscles to gauge mimicry activity: *Zygomaticus Major* ("smiling muscle" that lifts up the corners of the mouth) and *Corrugator Supercilii* ("frowning muscle" that furrows the brow). The results revealed that perceivers adapted their physiological EMG responses according to their own power level, the status level of the target, and the emotion of the target's expression: With frowning, all perceivers (regardless of their own power state) responded with an increased *Corrugator Supercilii* response to angry high-power targets, compared to low-power targets. With smiling, low-power participants smiled back to all target expressions (happiness and anger). Interestingly though, high-power participants only exhibited standard smile mimicry towards low-power targets but did not mimic the smiles of high-power targets. Instead, high-power participants smiled more when those high-power targets expressed anger. Critically, the experimental paradigm also controlled for more low-level factors that could have confounded the EMG results (i.e., attention, mood, and demand-effects), and no differences between the perceiver power conditions were found.

These findings are interesting because they demonstrate that spontaneous patterns of facial responding (detected by sensitive physiological measures of muscle activation) shift according to contextual cues of social hierarchy. Further, they highlight two important points: First, even when controlling for simple perceptual variables, these higher-level hierarchical factors influenced (and reversed, in some cases) normal patterns of facial mimicry. Although most direct-matching theories would predict a more straightforward correspondence between perceiver and target expression, these results suggest that spontaneous facial mimicry can be socially driven, even at the most basic level, whereby interaction goals, emotional appraisals, and situational constraints all converge in constructing the perceiver's "appropriate" mimicry response (Hess & Fischer, 2013). And second, the way in which perceivers recruit these responses seems to be largely dependent on their relative relationship with the target (along with the emotion being displayed). Even though many power theories assume that high- and low-power perceivers respond differently according to the status level of the target (e.g., Côté et al., 2011; Fiske, 1993; Guinote, 2010), this "interactive" perspective had yet to be shown to be so influential in breaking down the direct-matching patterns of facial mimicry. In sum, the findings by Carr et al. (2014) are most useful in showing that spontaneous facial mimicry responses are fundamentally reliant on relative power relationships between the perceiver and target, along with their mutual perceptions of the shifts and changes in this dynamic (Mast, 2010). Critically though, high-level social variables (such as hierarchy) are able to influence basic psychological and physiological function, particularly in an emotional context.

Reflexive and context-dependent facial responses in human–robot interaction

The discussion above highlights the sensitivity of the mimicry process to conceptual influences (and to the larger social meaning). This message is reinforced and extended by recent work from our laboratory, using state-of-the-art robots and androids. Note that research with such artificial agents allows systematic testing of agent attributes that are necessary for mimicry. It can also inform theoretical questions of robotics, such as synchronization between robotic and human agents, the role of emotions in human–robot interaction, and the role of androids' physical presence on cognitive and emotional responses. Answering these questions is of practical importance, as there is substantial and growing interest in developing such agents for healthcare, education, and customer service purposes (Coradeschi et al., 2006). Such development is costly, and the success of these agents depends on the naturalness of interaction with their human users. In turn, knowing how to elicit natural, spontaneous human mimicry could facilitate meaningful social engagement between human users and androids.

One question about mimicry that is particularly suitable to exploration with androids is the role of agent-perceiver similarity. Most mimicry theories assume that spontaneous imitation occurs when the observed agent is "similar" to a human. Yet "human-likeness" is a complex, multi-faceted concept, and the relevant dimensions of similarity can dynamically vary – which matters for predicting when such agents elicit mimicry. Specifically, many experiments and theoretical perspectives highlight that mimicry is influenced by: (a) visual similarity (Likowski et al., 2008; Nadel et al., 2006; Press, Bird, Flach, & Heyes, 2005; Weyers, Mühlberger, Hefele, & Pauli, 2006), (b) psychological or "intentional" similarity (Goldman & Sripada, 2005), (c) similarity in type or biological nature of motion (Calvo-Merino, Grèzes, Glaser, Passingham, & Haggard, 2006; Chaminade, Franklin, Oztop, & Cheng, 2005), and (d) emotional similarity (i.e., relatability, liking and comfort; Bourgeois & Hess, 2008; Likowski et al., 2008). In order to examine these different components, we recently conducted a series of studies using human, android, and robot targets. Some of these experiments focused on facial expressions, whereas others focused on gesture.

Expressive androids

Two studies examined spontaneous mimicry to android and human emotional expressions of anger and happiness (Hofree, Ruvolo, Bartlett, & Winkielman, 2014). In both studies, we employed a state-of-the-art android (Hanson's Einstein) programmed to perform realistic human facial expressions (more details on the android in Wu, Butko, Ruvulo, Bartlett, & Movellan, 2009). Both experiments followed the same basic paradigm, where participants were first told to simply watch the agent (*spontaneous* mimicry) and, in the second block, were instructed to mimic the agent (*deliberate* mimicry). In each block, participants viewed randomized presentations of both happy and angry expressions, and facial mimicry was measured using EMG over the *Zygomaticus Major* and *Corrugator Supercilii* muscles. In addition, we collected ratings on comfort and human-likeness for the agent, as well as psychological human attributes, such as intentionality, mental states, and emotions (using the IDAQ; Waytz, Cacioppo, & Epley, 2010). The critical difference between Study 1 and Study 2 was the mode of android presentation (i.e., video vs. direct presence).

In Study 1, participants viewed videos of either Einstein or an age-matched human control displaying emotional expressions. As expected, all participants spontaneously mimicked the human control. More interestingly, this study found evidence of spontaneous mimicry of Einstein, but this was observed only amongst participants who rated the android high on human-likeness in terms of *physical similarity*. Importantly, ratings of comfort with the android did not influence mimicry reactions, suggesting that in this case emotional relatability was not the critical factor. Further, ratings of *psychological similarity* to humans were very low for the android, as compared to the human control, and to other living creatures, such as reptiles, fish, and mammals. In sum, this study suggests that perceived physical similarity (not emotional or psychological ones) plays an important role in spontaneous mimicry reactions.

To further investigate this, we conducted Study 2, where participants saw the same android, but now Einstein was physically present in the room with them. Participants sat facing the actual android while it randomly produced both happy and angry expressions. Once again, participants were first told to just watch it (spontaneous condition) and, after that, to deliberately mimic the android (voluntary condition). Participants rated the android on similar measures as used in Study 1. A comparison of ratings across Studies 1 and 2 highlights that physical presence makes the android appear significantly more humanlike than its video counterpart, yet more emotionally discomforting and less psychologically humanlike. Nonetheless, participants reliably mimicked the android. Specifically, amplitude and synchronization analyses using actual values of electricity supplied to android's motors (i.e., activity generated from the individual servos moving Einstein's face) and EMG activity demonstrated that these spontaneous mimicry reactions shared similar time-flows to those of the android's expression. That is, while they lagged shortly after the android initialized an expression (as expected), they had similar onset, offset, and duration features. Together these studies demonstrate the power of physical presence on mimicry and other social behaviours. More specifically, for non-human agents such as androids, physical presence can influence attribution of human-likeness, which we found to be associated with a greater likelihood of mimicry reactions. Finally, these studies suggest that although psychological similarity and emotional comfort may play an important role in mimicry and other social behaviours, it is not necessary for spontaneous mimicry.

Androids and gestures

In order to further understand the role of observed agent features on motor simulation, we have recently explored the role of changes in appearance similarity and motion similarity (Hofree, Urgen, Winkielman, & Saygin, 2015). In this study, we took advantage of humanoid robots with different degrees of human-likeness in appearance and movement that were performing simple arm movements (e.g., waving, cleaning, etc.). The agents were a human adult (biological appearance and biological motion), a robot (mechanical appearance and mechanical motion), and an android (biological appearance, but mechanical motion). The android was Repliee Q2. The human was the woman whose appearance Repliee Q2 was modelled after. The robot was the same Repliee Q2 stripped of surface human-like features (such as skin, hair, and clothes – any of these features that could not be removed were covered; for more information on the original stimuli, see Saygin, Chaminade, Ishiguro, Driver, & Frith, 2011). Moreover, the robot and android displayed identical motion kinematics, since they were in fact the same robot with different perceptual features. Muscle activity in both participants' arms was measured with EMG while they either (a) merely observed the three agents produce actions with their right arm, or (b) when they were explicitly told to imitate these same actions. The results showed that participants faithfully imitated all agents with their dominant (right) arm when explicitly told to do so. More interestingly, participants also mirrored these agents with their left arm, even when passively observing the actions. Furthermore, muscle activity was sensitive to differences in motion dynamics: Participants mimicked the human with greater intensity than both the identical-looking android and the non-human-appearing robot. These results suggest that motor simulation is not limited to observation and imitation of agents with a biological appearance, but that this phenomenon is also present in response to robotic agents. On the other hand, the viewed agent's motion may play an important role, especially for action observation.

Androids in context

As mentioned, mimicry to emotional expressions also depends on social cues in the perceiver's environment. For example, when playing a game with an opponent, watching that opponent smile might not elicit a smile from you, since the smile signals that he/she is winning, and you might be losing. It is not yet clear how our emotional processes interact with automatic mimicry reactions, yet there is evidence that mimicry is difficult to inhibit (Cook, Bird, Lünser, Huck, & Heyes, 2012) and can slow down non-mimicking responses (Brass, Bekkering, & Prinz, 2001). On the other hand, research suggests that we are very attentive to our environment and that our responses to even unconscious cues can be influenced by the current context (Tamir, Robinson, Clore, Martin, & Whitaker, 2004). Although it appears that humanlike androids elicit automatic mimicry reactions, it is not clear whether these more complex emotional responses would occur when faced with an android. In order to address these questions, we conducted another study with the same android, Einstein.

In this study, participants played repeated dice games with the android. In one block, participants were told that Einstein was their teammate (cooperative block), and in the second block, that he was their opponent (competitive block). Each game depended purely on chance, and the outcome was displayed either on the computer screen or through Einstein's facial expressions (i.e., happy "smiling" when winning, sad "frowning" when losing). Participants' facial expressions were measured using EMG, as before, over the Zygomaticus Major and Corrugator Supercilii.

Overall, participants responded facially to the "expressions" of the android and they did so in a way that expressed their own emotional reactions to the valence of the outcome. That is, participants smiled more when they themselves won, and frowned more when they themselves lost. Critically, though, participants displayed these expressions even when the android's expressions communicating the outcome were *incongruent* with their own, such as was the case during the competitive block (where android's smile communicated participants' loss, and his frown communicated participants' gain). Interestingly, these facial reactions did not differ in timing or magnitude from those in the cooperative block. Furthermore, these reactions were weaker when the same outcome information was displayed on the screen, suggesting that participants are more expressive when viewing the android's actual facial movements communicating the outcome.

In conclusion, this study suggests that basic, direct mimicry reactions can be overridden or transformed in certain situations. This has been previously discussed in the context of work on reduction of basic mimicry to out-groups (e.g., Bourgeois & Hess, 2008; Likowski et al., 2008). Interestingly, the current studies suggest that rather than "suppressing" or overshadowing basic mimicry reaction, the social context can fundamentally reshape them (as in Carr et al., 2014). Specifically, our facial behaviours can reflect the *meaning* behind the observed expression, not just the perceptual features of the expression itself (e.g., we not only fail to mimic a smile if that expression carries implicit negative consequences, but we actively do the opposite – frown). Finally, although the android's emotional expression provided a very simple cue (winning/losing) that was identical to the information conveyed on the screen, it elicited greater expressivity. This suggests that our emotional reaction to information is strengthened when that information is conveyed through a face rather than on a screen.

Taking the just-discussed several studies on androids together, they suggest that artificial agents can elicit varied reactions, depending on the attributes of the androids and the context of the interaction. It appears that low-level mimicry reactions are mostly sensitive to how physically humanlike the android appears, how present it is, and basic biological properties of its movement. However, it is *also* clear that broader context can fundamentally reshape even the most basic and rapid reactions to android targets. This once again highlights the role of considering mimicry in the context of the broader social context, along with the inherent "intelligence" of the underlying process.

Third-party interaction: mimicry and "smart" social cognition

All the studies described so far concerned mimicry within a dyad. However, perhaps the strongest evidence for the role of social context comes from our work on inferences from human gestural mimicry as observed by third parties. This is important because social contexts in which mimicry occurs can also include situations where "outside" people are watching others' interactions, and these observers can then use information about who mimics whom when making basic social judgements. In fact, some previous work has shown that in situations like this, mimicry can serve as a visible and viable social cue to third-party observers who use this information to infer a variety of social traits, including the degree of affiliation within the dyad (Grahe & Bernieri, 1999). Critically, mimicry seems to inform observers' judgements in subtle, complex ways, "mirroring" the intelligence that we have seen in mimicry production, which we will demonstrate with a few illustrative examples.

In a now-classic study, third-party observers used mimicry to guess whether members of a party are socially related (Bernieri, 1988). Recently, we have shown that observers draw more complex inferences from observed mimicry by taking into account the quality of the interaction (Kavanagh, Suhler, Churchland, & Winkielman, 2011). Specifically, we found that if a target person mimics a model who is rude to the target, third-party observers of this interaction will judge the mimicker as social incompetent, as compared to a target who refrains from spontaneous mimicry. In fact, the mimicker was rated as less competent than the non-mimicker, reversing the usually observed benefit of mimicry. Notably, this occurs even though observers do not explicitly notice the presence of mimicry. This finding neatly contrasts with the general belief that greater mimicry tends to confer benefits (greater liking, greater tipping, greater rapport). However, our phenomenon of "disadvantageous mimicry" makes sense from a theoretical perspective. If a person chooses to mimic (i.e., attempts to affiliate with) a rude model, the person does not know "how to pick his friends," or in other words, he or she may be lacking social competence.

In general, a rational observer can take an act of mimicry (or non-mimicry) as a window into the mimicker's assessment of a social situation, given a larger social context. Kavanagh and colleagues (2013) have illustrated this point by showing that observers' judgements reflect not only whether people mimic or not but also the reputation of the model and whether the mimicker is aware of the model's reputation. Specifically, in this study, participants observed a dyadic interaction in which a target mimicked or did not mimic a model. Prior to observation, the model's honesty was either defamed or praised, in front of some (but not other) targets. Observers always knew the model's reputation *and* which targets were aware of the model's reputation. Results showed that observers' use of mimicry in trust judgements was quite sophisticated and reflected not just the presence of mimicry but also the model's moral reputation. Critically, these judgements were further influenced by observers' knowledge of the target's awareness for the model's reputation. This led observers to rate targets as trustworthy when they mimicked untrustworthy models, but only when the observers knew that the model reputation was unknown to the target.

In conclusion, it appears that third-party observation of mimicry reflects highly sophisticated, context-sensitive, yet still implicit processes. Of course, future research is needed to determine to what extent the actual *interactants* in the dyad share this same level of sophistication as external third-party observers, when making social inferences from the observation of mimicry (or lack thereof). However, in the context of previously discussed studies using manipulations of social power, group membership, and competitive versus cooperative contexts, we should expect as much (if not more) "intelligence" in the mimicry production and interpretation within the interacting dyad. This question of intelligence becomes crucial, as we move on to the discussion of atypical mimicry processes.

Spontaneous mimicry and atypical social behaviour: the case of autism

So far, we have surveyed a variety of ways in which spontaneous mimicry functions in everyday social cognition. We have argued that a full analysis of this phenomenon requires consideration of isolated sensori-motor and emotional processes, as well as conceptual influences that occur within the larger social context. In this section, we will argue that our analysis can also be usefully applied to understanding apparent deficits or atypical forms of social processing. Here, we will consider the specific case of autism – a significant clinical condition, whereby impairments in social and emotional functioning play a fundamental role.

Let us first offer a short reminder and some qualifications: Recall that Autism Spectrum Disorders (ASD) represent a set of complex and multi-faceted conditions characterized by a mosaic of deficits in three general areas: (*a*) *social interaction*, such as lack of social interest, social skills, or theory-of-mind, (*b*) *communicative skills*, including pragmatic language, and (*c*) *behavioural abnormalities*, as with the presence of restricted, repetitive, and stereotyped patterns of behaviours, interests, and activities (American Psychiatric Association, 1994). Critically, autism is a very complex disorder. In fact, there is no identified biological cause of autism, and there is no single causal explanation, at any level, that is able to explain all aspects of the syndrome. Further, the behavioural manifestations of this disorder vary in severity (low- and high-functioning ASDs) and heterogeneity of cognitive profile (e.g., language, intelligence, emotion, etc.). Unfortunately, different profiles of ASDs are often lumped together when reporting findings, sometimes obscuring the information about the level of functioning for which the findings are relevant. This matters because high-functioning individuals represent around 25 per cent of the total ASD population, yet they make up the majority of the participants in published studies. As such, any generalizations must be made with extreme caution. Yet, there are some reasonably consistent data emerging in the domain of spontaneous mimicry (but see Southgate & Hamilton, 2008), but it is worth noting that they may not generalize to intentional mimicry (Rogers & Williams, 2006).

Atypical spontaneous mimicry of non-emotional stimuli

Some early evidence about atypicalities in spontaneous mimicry comes from studies using gestures. As an example, in one study, ASD individuals and matched controls were asked to simply view videos of a person executing simple actions, or to perform the same actions (Oberman et al., 2005). During these tasks, the experimenters recorded mu wave suppression, an electroencephalography (EEG) index of activity in the primary motor cortex, which has been proposed to be indicative of activity in the premotor "mirror neuron area" during the observation of action. Typically developing individuals showed mu wave suppression to both the execution and observation of action; however, individuals with ASD only showed mu wave suppression when performing their own actual movement, but not when observing movement (see also Nishitani, Avikainen, & Hari, 2004, for similar results with MEG).

Consistent with the social psychological literature on the role of self–other overlap in mimicry phenomena, ASD impairments might relate to a deficit in mapping the representation of the observed action to the self. Théoret et al. (2005) asked typical and ASD groups to view videos of index-finger and thumb movements that were directed either towards or away from the participants. During these tasks, the experimenters recorded motor-evoked potentials (MEP) induced by single-pulse TMS. In the typical group, both participant-directed and other-directed actions increased MEPs recorded from the participant's muscles, suggesting spontaneous mirroring. However, the ASD group showed increased MEPs only when viewing actions directed towards the participant, but not when viewing actions directed away from the participant. This suggests that ASD participants' mirroring failures might be due to a reduction in self–other mapping. Consistent with these results, ASD children show a typical degree of mu suppression (EEG index of "mirroring" activity) in response to an action performed by a family member, or the participant himself, but not to the same action performed by a stranger (Oberman, Ramachandran, & Pineda, 2008). Interestingly, more recent studies have argued that ASD subjects often show less mimicry modulations after social manipulations, suggesting perhaps that in their case, mimicry is less related to representation of the self (e.g., Cook & Bird, 2012). There have also been reports where ASD participants demonstrate intact imitation of both hand actions (Bird, Leighton, Press, and Heyes, 2007) and facial expressions (Press, Richardson, & Bird, 2010; also see Cook, Brewer, Shah, & Bird, 2014). Therefore, while much evidence suggests that mirroring deficits in ASD subjects might be due (at least in part) to decrements in self–other mappings, further work should be done to explore the relationship between these "mirroring" and "mentalizing" processes, especially when they become dissociated (e.g., ASD subjects can show *hyper*imitation along with less brain activation in mental state attribution areas, like mPFC and TPJ; Spengler, Bird, & Brass, 2010).

Reduction and delay in spontaneous mimicry of emotional stimuli

A similar picture of impairments emerges from the literature on facial expressions. In contrast to typical participants, autistic individuals do not spontaneously reproduce (mimic) facial expressions when they "just watch" them, without any prompts to recognize the expressions or to react to them (Beall, Moody, McIntosh, Hepburn, & Reed, 2008; McIntosh, Reichmann-Decker, Winkielman, & Wilbarger, 2006; Stel, van den

Heuvel, & Smeets, 2008). But again, this deficit is somewhat conditional – for instance, when autistic individuals are explicitly asked to focus on recognizing expressions, their mimicry is present, albeit significantly delayed (Oberman, Winkielman, & Ramachandran, 2009). These and related findings fuel a debate whether any emotional mimicry deficits are primary, or result from attentional and motivational factors (Wang & Hamilton, 2012).

But, whatever their origin, why do ASD mimicry impairments matter? First, as discussed previously, others respond to the presence of mimicry, both as members of the interacting dyad and as third-party observers. Comparatively, ASD individuals could suffer direct and indirect social consequences from not having these tendencies. Second, as also discussed above, spontaneous mimicry may facilitate emotion-recognition. If so, mimicry deficits may hinder recognition of facial expressions, at least under some conditions. One clue to this comes from a study where the performance of ASD individuals was compared on easy and difficult emotion-recognition tasks (Clark, Winkielman, & McIntosh, 2008). More specifically, in the difficult condition, participants were shown images for durations in the range of micro-expressions (15 and 30 milliseconds). Participants detected (*a*) if emotional faces were happy or angry, (*b*) if neutral faces were male or female, and (*c*) if neutral images were animals or objects. ASD individuals performed selectively worse on emotion extraction from faces (60 per cent vs. approximately 75 per cent for control groups). There were no group differences on gender or animal-object tasks, with groups all performing around 65–70 per cent. Importantly, there were no group differences in accuracy, which was perfect (100 per cent) on any type of stimuli when pictures were presented for a longer duration (3 seconds). Crucially however, note that the good performance of ASD participants may come from using different, non-embodied strategies. This conclusion is suggested by Rutherford and McIntosh (2007), since they showed that individuals with ASD use facial features for a rule-based strategy, accepting expressions as "valid" even when such expressions had extremely exaggerated features (e.g., sadness with lips curled down to a biologically unrealistic degree). A recent study reached a similar conclusion from an observation that ASD participants show reduced emotional reactivity to very briefly presented expressions, suggesting processing using more descriptive routes (Nuske et al., 2014). In short, it appears that ASD individuals use a disembodied approach to emotion-perception, rather than one that employs embodied simulation of real-life, biologically constrained expressions (for a fuller review of theory and evidence in this area, see Winkielman, McIntosh, & Oberman, 2009).

Training mimicry

If it is indeed true that embodiment is contributing to recognition, it should be possible to improve individuals' real-life emotional communication skills by training their sensorimotor responses. Success in such a programme would also provide a powerful example of how theories of social cognition can inform and facilitate actual interpersonal behaviour. One domain where this can be easily achieved is facial mimicry, where quick motor reactions to faces are developed by frequent pairing of a specific stimulus and motor response (e.g., smile-to-smile, frown-to-frown, etc.). In fact, we recently tested this idea in our laboratory by using a training paradigm in which typical participants produce facial expressions in response to schematic facial stimuli (Deriso et al., 2012). The initial results are encouraging and suggest that facial imitation training may indeed improve facial recognition. Future studies in our laboratory (and related laboratories) will extend these interventions to participants with autism. One reason to expect that this may be beneficial are earlier findings suggesting that ASD participants show improvement in face perception after playing face-related video games (Tanaka et al., 2010). We are also planning an intervention programme with the earlier-described humanoid robot that makes realistic facial expressions (Wu et al., 2009). We hypothesize that these perception–action pairings will enhance the ability of ASD participants to quickly mirror facial expressions, which in turn may facilitate their recognition of emotional faces. Of course, the hope here is that being able to mimic will make others judge ASD individuals as more socially skilled. However, as we have argued throughout the chapter, the question of "social intelligence" of mimicry is critical, since direct "mirroring" is often inappropriate in many contexts. Thus, before making any practical recommendations, we need to more fully understand the underlying social and emotional dynamics of mimicry. One promising cue comes from research on the connection between mimicry and reward, which we discuss next.

The role of reward processes in mimicry, and a clue to studying imitation deficits in autism

As mentioned, in many contexts, ASD individuals' spontaneous mimicry of emotional facial expressions is reduced. Interestingly, ASD is also characterized by a largely atypical response to social rewards (Chevallier, Kohls, Troiani, Brodkin, & Schultz, 2012; Dawson et al., 2002; Dichter, Richey, Rittenberg, Sabatino, & Bodfish, 2012; Kohls et al., 2012; Scott-Van Zeeland, Dapretto, Ghahremani, Poldrack, & Bookheimer, 2010). The set of studies discussed next provide a theoretical framework to consider how these two deficits may be related to each other. Before we do so, let us again remind, we have done throughout the chapter, that mimicry can be influenced by context both when it operates in a more direct, automatic, fashion (e.g., when imitation is easily modifiable in a "dumb" fashion, based off lower-level stimulus cues) or more rational, indirect fashion (e.g., when imitation flexibly adapts in a "flexible" way to the specific social demands of the situation at hand). Some example moderators of these "dumb" and "smart" imitative patterns include social variables such as liking (Likowski et al., 2008; Stel et al., 2010), social competition (Carr et al., 2014; Lanzetta & Englis, 1989; Weyers et al., 2009), and group membership (Yabar, Johnston, Miles, & Peace, 2006). Now note that all of these processes effectively alter the reward value attached to the stimulus – that is, liking is related to how rewarding a person is, and being part of the same group/team can make the in-group member more rewarding than the out-group member, suggesting that reward may influence the degree of spontaneous mimicry. This idea was directly tested in a psychophysiological study, which found that spontaneous facial mimicry (measured using facial EMG) was modulated by the reward value of different stimuli (Sims, van Reekum, Johnstone, & Chakrabarti, 2012). In this experiment, neutral faces were conditioned with high and low rewards using an implicit conditioning task, instantiated through a card game. In the test phase, participants saw happy and angry expressions made by these same faces, while facial EMG was recorded from congruent muscles to measure spontaneous facial mimicry. This study found that more rewarding faces were associated with greater spontaneous mimicry, compared to less rewarding faces. This observation was true only for mimicry of happy faces, and not for angry faces, similar to observations made by Hofree and colleagues (Hofree et al., 2014). Crucially, this reward-dependent modulation of spontaneous mimicry of happy faces was inversely related to autistic traits (i.e., individuals high in autistic traits showed little difference in the extent of spontaneous mimicry for high vs. low rewarding faces, while this difference was pronounced in those with low autistic traits). In a separate sample of individuals who underwent an identical conditioning phase, brain activity was measured using fMRI during the testing phase. This study found that the functional connectivity between the nucleus accumbens (coordinates identified using a meta-analysis of studies of reward processing; Liu, Hairston, Schrier, & Fan, 2011) and the inferior frontal gyrus (coordinates identified using a meta-analysis of studies on mimicry; Caspers, Zilles, Laird, & Eickhoff, 2010) was inversely proportional to autistic traits, in response to happy faces conditioned with high reward compared to those conditioned with low reward. Thus, both of these studies found that autistic traits modulated the impact of reward on spontaneous facial mimicry.

This relationship between autistic traits and the reward-dependent modulation of mimicry was further tested using hand stimuli in a task developed by Heyes and colleagues (e.g., Press et al., 2005). In this task, two human hand silhouettes were conditioned with high and low rewards using an implicit conditioning task as described above. In the test phase, participants were asked to make a pre-specified movement ("close" or "open"), while a hand stimulus was presented simultaneously on screen, which was making a congruent or incongruent movement. The difference in reaction time to congruent vs. incongruent stimuli was measured as a proxy metric of automatic imitation. Autistic traits were found to be inversely related to the reward-dependent modulation of automatic mimicry of human hands (Haffey, Press, O'Connell, & Chakrabarti, 2013). Interestingly, this result was true only for human hands and not for robot hands, which were used as a control condition to test whether the reward-dependent modulation of automatic mimicry extended to non-human stimuli.

Generally, these studies suggest that autistic traits modulate the link between reward processing and spontaneous mimicry of social stimuli. This suggestion provides a potential theoretical bridge between studies that suggest a mirror system deficit in autism (Beall et al., 2008; Dapretto et al., 2006; McIntosh et al., 2006), and those that do not (Bird et al., 2007; Dinstein et al., 2010). Here, the idea is that the autistic phenotype is not characterized by a circumscribed deficit of the mirror system, but one of atypical modulation between the mirror system and the reward response to social stimuli. This view is in agreement with a recently suggested framework, which suggests atypical top-down modulation of mimicry in autism (Wang & Hamilton, 2012).

Summary and conclusion

Successful social interaction hinges on a number of psychological mechanisms. One of them appears to be the ability of people to spontaneously mimic others. In this chapter, we argued that this ability reveals how our perceptual and conceptual mind is grounded in embodied, somatosensory processes. Further, we have argued that mimicry, as a form of embodiment, is not just a byproduct of perception–action links, but instead, can sometimes play a constitutive role in information processing. Moreover, we have posited that spontaneous mimicry can (under some conditions) manifest features of an automatic and associative process (i.e., "dumb" mimicry), but still can be helpful in basic recognition tasks and influence memory performance and judgements.

Concurrently, we have highlighted many "smart" features of spontaneous mimicry, whereby its production is sensitive to a variety of social and emotional variables, when dealing with people but also artificial entities, such as androids. Further, we have demonstrated that the perception of mimicry is also attuned to these contextual cues and that they can be used to draw complex inferences. Finally, we discussed the implications of this work for developmental disorders, such as autism. We highlighted that part of the atypicality here may reflect differences at the level of basic perception–action links (and suitable to relevant interventions at that level), but also that ASD participants reveal a complex pattern of modulation by social and affective variables.

In conclusion, the picture of spontaneous mimicry that emerges from our chapter may seem rather complex – a conclusion that is surprising to us, given that our own work started as a fascination with mimicry as a seemingly simple and tractable, yet widespread and important process. But the mind is a complex entity, which consistently reveals itself to science in new ways. Further, the complexity here gives a testimony to the sophistication of the social mind even at its most spontaneous, fast, and implicit manifestation. Going forward, we hope that the insights highlighted here both enlighten and encourage further explorations of this fascinating process, in both typical and atypical individuals.

References

Adolphs, R., Damasio, H., Tranel, D., Cooper, G., & Damasio, A. R. (2000). A role for somatosensory cortices in the visual recognition of emotion as revealed by three-dimensional lesion mapping. *Journal of Neuroscience, 20,* 2683–2690.

American Psychiatric Association. (1994). *Diagnostic and statistical manual of mental disorders* (4th ed.). Washington, DC: Author.

Anderson, J. R. (1983). *The architecture of cognition.* Cambridge, MA: Harvard University Press.

Anderson, J. R., Myowa–Yamakoshi, M., & Matsuzawa, T. (2004). Contagious yawning in chimpanzees. *Proceedings of the Royal Society of London. Series B: Biological Sciences, 271*(Suppl. 6), S468–S470.

Barsalou, L. W. (1999). Perceptual symbol systems. *Behavioral and Brain Sciences, 22,* 577–660.

Barsalou, L. W. (2008). Grounded cognition. *Annual Review of Psycholology, 59,* 617–645.

Beall, P. M., Moody, E. J., McIntosh, D. N., Hepburn, S. L., & Reed, C. L. (2008). Rapid facial reactions to emotional facial expressions in typically developing children and children with autism spectrum disorder. *Journal of Experimental Child Psychology, 101,* 206–223.

Bernieri, F. (1988). Coordinated movement and rapport in teacher–student interactions. *Journal of Nonverbal Behavior, 12*, 120–138.

Bird, G., Leighton, J., Press, C., & Heyes, C. (2007). Intact automatic imitation of human and robot actions in autism spectrum disorders. *Proceedings of the Royal Society B: Biological Sciences, 274*, 3027.

Blairy, S., Herrera, P., & Hess, U. (1999). Mimicry and the judgment of emotional facial expressions. *Journal of Nonverbal Behavior, 23*, 5–41.

Bornemann, B., Winkielman, P., & van der Meer, E. (2012). Can you feel what you do not see? Using internal feedback to detect briefly presented emotional stimuli. *International Journal of Psychophysiology, 85*, 116–124.

Bourgeois, P., & Hess, U. (2008). The impact of social context on mimicry. *Biological Psychology, 77*, 343–352.

Brass, M., Bekkering, H., & Prinz, W. (2001). Movement observation affects movement execution in a simple response task. *Acta Psychologica, 106*(1–2), 3–22.

Buck, R. (1980). Nonverbal behavior and the theory of emotion: The facial feedback hypothesis. *Journal of Personality and Social Psychology, 38*, 811–824.

Calder, A. J., Keane, J., Cole, J., Campbell, R., & Young, A. W. (2000). Facial expression recognition by people with Möbius syndrome. *Cognitive Neuropsychology, 17*, 73–87.

Calvo-Merino, B., Grèzes, J., Glaser, D. E., Passingham, R. E., & Haggard, P. (2006). Seeing or doing? Influence of visual and motor familiarity in action observation. *Current Biology, 16*, 1905–1910.

Carr, L., Iacoboni, M., Dubeau, M. C., Mazziotta, J. C., & Lenzi, G. L. (2003). Neural mechanisms of empathy in humans: a relay from neural systems for imitation to limbic areas. *Proceedings of the National Academy of Sciences, 100*, 5497–5502.

Carr, E. W., Winkielman, P., & Oveis, C. (2014). Transforming the mirror: Power fundamentally changes facial responding to emotional expressions. *Journal of Experimental Psychology: General, 143*, 997–1003.

Caspers, S., Zilles, K., Laird, A. R., & Eickhoff, S. B. (2010). ALE meta-analysis of action observation and imitation in the human brain. *Neuroimage, 50*, 1148–1167.

Chaminade, T., Franklin, D. W., Oztop, E., & Cheng, G. (2005). Motor interference between humans and humanoid robots: Effect of biological and artificial motion. In *The 4th International Conference on Development and Learning, 2005. Proceedings* (pp. 96–101).

Chevallier, C., Kohls, G., Troiani, V., Brodkin, E. S., & Schultz, R. T. (2012). The social motivation theory of autism. *Trends in Cognitive Sciences, 16*, 231–239.

Clark, A. (1999). An embodied cognitive science? *Trends in Cognitive Sciences, 3*, 345–351.

Clark, T. F., Winkielman, P., & McIntosh, D. N. (2008). Autism and the extraction of emotion from briefly presented facial expressions: stumbling at the first step of empathy. *Emotion, 8*, 803–809.

Collins, A. M., & Loftus, E. F. (1975). A spreading-activation theory of semantic processing. *Psychological Review, 82*, 407–428.

Cook, J. L., & Bird, G. (2012). Atypical social modulation of imitation in autism spectrum conditions. *Journal of Autism and Developmental Disorders, 42*, 1045–1051.

Cook, R., Johnston, A., & Heyes, C. (2013). Facial self-imitation objective measurement reveals no improvement without visual feedback. *Psychological Science, 24*, 93–98.

Cook, R., Bird, G., Catmur, C., Press, C., & Heyes, C. (2014). Mirror neurons: From origin to function. *Behavioral and Brain Sciences, 37*, 177–241.

Cook, R., Bird, G., Lünser, G., Huck, S., & Heyes, C. (2012). Automatic imitation in a strategic context: Players of rock–paper–scissors imitate opponents' gestures. *Proceedings of the Royal Society B: Biological Sciences, 279*, 780–786.

Coradeschi, S., Ishiguro, H., Asada, M., Shapiro, S. C., Thielscher, M., Breazeal, C., ... Ishida, H. (2006). Human-inspired robots. *IEEE Intelligent Systems, 21*, 74–85.

Côté, S., Kraus, M. W., Cheng, B. H., Oveis, C., Van der Löwe, I., Lian, H., & Keltner, D. (2011). Social power facilitates the effect of prosocial orientation on empathic accuracy. *Journal of Personality and Social Psychology, 101*, 217–232.

Csibra, G., & Gergely, G. (2009). Natural pedagogy. *Trends in Cognitive Sciences, 13*, 148–153.

Damasio, A. R. (1999). *The feeling of what happens: Body and emotion in the making of consciousness*. New York: Harcourt Brace.

Dapretto, M., Davies, M., Pfeifer, J., Scott, A., Sigman, M., Bookheimer, S., & Iacoboni, M. (2006). Understanding emotions in others: Mirror neuron dysfunction in children with autism spectrum disorders. *Nature Neuroscience, 9*, 28–30.

Dawson, G., Carver, L., Meltzoff, A. N., Panagiotides, H., McPartland, J., & Webb, S. J. (2002). Neural correlates of face and object recognition in young children with autism spectrum disorder, developmental delay, and typical development. *Child Development, 73*, 700–717.

Deriso, D., Susskind, J., Tanaka, J., Winkielman, P., Herrington, J., Schultz, R., & Bartlett, M. (2012). Exploring the facial expression perception-production link using real-time automated facial expression recognition. In A. Fusiello, V. Murino & R. Cucchiara (Eds.), *Computer vision – ECCV 2012. workshops and demonstrations* (Vol. 7584, pp. 270–279): Berlin Heidelberg: Springer.

Dichter, G. S., Richey, J. A., Rittenberg, A. M., Sabatino, A., & Bodfish, J. W. (2012). Reward circuitry function in autism during face anticipation and outcomes. *Journal of Autism and Developmental Disorders, 42*, 147–160.

Dimberg, U. (1982). Facial reactions to facial expressions. *Psychophysiology, 18*, 643–647.

Dimberg, U., Thunberg, M., & Grunedal, S. (2002). Facial reactions to emotional stimuli: Automatically controlled emotional responses. *Cognition and Emotion, 16*, 449–472.

Dimberg, U., Thunberg, M., & Elmehed, K. (2000). Unconscious facial reactions to emotional facial expressions. *Psychological Science, 11,* 86–89.

Dinstein, I., Thomas, C., Humphreys, K., Minshew, N., Behrmann, M., & Heeger, D. J. (2010). Normal movement selectivity in autism. *Neuron, 66,* 461–469.

Fiske, S. T. (1993). Controlling other people: The impact of power on stereotyping. *American Psychologist, 48,* 621–628.

Fodor, J. A. (1975). *The language of thought (Vol. 5).* Harvard University Press.

Galinsky, A. D., Gruenfeld, D. H., & Magee, J. C. (2003). From power to action. *Journal of Personality and Social Psychology, 85,* 453–66.

Goldman, A. I., & Sripada, C. S. (2005). Simulationist models of face-based emotion recognition. *Cognition, 94,* 193–213.

Grahe, J. E., & Bernieri, F. J. (1999). The importance of nonverbal cues in judging rapport. *Journal of Nonverbal Behavior, 23,* 253–269.

Guinote, A. (2010). The situated focus theory of power. In A. Guinote and T. Vescio (Eds.). *The social psychology of power.* New York: Guilford Press.

Haffey, A., Press, C., O'Connell, G., & Chakrabarti, B. (2013). Autistic traits modulate mimicry of social but not nonsocial rewards. *Autism Research, 6,* 614–620.

Halberstadt, J., Winkielman, P., Niedenthal, P. M., & Dalle, N. (2009). Emotional conception: How embodied emotion concepts guide perception and facial action. *Psychological Science, 20,* 1254–1261.

Hess, U., & Fischer, A. (2013). Emotional mimicry as social regulation. *Personality and Social Psychology Review, 17,* 142–157.

Hofree, G., Ruvolo, P., Bartlett, M. S, & Winkielman, P. (2014). Bridging the mechanical and the human mind: Spontaneous mimicry of a physically present android. *PLoS ONE, 9:* e99934.

Hofree, G., Urgen, B. A., Winkielman, Pi., & Saygin, A. P. (2015). Observation and imitation of actions performed by humans, androids and robots: An EMG study. *Frontiers in Human Neuroscience, 9,* 364.

Kanwisher, N., McDermott, J., & Chun, M. M. (1997). The fusiform face area: A module in human extrastriate cortex specialized for face perception. *The Journal of Neuroscience, 17,* 4302–4311.

Kavanagh, L. C., Suhler, C. L., Churchland, P. S., & Winkielman, P. (2011). When it's an error to mirror: The surprising reputational costs of mimicry. *Psychological Science, 22,* 1274–1276.

Kavanagh, L., Bakhtiari, G., Suhler, C., Churchland, P., Holland, R. W., & Winkielman, P. (2013). What they don't know might help them: A demonstration of subtle social inference from mimicry. *Proceedings of the 35th Annual Conference of the Cognitive Science Society.* Berlin, Germany: Cognitive Science Society.

Keltner, D., Gruenfeld, D. H., & Anderson, C. (2003). Power, approach, and inhibition. *Psychological Review, 110,* 265–284.

Keysers, C., Kaas, J. H., & Gazzola, V. (2010). Somatosensation in social perception. *Nature Reviews Neuroscience, 11,* 417–428.

Kohls, G., Schulte-Rüther, M., Nehrkorn, B., Müller, K., Fink, G. R., Kamp-Becker, I., … Konrad, K. (2012). Reward system dysfunction in spectrum disorders. *Social Cognitive and Affective Neuroscience*, http://doi:10.1093/scan/nss033.

Lanzetta, J. T., & Englis, B. G. (1989). Expectations of cooperation and competition and their effects on observers' vicarious emotional responses. *Journal of Personality and Social Psychology, 56*, 543–554.

Leighton, J., Bird, G., Orsini, C., & Heyes, C. (2010). Social attitudes modulate automatic imitation. *Journal of Experimental Social Psychology, 46*, 905–910.

Likowski, K. U., Mühlberger, A., Seibt, B., Pauli, P., & Weyers, P. (2008). Modulation of facial mimicry by attitudes. *Journal of Experimental Social Psychology, 44*, 1065–1072.

Liu, X., Hairston, J., Schrier, M., & Fan, J. (2011). Common and distinct networks underlying reward valence and processing stages: A meta-analysis of functional neuroimaging studies. *Neuroscience & Biobehavioral Reviews, 35*, 1219–1236.

Maringer, M., Krumhuber, E. G., Fischer, A. H., & Niedenthal, P. M. (2011). Beyond smile dynamics: Mimicry and beliefs in judgments of smiles. *Emotion, 11*, 181–187.

Lundqvist, L. O., & Dimberg, U. (1995). Facial expressions are contagious. *Journal of Psychophysiology, 9*, 203–211.

Mast, M. S. (2010). Interpersonal behaviour and social perception in a hierarchy: The interpersonal power and behaviour model. *European Review of Social Psychology, 21*, 1–33.

McIntosh, D. N. (1996). Facial feedback hypotheses: Evidence, implications, and directions. *Motivation and Emotion, 20*, 121–147.

McIntosh, D. N., Reichmann Decker, A., Winkielman, P., & Wilbarger, J. L. (2006). When the social mirror breaks: Deficits in automatic, but not voluntary, mimicry of emotional facial expressions in autism. *Developmental Science, 9*, 295–302.

Mesoudi, A. (2009). How cultural evolutionary theory can inform social psychology and vice versa. *Psychological Review, 116*, 929–952.

Molenberghs, P., Cunnington, R., & Mattingley, J. B. (2012). Brain regions with mirror properties: A meta-analysis of 125 human fMRI studies. *Neuroscience & Biobehavioral Reviews, 36*, 341–349.

Moody, E. J., McIntosh, D. N, Mann, L. J., & Weisser, K. R. (2007). More than mere mimicry? The influence of emotion on rapid facial reactions to faces. *Emotion, 7*, 447–457.

Nadel, J., Simon, M., Canet, P., Soussignan, R., Blancard, P., Canamero, L., & Gaussier, P. (2006). Human responses to an expressive robot. In *Proceedings of the sixth international workshop on epigentic robotics* (Vol. *128*, pp. 79–86). Lund University Cognitive Studies.

Neumann, R., Schulz, S., Lozo, L., & Alpers, G. (2014). Automatic facial responses to near-threshold presented facial displays of emotion: Imitation or evaluation. *Biological Psychology, 96*, 144–149.

Niedenthal, P. M., Brauer, M., Halberstadt, J., & Innes-Ker, A. H. (2001). When did her smile drop? Facial mimicry and the influences of emotional state on the detection of change in emotional expression. *Cognition and Emotion, 15,* 853–864.

Niedenthal, P. M., Barsalou, L. W., Winkielman, P., Krauth-Gruber, S., & Ric, F. (2005). Embodiment in attitudes, social perception, and emotion. *Personality and Social Psychology Review, 9,* 184–211.

Nishitani, N., Avikainen, S., & Hari, R. (2004). Abnormal imitation-related cortical activation sequences in Asperger's syndrome. *Annals of Neurology, 55,* 558–562.

Nuske, H., Vivanti, G., Hudry, K., & Dissanayake, C. (2014). Pupillometry reveals reduced unconscious emotional reactivity in autism. *Biological Psychology, 101,* 24–35.

Oberman, L. M., Hubbard, E. M., McCleery, J. P., Altschuler, E. L., Ramachandran, V. S., & Pineda, J. A. (2005). EEG evidence for mirror neuron dysfunction in autism spectrum disorders. *Cognitive Brain Research, 24,* 190–198.

Oberman, L. M., Ramachandran, V. S., & Pineda, J. A. (2008). Modulation of mu suppression in children with autism spectrum disorders in response to familiar or unfamiliar stimuli: The mirror neuron hypothesis. *Neuropsychologia, 46,* 1558–1565.

Oberman, L. M., Winkielman, P., & Ramachandran, V. S. (2007). Face to face: Blocking facial mimicry can selectively impair recognition of emotional expressions. *Social Neuroscience, 2,* 167–178.

Oberman, L. M., Winkielman, P., & Ramachandran, V. S. (2009). Slow echo: Facial EMG evidence for the delay of spontaneous, but not voluntary, emotional mimicry in children with autism spectrum disorders. *Developmental Science, 12,* 510–520.

Pitcher, D., Garrido, L., Walsh, V., & Duchaine, B. C. (2008). Transcranial magnetic stimulation disrupts the perception and embodiment of facial expressions. *The Journal of Neuroscience, 28,* 8929–8933.

Press, C., Richardson, D., & Bird, G. (2010). Intact imitation of emotional facial actions in autism spectrum conditions. *Neuropsychologia, 48,* 3291–3297.

Press, C., Bird, G., Flach, R., & Heyes, C. (2005). Robotic movement elicits automatic imitation. *Cognitive Brain Research, 25,* 632–640.

Preston, S. D., & De Waal, F. (2002). Empathy: Its ultimate and proximate bases. *Behavioral and Brain Sciences, 25,* 1–20.

Pylyshyn, Z. W. (1984). *Computation and cognition.* Cambridge, MA: MIT Press.

Rives Bogart, K., & Matsumoto, D. (2010). Facial mimicry is not necessary to recognize emotion: Facial expression recognition by people with Moebius syndrome. *Social Neuroscience, 5,* 241–251.

Rogers, S. J., & Williams, J. H. G. (2006). *Imitation and the social mind: Autism and typical development.* New York: Guilford Press.

Rutherford, M. D., & McIntosh, D. N. (2007). Rules versus prototype matching: Strategies of perception of emotional facial expressions in the autism spectrum. *Journal of Autism and Developmental Disorders, 37,* 187–196.

Rychlowska, M., Cañadas, E., Wood, A., Krumhuber, E. G., Fischer, A., & Niedenthal, P. M. (2014). Blocking mimicry makes true and false smiles look the same. *PLoS One, 9,* e90876.

Saygin, A. P., Chaminade, T., Ishiguro, H., Driver, J., & Frith, C. (2011). The thing that should not be: Predictive coding and the uncanny valley in perceiving human and humanoid robot actions. *Social Cognitive and Affective Neuroscience,* http://doi:10.1093/scan/nsr025.

Schubert, T. W., & Semin, G. R. (2009). Embodiment as a unifying perspective for psychology. *European Journal of Social Psychology, 39,* 1135–1141.

Scott-Van Zeeland, A. A., Dapretto, M., Ghahremani, D. G., Poldrack, R. A., & Bookheimer, S. Y. (2010). Reward processing in autism. *Autism Research: Official Journal of the International Society for Autism Research, 3,* 53–67.

Sims, T. B., van Reekum, C. M., Johnstone, T., & Chakrabarti, B. (2012). How reward modulates mimicry: EMG evidence of greater facial mimicry of more rewarding happy faces. *Psychophysiology, 49,* 998–1004.

Southgate, V., & Hamilton, A. F. de C., (2008). Unbroken mirrors: Challenging a theory of autism. *Trends in Cognitive Sciences, 12,* 225–229.

Spengler, S., Bird, G., & Brass, M. (2010). Hyperimitation of actions is related to reduced understanding of others' minds in autism spectrum conditions. *Biological Psychiatry, 68,* 1148–1155.

Stel, M., & van Knippenberg, A. (2008). The role of facial mimicry in the recognition of affect. *Psychological Science, 19,* 984–985.

Stel, M., van Baaren, R. B., Blascovich, J., van Dijk, E., McCall, C., Pollmann, M. M., . . . Vonk, R. (2010). Effects of a priori liking on the elicitation of mimicry. *Experimental Psychology, 57,* 412.

Stel, M., van den Heuvel, C., & Smeets, R. C. (2008). Facial feedback mechanisms in autistic spectrum disorders. *Journal of Autism and Developmental Disorders, 38,* 1250–1258.

Tamir, M., Robinson, M. D., Clore, G. L., Martin, L. L., & Whitaker, D. J. (2004). Are we puppets on a string? The contextual meaning of unconscious expressive cues. *Personality and Social Psychology Bulletin, 30,* 237–249.

Tanaka, J. W., Wolf, J. M., Klaiman, C., Koenig, K., Cockburn, J., Herlihy, L., . . . & Schultz, R. T. (2010). Using computerized games to teach face recognition skills to children with autism spectrum disorder: The Let's Face It! program. *Journal of Child Psychology and Psychiatry, 51,* 944–952.

Théoret, H., Halligan, E., Kobayashi, M., Fregni, F., Tager-Flusberg, H., & Pascual-Leone, A. (2005). Impaired motor facilitation during action observation in individuals with autism spectrum disorder. *Current Biology, 15,* R84–R85.

Tiedens, L. Z., & Fragale, A. R. (2003). Power moves: Complementarity in dominant and submissive nonverbal behavior. *Journal of Personality and Social Psychology, 84,* 558–568.

Tomasello, M., Kruger, A. C., & Ratner, H. H. (1993). Cultural learning. *Behavioral and Brain Sciences, 16,* 495–511.

Wang, Y., & Hamilton, A. F. de C. (2012). Social top-down response modulation (STORM): A model of the control of mimicry in social interaction. *Frontiers in Human Neuroscience, 6.*

Waytz, A., Cacioppo, J., & Epley, N. (2010). Who sees human? The stability and importance of individual differences in anthropomorphism. *Perspectives on Psychological Science, 5*, 219–232.

Weyers, P., Mühlberger, A., Hefele, C., & Pauli, P. (2006). Electromyographic responses to static and dynamic avatar emotional facial expressions. *Psychophysiology, 43*, 450–453.

Weyers, P., Mühlberger, A., Kund, A., Hess, U., & Pauli, P. (2009). Modulation of facial reactions to avatar emotional faces by nonconscious competition priming. *Psychophysiology, 46*, 328–335.

Wilson, M. (2002). Six views of embodied cognition. *Psychonomic Bulletin & Review, 9*, 625–636.

Winkielman, P., McIntosh, D. N., & Oberman, L. (2009). Embodied and disembodied emotion processing: Learning from and about typical and autistic individuals. *Emotion Review, 1*, 178–190.

Winkielman, P., Niedenthal, P., Wielgosz, J., Eelen, J., & Kavanagh, L. C. (2015). Embodiment of cognition and emotion. In M. Mikulincer, P. R. Shaver, E. Borgida, & J. A. Bargh (Eds.), *APA handbook of personality and social psychology, Vol. 1. Attitudes and social cognition* (pp. 151–175). Washington, DC: APA.

Wu, T., Butko, N. J., Ruvulo, P., Bartlett, M. S., & Movellan, J. R. (2009). Learning to make facial expressions. In *Proceedings of the 2009 IEEE 8th International Conference on Development and Learning* (pp. 1–6). IEEE.

Yabar, Y., Johnston, L., Miles, L., & Peace, V. (2006). Implicit behavioral mimicry: Investigating the impact of group membership. *Journal of Nonverbal Behavior, 30*, 97–113.

Zajonc, R. B., & Markus, H. (1984). Affect and cognition: The hard interface. In C. E., Izard, J. Kagan, & R. B., Zajonc (Eds). *Emotions, cognition, and behavior* (pp. 73–102). New York: Cambridge University Press.

CHAPTER 9

The neurological basis of empathy and mimicry

Miriam Schuler, Sebastian Mohnke, and Henrik Walter

Empathy is thought to play a pivotal role in various phenomena in interpersonal contexts, such as social interaction, prosocial behaviour, and moral decision-making (Batson, 2009; de Vignemont & Singer, 2006; Walter, 2012). Research on empathy is presently enjoying a boom in popularity. Various approaches, from behavioural methods to cognitive neuroscience, have had varying degrees of success in attempting to elucidate the concept of empathy. In this, an important question arises – what exactly is empathy? The aim of this review is to provide an overview of recent literature on the phenomenon of empathy. The chapter is divided into three sections. The first section will map the theoretical framework of empathy and will focus on its conceptualization as well as related but distinct concepts, in particular mimicry. The second section will review neurocognitive approaches and probable modulation of neural and behavioural empathic responses. The concluding section will elaborate on recent data concerning the possible neurogenetic basis of empathy.

The theoretical framework of empathy

What is empathy?

Empathy denotes the ability to share another's affective and cognitive state. The process allows us to understand and predict the feelings, thoughts and actions of others. Accordingly, empathy forms a significant component of social interaction and emotional experience. Empathy can be found in different cultures and thus may be classified as a transcultural phenomenon underlying human interaction (Walter, 2012).

The term "empathy" was introduced into the English language in 1909 as a translation of the German word "Einfühlung" ("feeling into") and was mainly used in relation to "feeling into" art and nature (Titchener, 1909). Empathy quickly aroused interest among philosophers of the social and human sciences who regarded empathy as a mechanism for recognizing each other as minded creatures. Thenceforth, empathy further developed into a term describing the process of "inner imitation," which was based on a presumed innate disposition for motor mimicry. In other words, empathy was regarded as a tool by which the human mind was able to mirror mental activities or experiences of others through observations of their bodily or facial expressions (Stüber, 2008). Nowadays, empathy lacks a clear-cut definition, and the term is applied to a range of phenomena, from compassion for someone to knowing what the other person is feeling (Hodges & Klein, 2001). Thus, different theoretical approaches have been used to elucidate and define an overall concept of empathy (Batson, 2009; Singer & Lamm, 2009; Walter, 2012). For instance, the social psychologist Batson (2009) distinguishes eight conceptually different types of empathy. Most cognitive neuroscientists, in turn, regard empathy as an affective reaction in response to the observed or imagined affective state of someone else (Bernhardt & Singer, 2012; de Vignemont & Singer, 2006; Singer & Lamm, 2009). Accordingly, trying to explicitly define empathy or distinguish between various conceptions of empathy is a difficult undertaking. In contemporary research, the prevailing viewpoint is to distinguish between two main conceptions of empathy: cognitive empathy and affective empathy (Baron-Cohen & Wheelwright, 2004; Gonzalez-Liencresa, Shamay-Tsooryc, & Brüne, 2013; Walter, 2012; Ze, Thoma, & Suchan, 2014), which will be elaborated in the following section.

Cognitive empathy and affective empathy

Given the complex nature of a construct such as empathy, it seems reasonable to break the concept into its primary components. Several scholars have agreed upon two similarly weighted parts: affective empathy and cognitive empathy (Baron-Cohen & Wheelwright, 2004; Gonzalez-Liencresa et al., 2013; Walter, 2012; Ze et al., 2014).

Affective empathy is characterized by the following features: It is (a) an affective state, which is (b) elicited by observing, imagining, or inferring another person's affective state, (c) isomorphic (similar) to the other's affective state, and (d) oriented towards the other person. Additionally, affective empathy (e) includes some form of meta-knowledge about the self and the other, which allows the empathizer to identify the source of their own affective state as differing from the other person's affective state (de Vignemont & Singer, 2006; Singer & Lamm, 2009; Walter, 2012). However, it is important to note that opinions differ in terms of affective isomorphism as a defining criterion for affective empathy. Some conceptions of affective empathy only require some form of affective resonance instead of similar affective states in the empathizer and the observed person (e.g. Baron-Cohen & Wheelwright, 2004; Decety & Jackson, 2004; Dziobek et al., 2008). In actuality, affective empathy without isomorphism might be more closely related to real-life situations. For instance, when you see someone in despair after having lost his or her job, you might rather feel pity instead of despair (see the next section for an in-depth differentiation between these concepts). Nonetheless, including affective isomorphism as defining component of affective empathy is consistent with the current use in cognitive neuroscience (de Vignemont & Singer, 2006; Singer & Lamm, 2009; Walter, 2012).

The second variant is *cognitive empathy*, which refers to the ability to identify and understand the feelings of others, without implying that the empathizer shares the same affective state. Cognitive empathy is closely related to *Theory of Mind* (ToM). ToM relates to the ability to construct an internally imagined representation of another's affective or cognitive state that can be used to anticipate another's behaviour (Brüne, 2008). ToM can also be subdivided into a cognitive and an affective component. Cognitive ToM comprises the ability to comprehend cognitive states, whereas affective ToM refers to understanding affective states. Affective ToM is regarded as being more or less synonymous with cognitive empathy and is therefore oftentimes interchangeably used to describe this empathic process (Walter, 2012).

Let's consider an example to clarify the relations between affective empathy, cognitive empathy and ToM. Imagine you see a child on a playground, who is climbing up a climbing wall. You are aware that the intention of the child on the playground is to enjoy himself or herself (cognitive ToM). Suddenly, the child falls and begins to cry. Within a short time period, you focus your attention towards the child. You perceive the distressing state and understand what the child feels (cognitive empathy = affective ToM). Furthermore, next to understanding the distressing state, you are able to share the pain with the child (affective empathy).

It is important to realize that affective and cognitive empathy mostly co-occur in real life. For example, mentalizing the emotions of others (cognitive empathy = affective ToM) might elicit a comparable affective state in oneself (affective empathy) or vice versa, affective states of others might cause similar feelings in oneself (affective empathy), which then might lead to mentalizing the corresponding emotions (cognitive empathy = affective ToM) (Walter, 2012).

Notably, several pathologies are characterized by a lack of empathic abilities in either the affective or the cognitive domain. For instance, individuals with autism display impairments in cognitive, rather than in affective empathy. These empathy deficits have been quantified with test measures, such as the Empathy Quotient Questionnaire (Baron-Cohen & Wheelwright, 2004), and can be so severe that afflicted individuals show difficulties in understanding the perspective of others and recognizing their emotions (Brüne, 2008; Dziobek et al., 2008). Conversely, socially aversive personality dimensions, such as narcissism and psychopathy, are associated with affective empathy deficits. Accordingly, intact cognitive empathy combined with desensitization towards negative emotions of others might fuel the manipulative, uncaring nature and unresponsiveness to others' distress, which are crucial deficits evident in those with socially aversive personalities (Wai & Tiliopoulos, 2012).

Another way of approximating the concept of empathy is to define related but different concepts of empathy (Hodges & Klein, 2001). Hence, the purpose of the following section is to disentangle similarities and differences between empathy and related concepts.

Concepts related to but distinct from empathy

The concept of empathy is applied to a vast array of phenomena, ranging from perspective taking and mimicry to feelings of concern for others. These phenomena are closely linked to empathic responses, but they should not be equated with empathy. Nonetheless, the related concepts can co-occur with empathy and can indeed contribute to an empathic response (Hodges & Klein, 2001). In order to distinguish between associated phenomena and empathy, it is important to keep differences and similarities with empathy in mind (see Table 9.1 for an overview).

Empathy vs. mimicry

Mimicry is defined as the automatic imitation of affective behaviour, such as postures, movements, and vocalizations, which occurs without necessarily sharing the corresponding affective state (Hatfield, Cacioppo, & Rapson, 1993; Singer & Lamm, 2009; Walter, 2012). Mimicry highly facilitates social contact and communication (Chartrand & Bargh, 1999) and is regarded as reflection of the understanding of other people's emotions (Niedenthal, Mermillod, Maringer, & Hess, 2010; see also Stel, Chapter 2). People who are mimicked feel more comfortable and understood. It can therefore be said that mimicry strongly fosters closeness to others (Lakin, Chartrand, & Arkin, 2008). Mimicry is no defining feature of empathy, however, because it does not require the observer to be in an affective state (Hatfield et al., 1993; Singer & Lamm, 2009; Walter, 2012). Thus, unlike affective empathy, affective isomorphism does not apply to mimicry. Moreover, as mimicry occurs in an unconscious and automatic

Table 9.1 Essential components of empathy and related concepts.

	Affective behaviour	Affective experience	Affective isomorphy	Perspective taking	Self–other distinction	Other orientation	Prosocial motivation
Affective empathy	(+)	+	+	+	+	+	
Cognitive empathy (affective ToM)	(+)			+	+		
Cognitive ToM				+	+		
Emotional mimicry	+		+				
Emotional contagion	(+)	+					
Sympathy	(+)	+		+	+	+	+
Compassion	(+)	+		+	+	+	+
Personal distress	(+)	+			+		
Perspective taking				+			

Note. The table illustrates a suggestion for the decomposition of empathy and related concepts into their constituting subcomponents (Adapted from Walter, 2012).

manner, mimicry requires neither perspective taking nor self–other distinction.

In spite of these differences between empathy and mimicry, there are also various similarities linking both phenomena. Mimicry and empathy are both regarded as pervasive behaviours, which are found from young to old and across different cultures (Iacoboni, 2009). Furthermore, several studies support the notion that there is a positive correlation between the tendency to imitate others' behaviour and the ability to empathize with others (Chartrand & Bargh, 1999; Niedenthal, Barsalou, Winkielman, Krauth-Gruber, & Ric, 2005; Zajonc, Adelmann, Murphy, & Niedenthal, 1987, see also Sonnby-Borgström, Chapter 7). This suggests that by mimicking others, we are more easily able to feel and understand what other people feel. With this understanding, we are able to react sympathetically to the emotions of others. Moreover, even though mimicry has been described as automatic imitation of other people's affective behaviour, there is evidence that not only empathy but also mimicry can be modulated by the social context and type of affective expression (Hess & Bourgeois, 2006; McHugo, Lanzetta, & Bush, 1991, see also Hess et al., Chapter 5, and Winkielman et al., Chapter 8). For instance, Bourgeois and Hess (2008) investigated the impact of group membership and type of emotional expression on facial mimicry. The extent of facial mimicry was highly dependent on group membership. Specifically, positive emotions were mimicked regardless of group membership, whereas negative emotions were only imitated when shown by in-group members. Accordingly, just as empathy, mimicry seems to be susceptible to various modulation factors. Furthermore, on the neural level, empathy and mimicry have both been linked to the human mirror system (Iacoboni, 2009; Niedenthal et al., 2005). Mirror neurons fire both when we act and when we observe someone performing the same action (see below for an in-depth explanation; Gallese, Fadiga, Fogassi, & Rizolatti, 1996). Carr, Iacoboni, Dubeau, Mazziotta, and Lenzi (2003) investigated the neural mechanism of empathy and intentional mimicry in humans. Largely overlapping brain areas associated with the human mirror system and empathic processing were activated by both observation and intentional mimicry of emotional facial expressions, including the anterior insula (AI), inferior frontal gyrus (IFG), and ventral premotor area. Moreover, these brain areas showed greater activation during intentional mimicry compared to the passive observation of emotional facial expressions, suggesting that intentional mimicry affects emotion processing. However, here it must be noted that the existence and the role of the human mirror system are highly debated (see below; e.g. Turella, Pierno, Tubaldi, & Castiello, 2009). Nevertheless, empathy and mimicry seem to share some neural correlates.

In sum, mimicry and empathy both play a decisive role in social interaction. Both phenomena are pervasive, seem to share some neural correlates, and seem to be subject to modulation factors. However, in spite of these similarities, mimicry does not reach the level of complexity of empathy. Therefore, compared to empathy, mimicry should be regarded as basic form of an affective reaction (Walter, 2012).

Other phenomena related to, but distinct from empathy

Emotional contagion occurs if mere association leads to an affective state that matches the other's emotional state (Hatfield, Rapson, & Le, 2009; Hess & Blairy, 2001; Walter, 2012). For example, if infants hear other infants crying, they start to cry, or imitate a smile if someone directs a smile towards them. Emotional contagion as well as mimicry requires neither perspective taking nor self–other distinction. Therefore, just as mimicry, emotional contagion is regarded as a basic form of affective reaction (Singer & Lamm, 2009; Walter, 2012). Nonetheless, both phenomena play an important role in social interaction and communication, yet cannot explain the full scope of an empathic response (Hatfield et al., 2009; Lakin et al., 2008, see also Sonnby-Borgström, Chapter 7).

Sympathy and compassion denote feelings of concern for someone in distress and the wish to promote the other's well-being (Hastings, Miller, Kahle, & Zahn-Waxler, 2013). The most vital difference between empathy and the two concepts of sympathy and compassion is that neither of the latter phenomena requires affective isomorphism. For example, if you observe that someone is sad because of a broken relationship, you rather feel pity and concern than sadness. In addition, unlike empathy, sympathy and compassion are characterized by prosocial motivation. Prosocial motivation is an other-oriented motivation, which features the intention to help others (Decety, 2011; de Vignemont & Singer, 2006; Walter, 2012). Notably, empathy can lead to prosocial motivation, as well. However, there are cases in which empathy occurs without prosocial or even with an antisocial motivation. For example, a tormentor can use his empathic abilities in order to reach closer to his victims (Walter, 2012).

Another concept that must be distinguished from empathy is *personal distress*. Personal distress is a negative affective state that can be elicited by the affective state of someone else. Compared to sympathy and compassion, personal distress is more self- than other-oriented. For example, if the daily news portrays suffering people due to a natural disaster, you might change the channel, in order to alleviate your corresponding negative feelings. Accordingly, personal distress seems to promote an egoistic motivation with the aim of reducing one's own aversive state (Batson, Fultz, & Schoenrade, 1987; Decety & Lamm, 2009; Eisenberg & Eggum, 2009).

The final important related concept is *perspective taking*, which is described as "putting oneself mentally in the shoes of someone else" (Davis & Stone, 1995). Notably, perspective taking can elicit isomorphic as well as non-isomorphic states in the observer. The concept is therefore rather regarded as a cognitive mechanism underlying ToM, affective and cognitive empathy (Walter, 2012).

While in theory these constructs can be conceptualized in isolation, in day-to-day life situations a clear-cut differentiation between empathy and the above-mentioned concepts is difficult (Hodges & Klein, 2001). On that account, Singer and Lamm (2009, p. 82) proposed a hypothetical sequence of processes leading to empathy and associated behaviour patterns. Mimicry and emotional contagion are suggested to precede empathy, which in turn might be succeeded by sympathy and compassion. Sympathy and compassion in turn might lead to prosocial behaviour. Accordingly, empathy – by definition – needs to be distinguished from these related phenomena. However, in real-life and in phenomenal experience, there are various co-occurrences and mixing of phenomena (Walter, 2012).

Empathy and the brain

Is there a core neural network for generating an empathic response? Various scholars have addressed the question of how empathy is represented in the brain (Fan, Duncan, de Greck, & Northoff, 2011; Keysers, 2011; Lamm, Decety, & Singer, 2011; Van Overwalle, 2009). Research on the neural substrates of empathy is mainly governed by two different approaches: On the one hand, investigating shared neural circuits in the observed person and the observer versus inferences about mental states on the other (Engen & Singer, 2013; Van Overwalle & Baetens, 2009). In order to achieve a better grasp of recent neuroimaging data on empathy, the next section will briefly summarize these two views, which presently guide empathic response research, in order to provide insights into associated brain areas.

Different routes generating empathy

Shared neural circuits between empathizer and observed person

In order to shed light on how we understand cognitive and affective states in others, Preston and de Waal (2002) introduced the *perception-action model* of empathy. According to this model, the key to the question lies in automatically generated neural representations in the observer of an emotional state. More precisely, perception or imagination of an emotional state in another individual automatically activates in the observer the neural representations associated with that state, which in turn elicits autonomic and somatic responses that correspond to the observed state.

The perception-action model enjoys popularity among proponents of the *simulation theory* of other minds (Goldmann, 2006). The simulation theory considers neural representations as basis for understanding others' mental states. To be more specific, the theory postulates that we understand cognitive and emotional states and their expressions in others by means of internally simulating the same psychological state in ourselves. In other words, with the aid of our mental apparatus, we put ourselves mentally in the shoes of someone else to simulate their feelings and accordingly, form predictions and explanations about them. Likewise, we simulate the movements of someone else in order to understand what he or she is doing or intending. Consequently, both the perception-action model and the simulation theory consider shared neural representations to be essential components for social interaction and communication (Decety, 2011; Goldmann, 2006; Preston & de Waal, 2002).

The discovery of mirror neurons in the mid-1990s seemed to provide the perfect neurobiological mechanism for simulation (Gallese & Goldman, 1998; Rizzolatti & Arbib, 1998). Single cell recordings of the monkeys' premotor cortex (area F5) have shown that a class of neurons discharges not only when a monkey grasps or manipulates an object but also when a monkey observes someone else performing a similar gesture (Gallese et al., 1996). Subsequently, neurons with similar response properties as in the premotor cortex have also been recorded in the monkeys' anterior intraparietal area and in the primary motor cortex. On that account, mirror neurons have been assumed to aid in several functions, such as imitation, action understanding, and empathy (Gallese, 2001). Brain areas selective for both observed and executed movements have also been reported in functional neuroimaging (fMRI) studies of humans. Studies investigating motor phenomena in humans yielded brain areas of overlapping properties, which were homologues to areas in which mirror neurons were discovered in monkeys, including the ventral premotor cortex and the intraparietal area (Dinstein, Hasson, Rubin, & Heeger, 2007). However, given that fMRI is an indirect measure of neural activity, the ability for researchers to study the human mirror system is severely limited and thus can only be cautiously assumed. Notably, only one study provides direct evidence from single cell recording for a human mirror system (Cook, Bird, Catmur, Press, & Heyes, 2014). Mukamel,

Ekstrom, Kaplan, Iacoboni, and Fried (2010) recorded extracellular activity from medial frontal and temporal cortices while subjects perceived and performed hand-grasping movements and facial emotional expressions. Indirect evidence for an emotional human mirror system, in turn, has been postulated by a literature review including neuroimaging studies of pain, disgust, and touch. This review suggests that we activate similar circuits when observing sensations or emotions felt by others, and when experiencing these sensations and emotions ourselves. However, there does not seem to be a reliable mapping of specific emotions onto particular brain regions. Instead, experimental evidence suggests that emotion simulation seems to involve a conglomerate of affective, motor, and somatosensory components, which can then trigger emotional experience (Bastiaansen, Thioux, & Keysers, 2009).

Mental inferences

Another attempt to explain how we derive internal states of others has been proposed by proponents of the *theory theory* (Morton, 1980), which suggests that we possess a common-sense psychological theory, a so-called folk-psychology or Theory of Mind. With that ToM we infer mental states, comprehend intentions, and attempt to predict the future behaviour of others. It is hypothesized that the theory consists of various concepts (e.g. desires, beliefs) and governing principles of how the concepts interact. In addition, these concepts and ruling principles are either innately given or largely developed in childhood (Carruthers, 1996). Accordingly, in order to understand cognitive and affective states in others, we do not simulate the same psychological state in ourselves, but instead use our own set of concepts and principles concerning beliefs, desires, and behaviour in order to comprehend and explain mental states of others. Brain areas associated with ToM are the medial prefrontal regions, the bilateral superior temporal sulcus (STS) and temporo-parietal junctions (TPJ), posterior midline structures such as the posterior cingulate cortex and precuneus (PCC/pcu), and the temporal poles (Van Overwalle & Baetens, 2009; Walter, 2012).

By focusing on current neuroimaging paradigms in the field of generating empathic responses, the next section attempts to solve the theoretical debate on whether the understanding of cognitive and affective empathy is achieved by simulation or by a specific theory.

Investigations of the neural basis of empathy

The above-described approaches to empathy have different assumptions regarding how empathic responses are generated in the brain. Simulation theory is based on the assumption of shared neural representations, whereas theory theory focuses on mental inferences in order to understand the affective and cognitive states of others (Walter, 2012). Therefore, investigating the neural response pattern in neuroimaging studies might shed light on how empathy is represented in the brain.

Empathy has predominantly been studied in pain, as pain has been shown to reliably induce empathic responses (Morrison, Lloyd, di Pellegrino, & Roberts, 2004; Singer et al., 2004). First-hand pain experience activates prefrontal and posterior parietal cortices, primary and secondary somatosensory cortices (S1 and S2), anterior and medial cingulate cortex (ACC/MCC), insula and thalamic regions, as well as the periaqueductal grey (PAC) of the brainstem (Peyron, Laurent, & García-Larrea, 2000). During a functional imaging experiment, Singer and colleagues (2004) investigated brain activation corresponding to empathizing with the pain of others. In their study, volunteers experienced a painful stimulus and, in another session, perceived a cue that denoted that their loved one was receiving a comparably painful stimulation. Interestingly, bilateral AI, ACC, brainstem, and cerebellum activity was not only found when subjects received painful stimulation themselves but also when observing the signal that their loved one experienced pain. The data suggest that pain-related empathic responses seem to share the same neural networks that are recruited during the direct experience of pain. On that account, this experiment speaks in favour of shared neural networks between empathizer and observed person.

However, the question remains what the precise function of these structures is in generating an empathic response. Somatosensory regions and the posterior insula are thought to encode sensory-discriminative components of pain, such as stimulus intensity or location. Affective-motivational components of pain are assumed to be reflected in the activation of the anterior insula (AI) and ACC/MCC. Activation of posterior parietal and prefrontal cortices is thought to illustrate attentional and memory domains necessary for pain processing. Pain control, in turn, is expected to be mediated by thalamic regions and the PAC (Bernhardt & Singer, 2012; Peyron et al., 2000). Thus, generation of an empathic pain response seems to be subsumed by several brain regions. The following sections take a closer look at the individual brain areas and try to identify core empathy regions.

Cue- vs. picture-based research paradigms

A meta-analysis by Lamm et al. (2011) of fMRI studies investigating empathy for pain confirms the involvement of AI, ACC/MCC, S1, S2, and thalamic regions during the direct experience of pain. Furthermore, activation of the above-mentioned regions overlaps with the activation pattern for perceiving pain in others. More precisely, AI and ACC/MCC seem to be jointly activated by the direct and empathic experience of pain. Moreover, this meta-analysis contrasted previous experiments employing abstract visual cues to signal that another person present would undergo painful stimulation (cue-based paradigms) with studies that used affectively provoking material, such as pictures of body parts receiving pain (picture-based paradigms). The results indicate that depending on the type of experimental paradigm, the network of AI and ACC/MCC is co-activated with distinct brain regions. During cue-based paradigms, activation of somatosensory regions contralateral to the stimulated hand was only induced by self-related experience of pain and not by vicarious pain experience. In picture-based paradigms, S1 and S2 activity was observed during the other-related condition as well. However, activation in somatosensory regions was not lateralized to a hemisphere, and additionally, comparable S1 and S2 activation was also found for non-painful control pictures. Accordingly, somatosensory activation elicited by picture-based empathy for pain paradigms instead seems to be traced back to the perception of touch and movement of body parts and not to empathy for pain itself. Furthermore, compared to cue-based paradigms, picture-based paradigms showed relative activity increases in dorsolateral and dorsomedial PFC, bilateral inferior parietal cortex (IPC), and left inferior frontal gyrus (IFG), a network partly overlapping with the human mirror system. Conversely, cue-based paradigms engaged areas associated with inferring and representing mental states of the self and others (PCC/pcu, ventromedial prefrontal cortex (vmPFC), STS, TPJ). Taken together, this meta-analysis implies that picture-based paradigms trigger activation in the mirror network for the simulation of movements and goal-directed actions, which might serve as a basis for grasping the meaning of the situation presented in the picture. Activity might then be relayed on to the AI and ACC/MCC for the assessment of the affective-motivational component of the stimulus. Given that cue-based paradigms do not explicitly depict the pain of others, subjects are required to mentally infer the situation and its consequences, for example, by means of prior knowledge. Hence, the process of mental inferences is reflected in brain areas comprising the mentalizing network. Consequently, depending on the type of experimental condition and available information both the mirror system and the mentalizing network can be recruited together with AI and ACC/MCC in order to empathize with the pain of others (Lamm et al., 2011).

Affective-perceptual vs. cognitive-evaluative research paradigms

Another meta-analysis, comprising 40 fMRI studies on the neural bases of empathy, was performed by Fan et al. (2011). This analysis again assigned AI and ACC/MCC a central role in the generation of empathic responses. More precisely, Fan and colleagues (2011) detected three main activation clusters: The first cluster comprised the anterior MCC (aMCC), dorsal ACC (dACC), and supplementary motor area (SMA). The second and third cluster formed the left and right AI and IFG. Notably, activation in these brain areas was consistently observed independent of task and stimulus type. In other words, these so-called core regions of empathy were not only recruited when subjects empathized with others' pain, but also when experiencing the fear, happiness, disgust, and anxiety of others. In addition, Fan and colleagues (2011) contrasted affective-perceptual empathy experiments, in which subjects were required to observe the emotional or sensory state of others with cognitive-evaluative paradigms, during which subjects are explicitly asked to actively infer the emotional states of others. The right AI extending to the right IFG denoted higher activity during affective-perceptual empathy paradigms. Conversely, the left aMCC was more frequently activated in cognitive-evaluative paradigms. More differences in recruited brain areas were found at an uncorrected, less stringent threshold level ($p < .001$; *uncorrected*). Affective-perceptual empathy paradigms more frequently recruited the ventral part of the MCC (vMCC), extending to the right dACC, midbrain, and right dorsal medial thalamus (DMT). The left orbitofrontal cortex (OFC) and left DMT were more frequently engaged in cognitive-evaluative experiments. Accordingly, comparable to the results by Lamm and colleagues (2011), the meta-analysis by Fan and colleagues (2011) provides further evidence for core regions of empathy (AI and ACC/MCC), which are recruited irrespectively of the type of emotion or stimulus (see Figure 9.1).

Functional role of the implicated brain structures

A closer look at AI and ACC/MCC connectivity and functions clarifies the importance of these structures for the generation of empathy. The AI forms an important contributor in the integration of affect, sensation, and cognition (for reference see Kurth, Zilles, Fox, Laird, & Eickhoff, 2010). This integrative function is reflected in dense connections to PFC, OFC, and temporo-limbic regions. Moreover, the AI exhibits strong interconnections for bidirectional information flow. The cingulate cortex in turn is implicated in affective, cognitive, and motor control and assesses the motivational content of external and internal stimuli. The CC comprises several subparts, which display distinct connections and functions. For

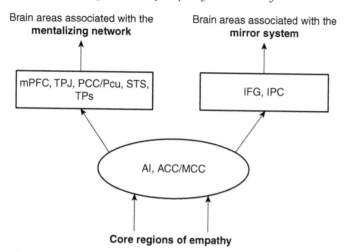

Empathy-related processing recruits, next to core regions of empathy, brain areas involved in mirror system and mentalizing network. Crucial for the co-recruitment of the mirror system or the mentalizing network is the context or the available information of the affective state of the person we are empathizing with. *Note*. mPFC: medial prefrontal cortex; TPJ: temporo-parietal junction; PCC/Pcu: posterior cingulate cortex and precuneus; STS: superior temporal sulcus; TPs: temporal poles; IFG: inferior frontal gyrus; IPC: intraparietal cortex; AI: anterior insula; ACC/MCC: anterior cingulate cortex and midcingulate cortex.

Figure 9.1 Brain areas involved in the generation of an empathic reaction.

instance, the rostral part of the ACC is densely connected to the lateral and orbital PFC. The dorsal part of the ACC and anterior MCC possess connections to sensorimotor regions, insula, amygdala, PAG, and ventral striatum. Accordingly, the AI and ACC/MCC in conjunction with limbic structures and several sub- and cortical regions form a densely connected network. Within that network, the AI seems to be the input region that integrates modality-specific information from several emotional states and contextual stimuli. Computations from the AI might then lead to predictions about emotions of others and the self. Subsequent value computations of the ACC/MCC, OFC, and ventral striatum help with response selection, action responses, and control. Consequently, location, dense connections, and functions of the AI and ACC/MCC render these regions ideal for the role of being core regions in the generation of empathy (Bernhardt & Singer, 2012).

In addition to the core empathy regions, different neuroanatomical circuits seem to subserve affective-perceptual and cognitive-evaluative forms of empathy. The right AI extending to the right IFG, dorsolateral, and dorsomedial PFC and IPC are associated with concrete, affective-perceptual paradigms of empathy. The IFG and IPC form part of the mirror network. Hence, simulation processes do seem to play a role in the induction of empathy – at least in affective-perceptual paradigms that show explicit visual cues of affectively provoking material. Both the abstract nature of cue-based stimuli and cognitive-evaluative paradigms require subjects to mentally infer the situation and its consequences. Therefore, structures associated with the mentalizing network are recruited, such as left aMCC, vmPFC, STS, TPJ, and PCC/pcu. The brain structures of the mentalizing network have been confirmed by several imaging studies that have directly assessed the process of mentalizing (Mohnke et al., 2014; Preston et al., 2007; Schnell, Bluschke, Konradt, & Walter, 2010; Walter et al., 2004; Walter el al., 2011). For instance, Walter and colleagues (2011) used a Cartoon Paradigm for the investigation of cognitive empathy (affective ToM). In this paradigm, subjects were presented with 16 cartoon stories outlined on three consecutive pictures. Subjects were required to judge changes of either the number of living beings from their own perspective (control condition) or changes in the affective state of the protagonist (affective ToM condition). Mentalizing about the emotions of the protagonist compared to visuospatial judgements corresponded with greater activation in the mentalizing network (dmPFC, TPJ, PCC/Pcu, anterior STS, temporal poles) as well as the limbic system (left amygdala and hippocampus).

Two roads to empathy

The two brain circuits comprising the mentalizing and the mirror neuron network have been linked to bottom-up and top-down processes in emotion generation (LeDoux, 1996; Walter, 2012). Bottom-up processes provide quick, low-level affective analyses of stimuli, whereas high-level, top-down functioning is induced by higher-order cognitive appraisal processes that rely on stored knowledge or contextual and situational information. Accordingly, the mirror-neuron system is associated with the low road to empathy, as induction of empathy in affective-perceptual paradigms showing explicit visual cues occurs more or less automatically in a stimulus-response fashion. On the other hand, generation of empathy via abstract visual cues or in cognitive-evaluative paradigms might best be illustrated by the high road. Hence, the mentalizing network is activated in a top-down manner in order to mentally infer the situation and its consequences. Notably, the cognitive understanding of a situation can lead to affective empathy as well (see Figure 9.2).

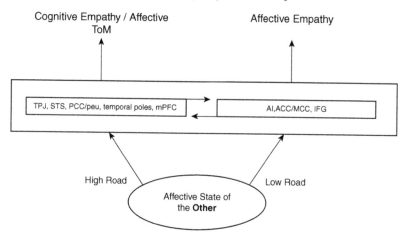

The affective state of another person can elicit activations in the observer either by quick bottom-up affective signals ("low road") or by higher-order cognitive appraisal processes that rely on stored knowledge or contextual and situational information ("high road"). The large rectangle schematically depicts the brain of the observing self and the small rectangles depict neural networks that have some specificity for the types of mental processes in the upper part. However, as indicated by the arrows between the small rectangles, these systems can be coactivated. *Note.* TPJ: temporo-parictal junction; STS: superior temporal sulcus; PCC/pcu: posterior cingulate cortex and precuneus; mPFC: medial prefrontal cortex; AI: anterior insula; ACC/MCC: anterior cingulate cortex and mideingulate cortex: IFG: inferior frontal gyrus.

(Adapted from Walter, 2012)

Figure 9.2 Brain circuits for empathy and ToM.

Findings by Fan and colleagues (2011) suggesting AI asymmetry in affective-perceptual and cognitive-evaluative paradigms might reflect the distinction between a low road and high road to empathy. The left AI seems to be implicated in both forms of empathic generation, the right AI, in turn, seems to be more frequently activated in affective-perceptual forms of empathy. Accordingly, the right AI has been proposed to be implicated in the processing of interoception and representations of bodily responses. Moreover, the right AI seems to be directly connected to the paralimbic circuit, consisting of striatal and OFC regions, which, in turn, is linked to core limbic structures, such as thalamus and amygdala. Therefore, it is likely that the paralimbic circuit is involved in the evaluation of "bottom-up" external and internal affective stimuli. Accordingly, the connection of the right AI to the paralimbic circuit and its associated processing mechanisms might be a crucial factor determining the preference of the right AI for affective-perceptual forms of empathy over cognitive-evaluative forms (Kober et al., 2008).

A word of caution is recommended given the fact that statements on shared neural activations are based on two fMRI activation maps of first-hand and vicarious experience of emotions. Specifically, overlapping clusters in two fMRI activation maps do not necessarily stem from the same neurons or neural networks. However, to date, no available human neuroimaging method directly measures activity of single neurons. Accordingly, more research is needed in order to determine whether activation maps are really shared on the neural level.

To conclude, current neuroimaging paradigms investigating the neural bases of empathy point to core empathy regions comprising the AI and ACC/MCC, which integrate information across various domains and allow selection of prospective responses. In addition, depending on the information provided in the task, two other systems seem to play a pivotal role in the generation of empathy: the mirror system and the mentalizing system. Remarkably, data suggests that the generation of empathy and subsequent overt behaviour can be modulated by various factors, such as the relationship with the observed person or contextual appraisal of the situation. On that account, the next section will examine factors influencing the generation of empathy on the neural and behavioural level.

Modulation of empathy

The generation of empathy is not a fixed or isolated process. On the contrary, the formation of empathy is subject to numerous modulation factors. Given this state of affairs, this section will examine individual differences, gender differences, attitudes towards others, perspective taking, and attention as modulating processes of empathic responses.

Singer and colleagues (2004) have shown that empathic responses are correlated with empathic traits, measured by self-report questionnaires, including the Interpersonal Reactivity Index (IRI, Davis, 1983). In addition, AI and dACC activity correlate with scores on the empathic concern subscale of the IRI during abstract cue-based paradigms. Jabbi, Swart & Keysers (2007) found similar correlations in fronto-insular regions and subscales of the IRI using a gustatory emotions paradigm. In other words, empathic traits seem to modulate empathic brain responses and subsequent behavioural outcomes.

Gender is a probable factor influencing the neural basis of empathy, as well as corresponding behaviours. For instance, Rueckert and Naybar (2008) found significantly higher scores on empathy questionnaires for women compared to men. Singer and colleagues (2006) found gender differences in neural processes underlying empathy during an economic trust game. Two confederates were instructed to play either fairly or unfairly in order to induce liking or disliking in the participants towards the confederates. Women showed neuronal activity in areas associated with pain when observing both a fair and an unfair person in pain. Men, on the contrary, showed activity in reward-related areas (nucleus accumbens of the ventral striatum; NAcc) when perceiving an unfair player in pain. Accordingly, empathic responses might – at least in men – be influenced by the evaluation of other people's social behaviour. However, it is still unclear to what extent gender affects empathy and its corresponding neural bases. In contrast to the findings of Singer et al. (2006), Lamm et al. (2011) reported no gender effects in their meta-analysis on empathy. To note, the meta-analysis by Fan et al. (2011) did not include gender in their calculations. Accordingly, further research is necessary in order to elucidate the role of gender differences in the processing of empathy as well as its neural bases.

Next to the attribution of specific traits to the target (fair vs. unfair), recent results also support the assumption that group membership and resulting attitudes towards others influence empathic responses. In accordance to this, Hein and colleagues (2010) reported stronger brain responses in the left AI when subjects perceived an in-group member as compared to an out-group member suffering pain. Moreover, subsequent willingness to help in-group and out-group members was correlated with the degree of AI response. Furthermore, consistent with the results of Singer and colleagues (2006), witnessing an out-group member in pain evoked activation in the reward-related right NAcc together with a decrease in empathy-related activation in left AI. In addition, participants who attributed less value to out-group members showed stronger NAcc activation compared to participants who viewed out-group members more positively. Hence, empathy-related responses seem to be modulated by the social evaluation of the observed person in pain. Furthermore, along with the results by Singer and colleagues (2006), activation in reward-related areas (NAcc) might reflect feelings of revenge or Schadenfreude, presumably counteracting empathic responses and ultimately preventing prosocial behaviour.

In addition, different forms of perspective taking can evoke variable behavioural and neural responses. The main focus of attention is on the distinction between imagine-other perspective and imagine-self conditions. The imagine-other perspective requires the participant to imagine the feelings and thoughts of the "to be observed" person. Contrary, the imagine-self perspective asks the subject to directly imagine oneself in the shoes of someone else (Batson, Early, & Salvarini, 1997). Lamm and colleagues (2007) reported different emotional consequences for the two forms of perspective taking. Adopting the perspective of the other promoted stronger empathic concern, whereas the imagine-self condition instead triggered personal distress and withdrawal (consistent with the self vs. other differentiation outlined above). Notably, the imagine-self perspective evoked stronger activity in brain areas associated with the affective response to potentially dangerous situations or pain, such as amygdala, insula, and aMCC. Thus, imaging oneself in the shoes of someone else might lead to a stronger aversive response, compared to imaging the feelings and thoughts of someone in the same situation.

Moreover, even relatively basic processes, such as the way we attend to the emotions of others, likely affect empathic responses. During an fMRI scanning session, Gu and Han (2007) presented subjects with pictures or cartoons of hands that were depicted in painful or neutral situations. Subjects were required to either rate the pain intensity presumably felt by the person whose hands were shown in the pictures or count the number of hands presented in the stimulus array. Relative to the neutral condition, ratings of painful situations elicited increased activation in areas associated with pain-related empathy (e.g. cingulate cortices, insula). Notably, neural activation related to the evaluation of painful consequences was absent when subjects were asked to count the number of hands depicted on the pictures. In other words, the counting task distracted the subjects from the painful aspects of the stimuli. On that account, the findings suggest that the simple perception of painful situations does not automatically evoke empathic brain responses. That is, activity of the network involved in empathic processing seems to depend upon top-down attentional processes.

In sum, there is extensive evidence that empathy can be modulated by several factors, such as person characteristics, perspective taking, and attention. Therefore, it is indispensable to keep these factors in mind when assessing individual differences in empathy and associated prosocial behaviour.

Empathy and genetics

In order to provide a complete overview on human empathy, it is important to outline recent data on a possible neurogenetic basis for empathy. To begin with, the question needs to be addressed on how to measure a genetic basis for empathy. Three methods have been applied in order to illustrate a genetic foundation. First, twin studies have been used to establish the heritability of certain phenotypes by separating phenotypic variations into environmental and genetic parts (Felson, 2014). Second, genetic association studies have sought to determine specific genes or polymorphisms contributing to a specific phenotype by trying to correlate individual differences or a disease status and genetic variation (Marchini, Donnelly, & Cardon, 2005). Third, a specialized form of genetic association that has recently been developed is called imaging genetics. Imaging genetics studies have used data on brain activation in specific circuits involved in certain psychological functions to elucidate genetic variation (Esslinger et al., 2009; Walter, Meyer-Lindenberg, & Heinz, 2013).

Knafo and Uzefovsky (2013) recently addressed the issue of direct evidence for a behavioural phenotype of empathy. They reviewed eight twin studies that assessed genetic and environmental contributions to individual differences in empathy. Except for one study, all studies reported genetic effects on empathy. More precisely, genetic factors accounted for 35 per cent of the variance of empathy. Six out of eight studies differentiated between cognitive and affective empathy and reported differing genetic contributions. Accordingly, genetic factors accounted for 30 per cent and 26 per cent of the variance, respectively. Remarkably, the meta-analysis revealed increasing heritability estimates for empathy with age and degree of emotional symptoms. Emotional symptoms were assessed by the Strengths and Difficulties Questionnaire (SDQ; Goodman, 1997) and can be referred to as worries, fears, or clingy behaviour. Furthermore, low economic status and medical risk decreased the genetic influence. Thus, genetic influences on individual differences in empathy do seem to exist, however, not in isolation. It is likely that they interact with environmental factors and age in a complex manner (Knafo & Uzefovsky, 2013).

What about specific genes contributing to the individual variance of empathy? First, obvious candidates are the neuropeptide hormones oxytocin and vasopressin, which have often been cited in the context of social cognition and behaviour (Heinrichs, von Dawans, & Domes, 2009; Skuse & Gallagher, 2011). Their expression and receptor density seem to influence female lactation, maternal attachment, pair bonding, and ejaculation (Donaldson & Young, 2008). Moreover, both neuropeptides seem to be implicated in various neurodevelopmental disorders (Francis et al., 2014) and in disorders hallmarked by impairments in socio-emotional functioning, such as autism spectrum disorder and schizophrenia (Montag et al., 2012). In addition, Domes and colleagues (2007) demonstrated that intranasal oxytocin improves the ability to infer affective mental states of others from social cues in the eye region, using the Reading the Mind in the Eyes Test (RMET; Baron-Cohen, Wheelwright, Hill, Raste, & Plumb, 2001). The RMET has also been used by Rodrigues and colleagues (2009), who investigated the influence of the naturally occurring genetic variation of the oxytocin receptor (OXTR) rs53576 on empathy and stress reactivity in humans. Oxytocin variant rs53576 carriers with one or two copies of the A-allele (AG/AA) expressed lower levels of behavioural and dispositional empathy than individuals homozygous for the G-allele of rs53576 (GG). Moreover, AA/AG carriers showed higher levels of physiological and dispositional stress reactivity during a startle anticipation task and an affective reactivity scale compared to GG carriers. The influence of genetic variations in the OXTR rs53576 gene on empathy has recently been confirmed by Smith and colleagues (2014). Smith and colleagues assessed 51 healthy male participants and found that oxytocin variant rs53576 GG carriers expressed higher levels of empathic concern as well as sympathetic and subjective arousal in response to perceiving harm in others compared to individuals with one or two copies of the A-allele (AG/AA). The findings on the OXRT rs53576 are supported by the fact that A-allele carriers of the OXTR rs53576 seem to display a statistically increased likelihood of an autism diagnosis (Wu et al., 2005). Preliminary evidence about the influence of the OXTR rs2254298 on self-rated affective empathy in schizophrenic subjects has been postulated by Montag et al. (2012). Specifically, schizophrenic patients carrying one or two copies of the OXTR rs2254298 A-allele displayed significantly more affective empathy levels, as determined by the IRI subscale "empathic concern," compared to those carrying two G-alleles. Moreover, OXTR rs2254298 significantly impacted general psychopathology scores indicated by the Positive and Negative Syndrome Scale (PANSS; Kay, Fiszbein, & Opler, 1987) for schizophrenia. Schizophrenic A-allele carriers showed significantly higher scores of PANSS general psychopathology compared to carriers of two G-alleles. Thus, the results suggest tentative findings for the involvement of OXTR rs2254298 variation in empathic functioning and symptom severity in schizophrenia.

Second, another candidate gene for a genetic basis for empathy is the 7-repeat polymorphism in the dopamine receptor gene (DRD4-III), which has been found to be implicated in susceptibility to parenting influences (Belsky & Pluess, 2009). Accordingly, Knafo and Uzefovsky (2013) reported a significant negative relationship between maternal negativity and empathic concern in children with the DRD4-III 7-repeat allele. This negative relationship was not found for children without the 7-repeat allele. Moreover, research findings by Poletti et al. (2013) tentatively refer to influences of dopaminergic transmission due to the catechol-O-methyltransferase (COMT) gene variation on perceived stress and neural correlates of empathy in schizophrenic patients. The COMT Val (108/158) Met (rs4680) polymorphism variably influences enzymatic activity, with the Val-allele being associated with higher enzymatic activity and subsequent decreased dopaminergic stimulation of post-synaptic neurons (Lachman et al., 1996). Thus, schizophrenic Val-allele carriers reported higher rates of distress, measured by the IRI subscale 'personal distress', compared to Met-allele carriers, and additionally showed lower BOLD neural responses in brain areas associated with empathic processing (Poletti et al., 2013). Hence, the size of the empathic reaction seems to be influenced by dopaminergic signal transmission.

Third, several scholars have suggested a link between serotonin (5-HT) and emotional reactivity (Beevers, Wells, Ellis, & McGeary, 2009; Hysek et al. 2013). In the context of empathic processing, the focal point of interest is on genetic variations in the promoter region of the 5-HT transporter gene (5-HTTLPL; Gyurak et al., 2013), which is implicated in the transcription of 5-HTT (Heils et al., 1996). Accordingly, in two recent independent studies on the effect of the 5-HTTLPL polymorphism, Gyurak and colleagues (2013) have shown that genetic variation of the 5-HTTLPR might be associated with differing emotional reactivity. Subjects with two short alleles of the 5-HTTLPR (SS-5-HTTLPR) reported more personal distress after watching films that portrayed others in distress, compared to participants with SL or LL variants of the 5-HTTLPR. Furthermore, subjects who were homozygous for the short allele displayed greater levels of anger and amusement and exhibited more emotional expressive behaviour while watching an embarrassing videotape, which depicted them singing. Hence, these two independent studies provide evidence that SS carriers of the 5-HTTLPR might be characterized by elevated emotional responses across different aspects of emotional reactivity. Referring to empathy, SS-carriers seem to display stronger empathic reactions and seem to experience more difficulties distinguishing their own from other people's emotions.

Finally, in a recently published imaging genetics study, Walter and colleagues (2011) investigated the effect of a genetic variant (rs1344706) of the gene ZNF804A on cognitive empathy. This genetic variant has been shown to be associated with schizophrenia and bipolar disorder with genome-wide support (O'Donovan et al., 2008; Williams et al., 2011). As ToM dysfunction on the behavioural and neural level has been reliably shown in patients with schizophrenia (Bora, Murat, & Pantelis, 2009; Mohnke et al., 2014), Walter and colleagues (2011) were motivated to explore the effect of the schizophrenia risk variant on activation of the mentalizing network. Accordingly, 109 healthy volunteers of both sexes completed the ToM cartoon task described above (mentalizing about the affective state of the other vs. counting the amount of living objects). With increasing number of risk alleles, dose brain activation decreased within the dmPFC, left posterior STS/TPJ, and PCC/Pcu. Importantly, the findings were recently replicated in an independent sample of 188 healthy controls (Mohnke et al., 2014). These results showed that healthy risk allele carriers of the genetic risk variant for schizophrenia display dysfunctional ToM network activation. That is to say, this genetic variant (rs1344706) of the gene ZNF804A is associated with dysfunction in the human ToM network. The results speak not only in favour of ToM abnormalities as being an intermediate phenotype of psychosis (Meyer-Lindenberg & Weinberger, 2006) but also empathize the role of genetic contributions to social cognition.

To conclude, the above-cited studies provide support for the genetic foundation of empathy. However, no single gene seems to be responsible for the entire extent of the empathic response. Conversely, the studies mentioned earlier point to different genes, each coding some form of empathic processing. The same applies to individual differences in empathic reactions that might be tracked back to genetic variations in various genes. Thus, understanding genetic contributions to individual differences in empathic processing takes on an important role in the exploration of abnormal and normal mental health. Consequently, neurogenetic approaches for empathy seem to be an interesting and valuable field for prospective studies on empathy.

Conclusion

Empathy research has evolved into a multidisciplinary field of interest in the last decade. Two main components of empathy can be identified: cognitive empathy and affective empathy. These two components need to be differentiated from related but distinct phenomena of empathy, such as mimicry. Mimicry and empathy have several features in common; however, an empathic reaction stands out due to its far more complex nature. Neuroimaging studies on empathy have consistently revealed that AI and ACC/MCC activation during vicarious experience of affective states, suggesting these structures are the core brain regions connected to empathy. Depending on the context and available information, empathy core regions are recruited with the mirror neuron network and brain structures associated with the mentalizing system. Hence, both simulation of affective states and mental inferences play an important role in the generation of empathy. Moreover, the generation of empathy is not a fixed process, but may be modulated by several factors, such as individual differences or attitudes towards the observed person. Recent neurogenetic studies on empathy suggest an involvement of candidate genes, related to oxytocin, dopamine, serotonin, and one schizophrenia risk variant.

However, even though research on empathy has begun to shed light on behavioural and neural underpinnings, there are still several remaining questions related to empathy. For instance, there is no universally accepted conceptualization of empathy. On that account the theoretical framework of empathy should be revised and handled with care, in order to allow for better comparisons between experimental designs and hypothetical constructs. In addition, the functional significance of shared representations should be scrutinized. In particular, the question of whether these shared activations illustrate simulation processes of affective states should be investigated with care. Moreover, the focus of future research efforts should not only be on network interactions and relevant subcomponents but also on the role of related phenomena, such as emotional mimicry, in order to enable deeper insights into the generation of empathy. In particular, special consideration should be paid to neurotransmitters, hormones, and presumed candidate genes that might be involved in vicarious experiences. Such fundamental insights into the process of generating empathy may ultimately be beneficial for therapeutic interventions.

References

Baron-Cohen, S., & Wheelwright, S. (2004). The empathy quotient: An investigation of adults with Asperger syndrome or high functioning autism, and normal sex differences. *Journal of Autism and Developmental Disorders, 34*, 163–175.

Baron-Cohen, S., Wheelwright, S., Hill, J., Raste, Y., & Plumb, I. (2001). The "Reading the Mind in the Eyes" Test, revised version: A study with normal adults, and adults with Asperger syndrome or high-functioning autism. *Journal of Child Psychology and Psychiatry, 42*, 241–251.

Bastiaansen, J. A., Thioux, M., & Keysers, C. (2009). Evidence for mirror systems in emotions. *Philosophical Transactions of the Royal Society B: Biological Sciences, 364*, 2391–2404.

Batson, C. D. (2009). These things called empathy: Eight related but distinct phenomena. In J. Decety & W. Ickes (Eds.), *The social neuroscience of empathy* (pp. 3–16). Cambridge, MA: MIT Press.

Batson, C. D., Early, S., & Salvarini, G. (1997). Perspective taking: Imagining how another feels versus imagining how you would feel. *Personality and Social Psychology Bulletin, 23*, 751–758.

Batson, C. D., Fultz, J., & Schoenrade, P. A. (1987). Distress and empathy: Two qualitatively distinct vicarious emotions with different motivational consequences. *Journal of Personality, 55*, 19–39.

Beevers, C. G., Wells, T. T., Ellis, A. J., & McGeary, J. E. (2009). Association of the serotonin transporter gene promoter region (5-HTTLPR) polymorphism with biased attention for emotional stimuli. *Journal of Abnormal Psychology, 118*, 670–681.

Belsky, J., & Pluess, M. (2009). Beyond diathesis stress: Differential susceptibility to environmental influences. *Psychological Bulletin, 135*, 885–908.

Bernhardt, B. C., & Singer, T. (2012). The neural basis of empathy. *Annual Review of Neuroscience, 35*, 1–23.

Bora, E., Murat, Y., & Pantelis, C. (2009). Theory of mind impairment in schizophrenia: Meta-analysis. *Schizophrenia Research, 109*, 1–9.

Bourgeois, P., & Hess, U. (2008). The impact of social context on mimicry. *Biological Psychology, 77*, 343–352.

Brüne, M. (2008). Soziale Kognition- Psychologie. In T. Kircher & S. Gauggel (Eds.), *Neuropsychologie der Schizophrenie: Symptome, Kognition, Gehirn* (pp. 347–356). Berlin: Springer-Verlag.

Carr, L., Iacoboni, M., Dubeau, M. C., Mazziotta, J. C., & Lenzi, G. L. (2003). Neural mechanisms of empathy in humans: A relay from neural systems for imitation to limbic areas. *Proceedings of the National Academy of Sciences, 100*, 5497–5502.

Carruthers, P. (1996). Simulation and self-knowledge: A defence of the theory-theory. In P. Carruthers & P. K. Smith (Eds.), *Theories of theories of mind*. Cambridge, UK: Cambridge University Press.

Chartrand, T. L., & Bargh, J. A. (1999). The chameleon effect: the perception-behavior link and social interaction. *Journal of Personality and Social Psychology, 76*, 893–910.

Cook, R., Bird, G., Catmur, C., Press, C., & Heyes, C. (2014). Mirror neurons: From origin to function. *Behavioral and Brain Sciences, 37*, 177–241.

Davis, M. (1983). Measuring individual differences in empathy: Evidence for a multidimensional approach. *Journal of Personality and Social Psychology, 44*, 113–126.

Davis, M., & Stone, T. (1995). *Mental simulations: evaluations and applications*. Oxford: Blackwell.

de Vignemont, F., & Singer, T. (2006). The empathic brain: how, when and why? *Trends in Cognitive Sciences, 10*, 435–441.

Decety, J. (2011). Dissecting the neural mechanisms mediating empathy. *Emotion Review, 3*, 92–108.

Decety, J., & Jackson, P. L. (2004). The functional architecture of human empathy. *Behavioral and Cognitive Neuroscience Reviews, 3*, 71–100.

Decety, J., & Lamm, C. (2009). Empathy versus personal distress: recent evidence from social neuroscience. In J. Decety & W. Ickes (Eds.), *The social neuroscience of empathy* (pp. 199–214). Cambridge, MA: MIT Press.

Dinstein, I., Hasson, U., Rubin, N., & Heeger, D. J. (2007). Brain areas selective for both observed and executed movements. *Journal of Neurophysiology, 98*, 1415–1427.

Domes, G., Heinrichs, M., Michel, A., Berger, C., & Herpertz, S. C. (2007). Oxytocin improves "mind-reading" in humans. *Biological Psychiatry, 61*, 731–733.

Donaldson, Z. R., & Young, L. J. (2008). Oxytocin, vasopressin, and the neurogenetics of sociality. *Science, 322*, 900–904.

Dziobek, I., Rogers, K., Fleck, S., Bahnemann, M., Heekeren, H. R., Wolf, O. T., & Antonio Convit, A. (2008). Dissociation of cognitive and emotional empathy in adults with Asperger syndrome using the multifaceted empathy test (MET). *Journal of Autism and Developmental Disorders, 38*, 464–473.

Eisenberg, N., & Eggum, N. D. (2009). Empathic responding: Sympathy and personal distress. In J. Decety & W. Ickes (Eds.), *The social neuroscience of empathy* (pp. 71–84). Cambridge, MA: MIT Press.

Engen, H. G., & Singer, T. (2013). Empathy circuits. *Current Opinion in Neurobiology, 23*, 275–282.

Esslinger, C., Walter, H., Kirsch, P., Erk, S., Schnell, K., Arnold., C., ... Meyer-Lindenberg, A. (2009). Genome-wide significant neurogenetic risk mechanisms for psychosis. *Science, 324*, 605-605.

Fan, Y., Duncan, N. W., de Greck, M., & Northoff, G. (2011). Is there a core neural network in empathy? An fMRI based quantitative meta-analysis. *Neuroscience and Biobehavioral Reviews, 35,* 903–911.

Felson, J. (2014). What can we learn from twin studies? A comprehensive evaluation of the equal environments assumption. *Social Science Research, 43,* 184–199.

Francis, S. M., Sagar, A., Levin-Decanini, T., Liu, W., Carter, C. S., & Jacob, S. (2014). Oxytocin and vasopressin systems in genetic syndromes and neuro-developmental disorders. *Brain Research, 580,* 199–218.

Gallese, V. (2001). The "shared manifold" hypothesis: From mirror neurons to empathy. *Journal of Consciousness Studies, 8,* 33–50.

Gallese, V., Fadiga, L., Fogassi, L., & Rizolatti, G. (1996). Action recognition in the premotor cortex. *Brain, 119,* 593–609.

Gallese, V., & Goldman, A. (1998). Mirror neurons and the simulation theory of mind-reading. *Trends in Cognitive Sciences, 2,* 493–550.

Goldmann, A. (2006). *Simulating minds: The philosophy, psychology, and neuroscience of mindreading.* Oxford, UK: Oxford University Press.

Gonzalez-Liencresa, C., Shamay-Tsooryc, S. G., Brüne, M. (2013). Towards a neuroscience of empathy: Ontogeny, phylogeny, brain mechanisms, context and psychopathology. *Neuroscience & Biobehavioral Reviews, 37,* 1537–1548.

Goodman, R. (1997). The strengths and difficulties questionnaire: A research note. *Journal of Child Psychology and Psychiatry, 38,* 581–586.

Gu, X., & Han, S. (2007). Attention and reality constraints on the neuronal processes of empathy for pain. *NeuroImage, 36,* 256–267.

Gyurak, A., Haase, C. M., Sze, J., Goodkind, M. S., Coppola, G., Lane, J., … Levenson, R. W. (2013). The effect of the serotonin transporter polymorphism (5-HTTLPR) on empathic and self-conscious emotional reactivity. *Emotion, 13,* 25–35.

Hastings, P. D., Miller, J. G., Kahle, S., & Zahn-Waxler, C. (2013). The neurobiological bases of empathic concern for others. In M. Killen & J. G. Smetana (Eds.), *Handbook of moral development,* 2nd Ed. (pp. 411–434). New York: Taylor & Francis Group.

Hatfield, E., Cacioppo, J. T., & Rapson, R. L. (1993). Emotional contagion. *Current Directions in Psychological Sciences, 2,* 96–99.

Hatfield. E., Rapson, R. L. & Le, Y. L. (2009). Emotional contagion and empathy. In J. Decety & W. Ickes (Eds.), *The social neuroscience of empathy* (pp. 19–30). Cambridge, MA: MIT Press.

Heils, A., Teufel, A., Petri, S., Stöber, G., Riederer, P., Bengel, D., & Lesch, K. P. (1996). Allelic variation of human serotonin transporter gene expression. *Journal of Neurochemistry, 66,* 2621–2624.

Hein, G., Silani, G., Preuschoff, K., Batson, D., & Singer T. (2010). Neural responses to ingroup and outgroup members' suffering predict individual differences in costly helping. *Neuron, 68,* 149–160.

Heinrichs, M., von Dawans, B., & Domes, G. (2009). Oxytocin, vasopressin, and human social behavior. *Frontiers in Neuroendocrinology, 30,* 548–557.

Hess, U., & Blairy, S. (2001). Facial mimicry and emotional contagion to dynamic emotional facial expressions and their influence on decoding accuracy. *International Journal of Psychophysiology 40*, 129–141.

Hess, U., & Bourgeois, P. (2006). *The social costs of mimicking – why we should not both look angry.* Article presented at the 7th Annual Meeting of the Society for Personality and Social Psychology, January 26–28th, Palm Springs, CA.

Hodges, S. D., & Klein, K. J. K. (2001). Regulating the costs of empathy: The price of being human. *Journal of Socio-Economic, 30*, 437–452.

Hysek, C. M., Schmid, Y., Simmler, L. D., Domes, G., Heinrichs, M., Eisenegger, C, . . . Liechti, M. E. (2013). MDMA enhances emotional empathy and prosocial behavior. *Social Cognitive and Affective Neuroscience*, http://doi:10.1093/scan/nst161.

Iacoboni, M. (2009). Imitation, empathy, and mirror neurons. *Annual Review of Psychology, 60*, 653–670.

Jabbi, M., Swart, M., & Keysers, C. (2007). Empathy for positive and negative emotions in the gustatory cortex. *NeuroImage, 34*, 1744–1753.

Kay, S. R., Fiszbein, A., & Opler, L. A. (1987). The positive and negative syndrome scale (PANSS) for schizophrenia. *Schizophrenia Bulletin, 13*, 261–276.

Keysers, C. (2011). *The empathic brain.* Social Brain Press.

Knafo, A., & Uzefovsky, F. (2013). Variation in empathy. The interplay of genetic and environmental factors. In M. Legerstee, D. W. Haley & M. H. Bornsein (Eds.), *The Infant Mind: Origins of the Social Brain* (pp. 97–122). New York, NY: Guilford Press.

Kober, H., Barrett, L. F., Joseph, J., Bliss-Moreau, E., Lindquist, K., & Wager, T. D. (2008). Functional grouping and cortical–subcortical interactions in emotion: A meta-analysis of neuroimaging studies. *NeuroImage, 42*, 998–1031.

Kurth, F., Zilles, K, Fox, P. T., Laird, A. R., & Eickhoff, S. B. (2010). A link between the systems: functional differentiation and integration within the human insula revealed by meta-analysis. *Brain Structure and Function, 214*, 519–534.

Lachman, H. M., Papolos, D. F., Saito, T., Yu, Y. M., Szumlanski, C. L., & Weinshilboum, R. M. (1996). Human catechol-O-methyltransferase pharmaco-genetics: Description of a functional polymorphism and its potential application to neuropsychiatric disorders. *Pharmacogenetics, 6*, 243–250.

Lakin, J. L., Chartrand, T. L., & Arkin, R. M. (2008). I am too just like you: Nonconscious mimicry as an automatic behavioral response to social exclusion. *Psychological Science, 19*, 816–822.

Lamm, C., Batson, C. D., & Decety, J. (2007). The neural substrate of human empathy: Effects of perspective-taking and cognitive appraisal. *Journal of Cognitive Neuroscience, 19*, 42–58.

Lamm, C., Decety, J., & Singer, T. (2011). Meta-analytic evidence for common and distinct neural networks associated with directly experienced pain and empathy for pain. *NeuroImage, 54*, 2492–2502.

LeDoux, J. (1996). *The emotional brain*. New York, NY: Simon & Schuster.

Marchini, J., Donnelly, P., & Cardon, L. R., (2005). Genome-wide strategies for detecting multiple loci that influence complex diseases. *Nature Genetics, 37,* 413–417.

McHugo, G. J., Lanzetta, J. T., & Bush, L. K., (1991). The effect of attitudes on emotional reactions to expressive displays of political leaders. *Journal of Nonverbal Behavior, 15,* 19–41.

Meyer-Lindenberg, A., & Weinberger, D. R. (2006). Intermediate phenotypes and genetic mechanisms of psychiatric disorders. *Nature Reviews Neuroscience, 7,* 818–827.

Mohnke, S., Erk, S., Schnell, K., Schütz, C., Seiferth, N., Grimm, O., . . . Walter, H. (2014). Further evidence for the impact of a genome-wide- supported psychosis risk variant in ZNF804A on the theory of mind network. *Neuropsychopharmacology, 39,* 1196–1205.

Montag, C., Brockmann, E. M., Lehmann, A., Müller, D. J., Rujescu, D., & Gallinat, J. (2012). Association between oxytocin receptor gene polymorphisms and self-rated "empathic concern" in schizophrenia. *PloS one, 7,* e51882.

Morrison, I., Lloyd, D., di Pellegrino, G., & Roberts, N. (2004). Vicarious responses to pain in anterior cingulate cortex: Is empathy a multisensory issue? *Cognitive, Affective, & Behavioral Neuroscience, 4,* 270–278.

Morton, A. (1980). *Frames of mind: Constraints on the common-sense conception of the mental*. Oxford: Clarendon Press.

Mukamel, R., Ekstrom, A. D., Kaplan, J., Iacoboni, M., & Fried, I. (2010). Single-neuron responses in humans during execution and observation of actions. *Current Biology, 20,* 750–56.

Niedenthal, P. M., Barsalou, L. W., Winkielman, P., Krauth-Gruber, S., & Ric, F. (2005). Embodiment in attitudes, social perception, and emotion. *Personality and Social Psychology Review, 9,* 184–211.

Niedenthal, P. M., Mermillod, M., Maringer, M., & Hess, U. (2010). The Simulation of Smiles (SIMS) model: Embodied simulation and the meaning of facial expression. *Behavioral and Brain Sciences, 33,* 417–480.

O'Donovan, M. C., Craddock, N., Norton, N., Williams, H., Peirce, T., Moskvina, V., . . . Cloninger, C. R. (2008). Identification of loci associated with schizophrenia by genome wide association and follow-up. *Nature Genetics, 40,* 1053–1055.

Van Overwalle, F. (2009). Social cognition and the brain: A meta-analysis. *Human Brain Mapping, 30,* 829–858.

Van Overwalle, F., & Baetens, K. (2009). Understanding others' actions and goals by mirror and mentalizing systems: A meta-analysis. *NeuroImage, 48,* 564–584.

Peyron, R., Laurent, B., & García-Larrea, L. (2000). Functional imaging of brain responses to pain. A review and meta-analysis. *Clinical Neurophysiology, 30,* 263–288.

Poletti, S., Radaelli, D., Cavallaro, R., Bosia, M., Lorenzi, C., Pirovano, A., . . . Benedetti, F. (2013). Catechol-O-methyltransferase (COMT) genotype biases neural correlates of empathy and perceived personal distress in schizophrenia. *Comprehensive Psychiatry, 54,* 181–186.

Preston, S. D., Bechara, A., Damasio, H., Grabowski, T. J., Stansfield, R. B., Mehta, S., & Damasio, A. R. (2007). The neural substrates of cognitive empathy. *Social Neuroscience, 2,* 254–275.

Preston, S. D., & de Waal, F. (2002). Empathy: Its ultimate and proximate bases. *Behavioral and Brain Sciences, 2,* 254–275.

Rizzolatti, G., & Arbib, M. A. (1998). Language within our grasp. *Trends in Neuroscience, 21,* 188–194.

Rodrigues, S. M., Saslow, L. R., Garcia, N., John, O. P., & Keltner, D. (2009). Oxytocin receptor genetic variation relates to empathy and stress reactivity in humans. *Proceedings of the National Academy of Sciences of the United States of America, 106,* 21437–21441.

Rueckert, L., & Naybar, N. (2008). Gender differences in empathy: The role of the right hemisphere. *Brain and Cognition, 67,* 162–167.

Schnell, K., Bluschke, S., Konradt, B. & Walter, H. (2010). Functional relations of empathy and mentalizing: An fMRI study on the neural basis of cognitive empathy. *NeuroImage, 54,* 1743–1754.

Singer, T., & Lamm, C. (2009). The social neuroscience of empathy. *Annals of the New York Academy of Sciences, 1156,* 81–96.

Singer, T., Seymour, B., O'Doherty, J., Kaube, H., Dolan, R. J., & Frith, C. D. (2004). Empathy for pain involves the affective but not sensory components of pain. *Science, 303,* 1157–1162.

Singer, T., Seymour, B., O'Doherty, J. P., Stephan, K. E., Dolan, R. J., Frith, C. D. (2006). Empathic neural responses are modulated by the perceived fairness of others. *Nature, 439,* 466–469.

Skuse, D. H., & Gallagher, L. (2011). Genetic Influences on Social Cognition. *Pediatric Research, 69,* 85–91.

Smith, K. E., Porges, E. C., Norman, G. J., Connelly, J. J., & Decety, J. (2014). Oxytocin receptor gene variation predicts empathic concern and autonomic arousal while perceiving harm to others. *Social Neuroscience, 9,* 1–9.

Stüber, K. (2008). Empathy. In E. N. Zalta (Ed.), *The Stanford encyclopedia of philosophy.* Stanford: The Metaphysics Research Lab, Stanford University. Available at http://plato.stanford.edu/entries/empathy/.

Titchener, E. B. (1909). *Lectures on the experimental psychology of thought processes.* New York: Macmillan.

Turella, L., Pierno, A., Tubaldi, F., & Castiello, U. (2009). Mirror neurons in humans: Consisting or confounding evidence? *Brain and Language, 108,* 10–21.

Wai, M., & Tiliopoulos, N. (2012). The affective and cognitive empathic nature of the dark triad of personality. *Personality and Individual Differences, 2,* 794–799.

Walter, H. (2012). Social cognitive neuroscience of empathy: concepts, circuits, and genes. *Emotion Review, 4,* 9–17.

Walter, H., Adenzato, M., Ciaramidaro, A., Enrici, I., Pia, L., & Bara, B. G. (2004). Understanding intentions in social interaction: The role of the anterior paracingulate cortex. *Journal of Cognitive Neuroscience, 16,* 1854–1863.

Walter, H., Meyer-Lindenberg, A., & Heinz, A. (2013). Imaging genetics. In O. Gruber, P. Falkai, W. Gaebel & W. Rössler (Eds.), *Systemische Neurowissenschaften in der Psychiatrie. Methoden und Anwendungen in der Praxis* (pp. 308–326). Stuttgart: Kohlhammer.

Walter, H., Schnell, K., Erk, S., Arnold, C., Kirsch, P., Esslinger, C., . . . Meyer-Lindenberg, A. (2011). Effects of a genome-wide supported psychosis risk variant on neural activation during a theory-of-mind task. *Molecular Psychiatry, 16*, 462–470.

Williams, H. J., Craddock, N., Russo, G., Hamshere, M. L., Moskvina, V., Dwyer, S., . . . O'Donovan, M. C. (2011). Most genome-wide significant susceptibility loci for schizophrenia and bipolar disorder reported to date cross-traditional diagnostic boundaries. *Human Molecular Genetics, 20*, 387–391.

Wu, S., Jia, M., Ruan, Y., Lui, J., Guo, Y., Shuang, M., . . . Zhang, D. (2005). Positive association of the oxytocin receptor gene (OXTR) with autism in the Chinese Han population. *Biological Psychiatry, 58*, 74–77.

Zajonc, R. B., Adelmann, P. K., Murphy, S. T., & Niedenthal, P. M. (1987). Convergence in the physical appearance of spouses: An implication of the vascular theory of emotional efference. *Motivation and Emotion, 11*, 335–346.

Ze, O., Thoma, P., & Suchan, B. (2014). Cognitive and affective empathy in younger and older individuals, *Aging & Mental Health, 18*, 929–935, http://doi:10.1080/13607863.2014.899973.

CHAPTER 10

Conclusion: toward a better understanding of emotional mimicry

Ursula Hess and Agneta H. Fischer

The various contributors to this volume have provided evidence that mimicry can be seen as an empathic reaction, forming an important element in shared minds. This idea has been described in our "Emotional Mimicry in Social Context" view (Hess & Fischer, 2013, 2014), which states that the functions of emotional mimicry are basically social and hence vary with the characteristics of the relationship, the interaction partner, and the social goals in the specific situation. This view implies that emotional mimicry only occurs under specific circumstances, namely (a) when the mimicked expression is understood as an emotional signal directed at oneself, (b) when the expresser is perceived to have affiliative intent, and (c) when the mimicking person also has affiliative intent. It should thus be noted that in lab contexts, where a participant observes photos or videos containing facial expressions, mimicry occurs because the affiliative intent in such an experimental setting is a default stance and the expressions are implicitly considered to be directed at oneself.

This definition of emotional mimicry also points to a common misunderstanding about what is and what is not mimicry, because the various forms of mimicry cannot be defined on the basis of their form, but only on the basis of their functions. It may therefore be useful to distinguish at least two different phenomena (see also Hess & Fischer, 2013, 2014). One is a mimicry reaction in the traditional sense – a congruent expression that "mirrors" an observed reaction. The second is an emotional reaction to the other's expression, which is also congruent but not mirrored. Specifically, when one person shows a congruent nonverbal reaction in reaction to another person, this can, but need not necessarily, be considered mimicry. Take the example of anger. When a person shows anger in response to another's anger expression because of the implied insult, the two expressions are congruent, but do not represent mimicry. In such cases, the matching expression serves to assert dominance (as opposed to submission signaled by fear or an abasing smile) and thus cannot be seen as an indication of emotional mimicry. Similarly, showing congruent disgust to disgust can be seen as a sign of social rejection (Rozin, Haidt, & McCauley, 2008), not of affiliation. These congruent emotional displays are therefore not an imitation of, but rather *a reaction to*, the emotion of the other person. Thus, emotional mimicry should be defined on the basis of its function: it is the imitation of another's emotional display in order to understand and share the other's emotional perspective. The fact that there is evidence that emotional mimicry occurs independently of the specific nonverbal channel in which it is displayed (Hawk & Fischer, Chapter 6) further suggests that we may think of emotional mimicry as a form of re-enactment or simulation of the other's emotional perspective and hence as a process that is embedded in a larger social context. Importantly, once noted by the interaction partner, mimicry also plays a communicative role as a social regulator (Hess & Fischer, 2013, 2014; Hess, Houde, & Fischer, 2014).

Traditionally, mimicry has been considered to be a low-level process that is based on a direct perception-behavior link (Chartrand & Bargh, 1999), representing an automatic "low road" to empathy (Walter, 2012). Following the idea that mimicry is an automatic process based on changing appearances of facial muscles, Chartrand and Bargh (1999) speculated that "the effect [of mimicry] should occur among strangers when no affiliation goal is present" (p. 900). In this sense, mimicry was largely assumed to be a spontaneous unitary process – the implicit assumption being that mimicry occurs automatically and that all behaviors are mimicked to an equal degree under all circumstances, as long as they are perceived.

The Emotional Mimicry in Social Context view takes the meaning of the facial display as the key factor determining whether or not it is mimicked. It considers the central function of mimicry to be to shape social interactions in ways that interaction partners feel understood and liked. In other words, emotional mimicry reflects a sharing of minds (Oatley, Chapter 1) and empathic understanding (Schuler et al., Chapter 9). Neurological evidence supports the importance of this social interactional context (Schuler et al., Chapter 9).

Supporting the social functions of mimicry, more recently a number of factors have been found to moderate mimicry behavior. First, mimicry depends on the characteristics of the mimickee (Chapters 2, 3, 7, and 8). Individuals mimic liked interaction partners more than disliked ones, and they mimic positive and affiliative emotions more than aversive or hostile emotions. More generally, emotional mimicry is restricted to situations in which relationships are either affiliative or at least neutral.

Second, mimicry also depends on the personality characteristics of the mimicker (Sonnby-Börgstrom, Chapter 7). The tendency to mimic may be a stable part of the behavioral repertoire that can be used to regulate social interactions (Hess et al., Chapter 5). In this vein, it may be argued that emotional mimicry is related to the strength of a person's implicit affiliation motive. Hence, individuals who tend to mimic should report more satisfying social interactions, because they are likely to engage in positive social behaviors such as trying to please others, maintaining harmony with others, or showing affection to others. As mentioned earlier, Hess and Fischer (2014) argue for the need to distinguish between mimicry, that is, the imitation of another's behavior, and congruent emotional displays that are in fact not an imitation of, but rather *a reaction to*, the emotions of others. Thus, mimicry as a trait should be restricted to situations in which the mimicker has affiliative intent and the mimicked behavior is also affiliative. When congruent facial reactions to non-affiliative facial expressions are shown, these should be seen as reactive.

In sum, the Emotional Mimicry in Social Context model assumes that not everyone will mimic all expressions under all circumstances. In an affiliative context, individuals who have affiliative intentions should mimic those nonverbal signals that in turn signal affiliation, such as the emotions of happiness and sadness, but also affiliative body movements as recently shown by Kurzius and Borkenau (2015). In an antagonistic context or when individuals are not striving for affiliation, and when behaviors do not signal affiliation, congruent facial expressions may still occur, but they are more likely to be emotional reactions to the antagonistic behavior of the other person. In these contexts, opposite behaviors, such as smiling in response to pain or a frown in response to a smile – often referred to as counter-mimicry (Lanzetta & Englis, 1989; Weyers, Mühlberger, Kund, Hess, & Pauli, 2009) – also occur.

Two recent studies found evidence for this notion. Kurzius and Borkenau (2015) studied behavioral mimicry including smiles and frowns during cooperative and competitive tasks in a laboratory setting, whereas Mauersberger et al. (2015) studied emotional mimicry. Both studies postulated that affiliation-related personality characteristics would positively predict mimicry of positive behaviors or affiliative emotions, respectively, whereas non-affiliative traits such as neuroticism would be related to showing congruent negative behavior or non-affiliative emotions, respectively. They then predicted positive interaction outcomes as a function of the mimicry of positive/affiliative behaviors and negative outcomes for the negative/non-affiliative behaviors. Mauersberger et al. asked participants to keep a diary about their daily interactions, whereas Kurzius and Borkenau studied laboratory interactions. Figure 10.1 shows the general model underlying these predictions.

Despite these vast differences in approach, considerable congruence in findings emerged. Thus, neuroticism was linked to the imitation of

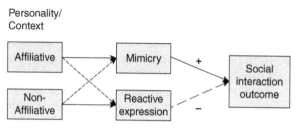

Figure 10.1 Antecedents and consequences of mimicry and reactive expressions.

negative behaviors, as well as to disgust mimicry, whereas agreeableness was linked to the imitation of positive behaviors and the affiliative emotion of sadness. In turn, the imitation of positive behaviors and sadness mimicry both increased liking and interaction satisfaction, respectively, whereas the imitation of negative behaviors and disgust mimicry decreased liking and interaction satisfaction. In sum, these findings show congruence between behavioral mimicry and emotional mimicry when interactionally meaningful measures of behavioral mimicry are taken.

These studies hint at the importance of distinguishing between the imitation of affiliative and non-affiliative behaviors. In particular, more research is needed to understand the role and function of showing congruent non-affiliative behaviors, which have so far only rarely been studied separately from affiliative behaviors. For example, the finding reported by Mauersberger et al. (2015) for congruent reactions to anger points to this need. It turns out that the outcome of anger imitation depends on the emotion regulation ability of the mimicker. When individuals high in emotion regulation ability show congruent anger, the social interaction outcome is positive, yet when individuals low in emotion regulation ability show congruent anger, the outcome is negative. Anger is an especially interesting emotion in this context, because it is linked, on the one hand, to aggression (Berkowitz, 1999) but also (in the form of "righteous" anger) to goal-conducive acts that redress injustice (Hess, 2014). As such, anger that is perceived as appropriate can have positive consequences, whereas anger that seems simply aggressive has negative consequences.

In sum, over and above the general notion that mimicry serves as "social glue," we need to understand better the specific types of glue and their proper application. Just as wood glue is useless for metal, and vice versa, we need to understand the specific consequences of the mimicry of specific behaviors. The line of research described earlier seems a fruitful way to better understand the function of mimicry for the mimicker: when does mimicry result in feeling better – or worse – about the other? The observation that the mimicry of sad expressions seems to be linked to more positive feelings on the part of the mimickee (Mauersberger et al., 2015) also suggests the importance of studying the "other side." In this context, it should be noted that laboratory research on mimicry has so far considered only single mimicry events (in the case of emotional mimicry) or aggregate observations (in the case of behavioral mimicry), yet clearly mimicry is a time series event, occurring in sequential steps. What happens if I mimic another person, but the person does not mimic me? Conversely, can we actually get into a runaway positive feedback loop, which ends in a catastrophic breakdown? Can phenomena such as hysterical laughter or panic be partly described in these terms? That hysterical laughter occurs mainly among friends and depends on eye contact may be one hint in that direction (Hess, Banse, & Kappas, 1993). In sum, the Emotional Mimicry in Social Context view promises to be a fruitful avenue for research on the understanding of important aspects of human interaction.

An important related phenomenon, which is considered in this book, is empathy (Chapters 7 and 9) and its relation to mimicry. The Emotional Mimicry in Social Context view considers an empathic stance a prerequisite for mimicry. But there are larger questions to consider. Classically, empathy described a process of "inner imitation," which was based on a presumed innate disposition for motor mimicry (Lipps, 1907). From this perspective, mimicry is a process that underlies empathy. However, in the intervening century the concept of empathy evolved and, as Schuler et al. (Chapter 9, this volume) note, "trying to explicitly define empathy or distinguish between various conceptions of empathy is a difficult undertaking." At the very least we need to distinguish between cognitive and affective empathy (e.g., Baron-Cohen & Wheelwright, 2004; Walter, 2012). In cognitive empathy the emphasis is on the ability to infer or label another person's feelings accurately. This can be done via perceptual processes such as pattern matching (Buck, 1984) or via perspective-taking (Kirouac & Hess, 1999). Ickes (1997) refers to empathic accuracy in this context. By contrast, affective empathy is defined as a process in which the perception of another's emotional state generates a matching state in the perceiver (de Waal, 2008). This process overlaps conceptually with emotional contagion (Hatfield, Cacioppo, & Rapson, 1994). However, unlike emotional contagion the affective state in empathy, while congruent with the affective state of the other, is still oriented toward the other and, importantly, the empathic person is aware of the source of the emotion (Lamm, Batson, & Decety, 2007) even though some theories describe affective empathy simply as a form of affective resonance (e.g., Baron-Cohen & Wheelwright, 2004). This second process – affective empathy – is more closely related to mimicry in that both involve affect. This also raises the possibility that the emotional contagion in empathy entrains the congruent expression of emotion in mimicry, and not vice versa as suggested by Lipps (1907) and later by Hatfield et al. (1994).

There is also evidence that empathic processes and (intentional) mimicry share neural substrates such as the anterior insula, inferior frontal gyrus, and ventral premotor area (see Schuler et al., Chapter 9). But this raises the issue of how intentional and unintentional mimicry relate to each other. As intentional and spontaneous facial expressions are innervated via separate neural pathways (Rinn, 1991), the two cannot simply be equated. However, research that relies on intentional mimicry tends not to discuss this issue. Walter (2012) concludes that, compared to empathy, mimicry is a more basic form of affective reaction. It seems reasonable to consider mimicry to be an index of (affective) empathy, but the actual relation between these processes is not well understood.

Even less well understood is the relation between mimicry and cognitive empathy. To the degree that mimicry relies on simulation, these two processes have something in common, because perspective-taking also involves simulation (see Decety & Lamm, 2006). When participants were asked to think about how another *person* may act next, activation of the Medial Prefrontal Cortex (MPFC) – an area associated with theory of mind – was found, suggesting that participants were attempting a mental simulation of the other's perspective. However, when they were asked to think about these same actions when performed by a computer the MPFC was not activated, suggesting that they did not attempt to understand the computer's "perspective" or state of mind through simulation (Gallagher, Jack, Roepstorff, & Frith, 2002; Rilling, Sanfey, Aronson, Nystrom, & Cohen, 2004). Also, some studies have reported evidence for more mimicry and personal distress, but less empathic concern, when people are instructed to engage in the more cognitive task of imagining themselves in the place of the other rather than imagining the feelings of the other (Lamm et al., 2007; Lamm, Porges, Cacioppo, & Decety, 2008).

Evidence that mimicry can facilitate emotion decoding (see Stel, Chapter 2; Niedenthal et al., Chapter 3) also relates the two processes. However, care must be taken here, as well. First, the evidence suggests that the facilitating effect of mimicry may well be restricted to happiness and/or difficult decoding tasks. In addition, there is evidence that the two might diverge. Thus, Hühnel, Fölster, Werheid, and Hess (2014) found that older participants showed some of the expected age-related deficits in emotion decoding (cognitive empathy) but none with regard to mimicry in a difficult decoding task. In fact, if anything, they were more likely than young participants to mimic emotion expressions. Taking the notion of affective and cognitive empathy further, the question that arises is to what degree mimicry is linked to the knowledge of other people's minds, as discussed by Oatley (Chapter 1) and Schilbach (Chapter 4).

In sum, future research is faced with the ambitious task of disentangling the related but different processes of empathy, perspective-taking, Theory of Mind, and mimicry. One important task in this process might, as alluded to by Schuler et al. (Chapter 9), be to develop clear and nonoverlapping definitions of these processes.

In conclusion, we believe that the Emotional Mimicry in Social Context model opens the door to a new and more differentiated view of mimicry as a social regulator. As outlined earlier, exciting research can be generated based on this model with the aim of better understanding the complex interplay that underlies social interactions.

References

Baron-Cohen, S., & Wheelwright, S. (2004). The empathy quotient: An investigation of adults with Asperger syndrome or high functioning autism and normal sex differences. *Journal of Autism and Developmental Disorders, 34*, 163–175.

Berkowitz, L. (1999). Anger. In T. Dalgleish & M. J. Power (Eds.), *Handbook of cognition and emotion* (pp. 411–428). New York, NY: John Wiley & Sons.

Buck, R. (1984). Nonverbal receiving ability. In R. Buck (Ed.), *The communication of emotion* (pp. 209–242). New York: Guilford Press.

Chartrand, T. L., & Bargh, J. A. (1999). The chameleon effect: The perception-behavior link and social interaction. *Journal of Personality and Social Psychology, 76*, 893–910.

de Waal, F. B. M. (2008). Putting the altruism back into altruism: The evolution of empathy. *Annual Review of Psychology, 59*, 279–300.

Decety, J., & Lamm, C. (2006). Human empathy through the lens of social neuroscience. *The Scientific World Journal, 6*, 1146–1163.

Gallagher, H. L., Jack, A. I., Roepstorff, A., & Frith, C. D. (2002). Imaging the intentional stance in a competitive game. *NeuroImage, 16*, 814–821.

Hatfield, E., Cacioppo, J. T., & Rapson, R. L. (1994). *Emotional contagion*. Madison, WI: C.W. Brown.

Hess, U. (2014). Anger is a positive emotion. In W. G. Parrott (Ed.), *The Positive Side of Negative Emotions* (pp. 55–75). New York, NY: Guilford Press.

Hess, U., Banse, R., & Kappas, A. (1993). *Hysterical laughter in the laboratory: Two studies on emotional contagion in an interactive setting*. Paper presented at the The 54th Annual Convention of The Canadian Psychological Association, Montreal, Canada.

Hess, U., & Fischer, A. (2013). Emotional mimicry as social regulation. *Personality and Social Psychology Review, 17*, 142–157.

Hess, U., & Fischer, A. (2014). Emotional mimicry: Why and when we mimic emotions. *Social and Personality Psychology Compass, 8*, 45–57.

Hühnel, I., Fölster, M., Werheid, K., & Hess, U. (2014). Empathic reactions of younger and older adults: No age related decline in affective responding. *Journal of Experimental Social Psychology, 50*, 136–143.

Ickes, W., & Simpson, J. A. (1997). Managing empathic accuracy in close relationships. In W. J. Ickes (Ed.), *Empathic accuracy* (pp. 218–250). New York: Guilford Press.

Kirouac, G., & Hess, U. (1999). Group membership and the decoding of nonverbal behavior. In P. Philippot, R. Feldman, & E. Coats (Eds.), *The social context of nonverbal behavior* (pp. 182–210). Cambridge, UK: Cambridge University Press.

Kurzius, E., & Borkenau, P. (2015). Antecedents and consequences of mimicry: A naturalistic interaction approach. *European Journal of Personality, 29*(2), 107–124.

Lamm, C., Batson, C. D., & Decety, J. (2007). The neural substrate of human empathy: Effects of perspective-taking and cognitive appraisal. *Journal of Cognitive Neuroscience, 19*, 42–58.

Lamm, C., Porges, E. C., Cacioppo, J. T., & Decety, J. (2008). Perspective taking is associated with specific facial responses during empathy for pain. *Brain Research, 1227*, 153–161.

Lanzetta, J. T., & Englis, B. G. (1989). Expectations of cooperation and competition and their effects on observers' vicarious emotional responses. *Journal of Personality and Social Psychology, 56*, 543–554.

Lipps, T. (1907). Das Wissen von fremden Ichen. In T. Lipps (Ed.), *Psychologische Untersuchungen* (Band 1, pp. 694–722). Leipzig: Engelmann.

Rilling, J. K., Sanfey, A. G., Aronson, J. A., Nystrom, L. E., & Cohen, J. D. (2004). The neural correlates of theory of mind within interpersonal interactions. *NeuroImage, 22*, 1694–1703.

Rinn, W. (1991). Neuropsychology of facial expression. In R. S. Feldman & B. Rimé (Eds.), *Fundamentals of nonverbal behavior* (pp. 3–30). Cambridge: Cambridge University Press.

Rozin, P., Haidt, J., & McCauley, C. R. (2008). Disgust. In M. Lewis, J. M. Haviland-Jones, & L. F. Barrett (Eds.), *Handbook of emotions* (3rd ed., pp. 757–776). New York, NY: Guilford Press.

Walter, H. (2012). Social cognitive neuroscience of empathy: Concepts, circuits, and genes. *Emotion Review, 4*(1), 9–17.

Weyers, P., Mühlberger, A., Kund, A., Hess, U., & Pauli, P. (2009). Modulation of facial reactions to avatar emotional faces by nonconscious competition priming. *Psychophysiology, 46*, 328–335.

Index

ACC/MCC, 49, 202, 204, 208, 214

affect program, 129

affective empathy, 40, 193, 194, 195, 206, 211, 212, 214, 226

affiliation, 4, 38, 53, 54, 58, 61, 84, 90, 91, 93, 95, 98, 101, 113, 176, 223, 224

affiliative, 2, 41, 52, 53, 54, 61, 83, 91, 92, 93, 94, 95, 97, 98, 99, 102, 103, 117, 222, 223, 224, 225

anterior insula AI, 3, 7, 197, 202, 204, 206, 207, 208, 209, 214, 227

alexithymia, 139

amygdala, 47, 49, 51, 75, 80, 137, 140, 205, 206, 207, 210

androids, 5, 171, 172, 173, 175, 176, 184

anger, 2, 12, 15, 17, 27, 30, 34, 35, 36, 37, 38, 51, 55, 56, 60, 63, 91, 92, 94, 97, 99, 102, 103, 111, 114, 116, 117, 129, 132, 148, 167, 169, 170, 172, 213, 222, 225

anxiety, 15, 17, 141, 142, 143, 145, 204

appraisals, 117, 170, 171, 206

ASD, 35, 36, 140

associative network, 164

attachment, 4, 8, 79, 142, 143, 145, 146, 150, 151, 211

Autistic Spectrum Disorder, 10, 18, 58, 63, 84, 140, 163, 164, 168, 178, 179, 180, 181, 182, 183, 184, 194, 211, 212

automatic, 3, 47, 48, 50, 60, 61, 63, 72, 74, 79, 80, 90, 95, 107, 115, 125, 126, 127, 130, 131, 137, 139, 141, 145, 147, 149, 150, 167, 174, 182, 183, 195, 197, 223

behavioural mimicry, 90, 91, 93, 101, 113

blocking mimicry, 4, 30, 31, 32, 59, 112, 132, 133

CERT, 59

cognitive empathy, 3, 27, 35, 138, 193, 194, 195, 206, 214, 226

competitive, 5, 95, 103, 140, 175, 177, 224

contempt, 30, 52

contextual view, 108

cooperative, 1, 5, 8, 11, 12, 13, 14, 44, 91, 95, 103, 140, 150, 175, 177, 224

Corrugator Supercilii, 29, 36, 37, 39, 50, 96, 99, 109, 110, 111, 140, 143, 144, 145, 170, 172, 175

counter-empathy, 91

cross-channel mimicry, 3, 5, 109, 110, 113, 114, 115, 117, 118, 119

Darwin, 44, 72

decoding, 45, 46, 54, 58, 59, 60, 61, 97, 146, 168, 218, 227

deliberate, 29, 172

disgust, 29, 30, 35, 38, 44, 54, 55, 91, 92, 94, 103, 111, 112, 114, 116, 118, 129, 132, 133, 201, 204, 223, 225

dominance, 52, 53, 54, 58, 91, 92, 94, 98, 222

dopamine, 212, 214

embodiment, 4, 5, 28, 37, 108, 116, 118, 163, 164, 165, 181, 183

emotion recognition, 29, 30, 31, 35

emotional contagion, 2, 7, 18, 28, 33, 52, 60, 72, 113, 130, 131, 133, 134, 137, 138, 139, 141, 146, 147, 148, 149, 159, 198, 199, 226

emotional mimicry, 2, 3, 4, 5, 72, 90, 91, 92, 93, 94, 96, 99, 100, 101, 102, 103, 107, 111, 113, 114, 117, 118, 119, 120, 180, 189, 196, 215, 222, 223, 224, 225, 226

empathic accuracy, 226
empathy, vii, 3, 4, 7, 12, 13, 16, 17, 18, 20, 22, 27, 29, 33, 34, 35, 37, 40, 80, 95, 115, 134, 138, 139, 140, 141, 146, 148, 149, 150, 192, 193, 194, 195, 196, 197, 198, 199, 200, 201, 202, 204, 205, 206, 207, 208, 209, 210, 211, 212, 213, 214, 218, 220, 221, 223, 226, 227, 228
evolution, 8, 11, 12, 13, 14, 15, 44, 79, 101, 129
eye contact, 39, 46, 55, 56, 57, 58, 61, 119, 195, 226
eye gaze, 56, 57, 83, 84

Facial Action Coding System (FACS), 111
facial electromyography (EMG), 36, 39, 49, 50, 56, 59, 77, 96, 99, 103, 127, 130, 136, 137, 138, 139, 140, 146, 167, 169, 170, 172, 173, 174, 175, 182
Facial Feedback Hypothesis, 4, 28, 131
fear, 14, 15, 16, 27, 29, 30, 32, 35, 44, 55, 56, 60, 91, 99, 102, 111, 129, 132, 143, 145, 148, 160, 204, 222
friends, 1, 5, 19, 92, 93, 94, 103, 177, 226
frown, 29, 30, 96, 116, 117, 129, 175, 181, 224

gender, 36, 146, 147, 149, 151, 154, 161, 180, 208
genetic, 127, 128, 136, 138, 143, 147, 210, 211, 212, 213, 214
goals, 1, 12, 14, 20, 73, 90, 94, 95, 96, 97, 98, 101, 103, 163, 170, 171, 222
guilt, 12, 32

happiness, 9, 12, 13, 14, 17, 20, 27, 28, 30, 31, 32, 34, 35, 36, 37, 38, 51, 55, 56, 57, 60, 93, 99, 101, 102, 103, 112, 117, 129, 132, 166, 167, 169, 170, 172, 204, 224, 227

identification, 17, 18, 19
inferior frontal gyrus (IFG), 50, 51, 84, 133, 134, 182, 197, 203, 204, 206, 227
insula, 48, 49, 50, 51, 133, 202, 205, 210

intentional, 162, 172
interactionist, 5, 73, 75, 76

lesion, 37, 48, 51, 168
Lipps, 28, 42, 45, 226

Matched Motor hypothesis, 5
Medial Prefrontal Cortex (MPFC), 75, 82, 84, 227
mentalizing network, 5, 79, 80, 85, 203, 206, 213
mimetic, 3, 8
mimicry, vii, 73, 199, 225
    emotional, 30, 94, 119, 152, 170, 187, 198
mirror neurons, 1, 3, 5, 10, 51, 56, 73, 76, 77, 79, 83, 84, 126, 133, 134, 135, 140, 149, 150, 154, 178, 183, 200, 206, 208, 214
Möbius syndrome, 35
modality, 108, 116, 117, 164, 165, 205
motor mimicry, 108, 111, 115, 133

norms, 12, 147, 162

Orbicularis Oculi, 39, 96, 99
other-directed, vii, 74, 75, 77, 141, 179
oxytocin, 211, 214

pain, 1, 2, 7, 39, 57, 91, 107, 116, 141, 194, 201, 202, 204, 209, 210, 219, 224
Parkinson's disease, 48
Perception-Action Model, 115, 170, 199
Perception-Behavior link, 27, 115, *See Perception-Action Model*
personal distress, 196, 198
perspective taking, 3, 8, 35, 141, 195, 197, 199, 208, 209, 210, 226, 227, 228
posterior cingulate cortex, 49, 50, 78, 79, 80, 201
postures, 2, 27, 39, 110, 119, 121, 125, 132, 138, 153, 195
power, 15, 92, 164, 170, 171, 173, 177
pupil, 77

Reading the Mind in the Eyes Test, 31, 211

recognition, 4, 27, 30, 31, 32, 33, 35, 37, 40, 48, 51, 54, 55, 56, 58, 60, 62, 79, 109, 110, 111, 112, 114, 118, 126, 163, 165, 166, 168, 180, 181, 183, 193, 195, 217

re-enactment, 28, 114, 165, 166, 223

reward, 45, 53, 82, 84, 97, 181, 182, 183, 209

robotics, 164, 171

sadness, 12, 14, 15, 16, 17, 18, 27, 29, 30, 31, 34, 35, 38, 55, 57, 60, 91, 97, 99, 101, 103, 111, 114, 116, 129, 132, 142, 148, 180, 198, 224, 225

schizophrenic, 212

scripts, 13

self-directed, vii, 74, 75, 77

serotonin, 213, 214

shared, 1, 3, 7, 8, 9, 12, 14, 15, 20, 98, 113, 173, 199, 200, 202, 207, 217, 222

sharing, 2, 3, 7, 10, 11, 12, 15, 16, 17, 19, 20, 22, 80, 83, 90, 97, 114, 140, 141, 223

SIMS model, 46, 47, 51, 52, 53, 54, 55, 58, 61, 62

simulation, 5, 18, 19, 20, 38, 40, 45, 47, 52, 54, 55, 56, 57, 58, 61, 62, 63, 73, 76, 116, 117, 133, 136, 149, 165, 166, 173, 180, 200, 201, 203, 206, 214, 217, 223, 227

SMA. *See* supplementaty motor area

smile, 4, 13, 28, 31, 32, 34, 36, 45, 46, 48, 49, 52, 53, 54, 55, 56, 58, 59, 60, 61, 62, 92, 96, 117, 175, 198, 222

smiles, 4, 13, 14, 32, 34, 58, 60, 61, 62, 76, 91, 92, 95, 108, 112, 125, 129, 132, 148, 162, 166, 167, 168, 169, 170, 174, 175, 181, 224

smiling Ziesmiles, 5, 9, 27, 28, 73, 76, 93, 94, 99, 109, 110, 112, 113, 114, 118, 132, 224

social context, 5, 54, 58, 61, 72, 90, 97, 118, 126, 137, 169, 175, 176, 177, 178, 197, 222, 223, 224, 226, 228

social cues, 174, 211

social hierarchy, 52, 91, 170, 171

social stimuli, 183

somatosensory cortices, 48, 202

spontaneous, 30, 32, 36, 37, 40, 48, 49, 50, 51, 74, 77, 84, 92, 102, 127, 128, 136, 139, 147, 149, 162, 163, 164, 165, 166, 168, 169, 170, 171, 172, 173, 176, 177, 178, 179, 180, 181, 183, 184, 223, 227

STORM model, 83, 84, 89

strangers, 90, 92, 93, 94, 102, 103, 223

sufficiency hypothesis, 131

supplementary motor area (SMA), 48, 49, 50, 204

sympathy, 1, 17, 18, 46, 198, 199

the Corrugator Supercilii, 96

Theory of Mind, 8, 9, 11, 19, 22, 178, 194, 201, 228

transcranial magnetic stimulation (TMS), 48, 168

understanding, 1, 4, 9, 11, 19, 27, 28, 29, 32, 33, 35, 36, 37, 39, 40, 73, 126, 140, 141, 148, 149, 150, 194, 195, 200, 223

ventral premotor area, 197, 200, 227

ventral striatum, 82, 205, 209

volitional facial paresis (VFP), 48, 50

vocalizations, 2, 38, 77, 110, 116, 119, 132, 195

voluntary, 48, 49, 50, 51, 60, 73, 77, 173

Zygomaticus Major, 36, 37, 39, 49, 50, 53, 56, 59, 96, 99, 109, 110, 132, 140, 145, 170, 172, 175

Lightning Source UK Ltd.
Milton Keynes UK
UKOW05n0844080517

300718UK00011BA/126/P